But I Can Learn

By Clair

The contents of this work including, but not limited to, the accuracy of events, people, and places depicted; opinions expressed; permission to use previously published materials included; and any advice given or actions advocated are solely the responsibility of the author, who assumes all liability for said work and indemnifies the publisher against any claims stemming from publication of the work.

All Rights Reserved
Copyright © 2023 by Clair

No part of this book may be reproduced or transmitted, downloaded, distributed, reverse engineered, or stored in or introduced into any information storage and retrieval system, in any form or by any means, including photocopying and recording, whether electronic or mechanical, now known or hereinafter invented without permission in writing from the publisher.

Dorrance Publishing Co
585 Alpha Drive
Pittsburgh, PA 15238
Visit our website at www.dorrancebookstore.com

ISBN: 979-8-88812-194-8
eISBN: 979-8-88812-694-3

Introduction

This is the story of a part of my life, only a part. While the essence of the story is true, it is also true that after fifty years it was impossible to always recall the exact details of events and conversations.

I dug deep into my emotional reserves, forced myself to go back and remember how I felt then, how I saw others react to me, what I was told and what I believed. I wrote this story from that.

Every line and every conversation may not be exactly true and factual, but it is still my story. As I lived it for many years.

I have, of course, changed names and some details to protect the privacy of others

And, despite the prologue, this is not a story about childhood sexual abuse. It also does not contain any graphic sexuality. It may still be difficult to read in some places, but I promise you it ends well!

Prologue – Illinois, 1952

I wonder what would happen if I took this hammer and hit my dad in the head with it.

I don't want to be here, in this upstairs space with my Dad. It sorta looks like an attic, but he's building two extra bedrooms for us kids up here. I'm the oldest and he says he needs my help. That's what he tells Mom. She believes him. But I don't like it here. I just hand him tools, hold boards sometimes, walk across the room to get something so he doesn't have to. Mostly it's boring.

Seems to be taking forever to get this done. Not like there's any hurry. We three kids are all in one room now, on the main floor. It's a big room, and the other kids are still pretty little. But I'm almost ten now, and don't play baby stuff anymore, so I think I'll like it when we all have more space. I'll have to share the room with my little sister, though, so it still won't be all mine. Still won't be a big girl room.

I am a big girl now, even though I'm so small for my age, the smallest one in my class. Dad says I'm growing up and have to help him take care of things.

I don't feel grown up. Why can't I remember stuff, like what tool Dad sent me to the basement for? They don't know, they can't see inside me, they can't see how crazy I am, how stupid I am. I'm ten and still wet the bed. I try and try and can't find what's wrong with me.

My brother is a little boy, but he wants to be a man. He keeps climbing up these stairs to see if he can help Dad build stuff, but he just gets yelled at, really yelled at. I'm embarrassed that I'm up here, a girl,

Clair

and he gets sent away, a boy. But I'm glad. I'm glad that he doesn't have to be here. Then he'd hate it as much as I do.

He'd hate being kissed like a grown up and having to pull down his pants and get kissed there. He'd hate it, I know he would. Just like me.

But if I took the hammer and hit Dad in the head then everybody would want to know why I killed my own dad, and then they'd know. That Dad does the kissing thing and that I don't like it. I'm supposed to like it. Dad says everybody likes it. So I know there's something really wrong with me and I am afraid.

Chapter 1 – Washington State, 1962

I didn't go to college after high school, I went to work. In an office. In the big city nearby. I had few skills, but I could type eighty words a minute with almost no errors and that counted for something in 1962.

Standing in the hall, staring at the office door, at the bumpy glass window, the stenciled letters announcing, "McCormick Publications." I clutched my purse, my sweater, the newspaper want-ads. Desperately needing this job, needing it to rescue me. Sure, this company only sold ads for small trade papers, and sure, I would only be keeping their paperwork in order, but I would have a paycheck every week. A paycheck so I could move out on my own, in an apartment, away from my dad. Taking a moment to compose myself, to straighten my shoulders, to look confident, to smile big, I stepped into the office.

No receptionist greeted me, only a pudgy, grey haired fellow, talking on the phone, pacing, going only as far as the cord would allow. I took the seat he motioned me to and looked around. Six desks, each with its own phone. Generic desks. No personal items. Only paper and pens and small newspapers, ashtrays and empty coffee cups. And dust. It smelled old and looked dingy.

As Mr. Pacing Man hung up the phone, I stood, extended my hand, introducing myself. "I've come to answer your ad, the one here in the newspaper. I'd like to apply for the job."

"Just call me Max," he insisted, extending his own hand for a fleeting moment, twirling a stubby cigar in the corner of his mouth. "Can you type, without too many errors I mean? Can you be here every day?"

"Yes, sir, I can do both of those things." I waited. Waited for a typing test, for more questions. Questions the library book had prepared me for. Answers I had practiced in front of the mirror. To get them right. So I would get the job.

He stood, not pacing then, only staring at me. "Ok, you're hired! Can you start now? That can be your desk, there's a ton of stuff to file, and if you can answer the phone now, I can make some sales."

This was the first day I sat at a desk, my own desk in a small office, doing work that would give me my first real paycheck.

I felt grown up, in control, proud. "I have taken this first step and I will soon be the boss of me," I said to myself. And I smiled.

∼

Two weeks later, holding a paycheck in my hand, I paid the first week's rent on a tiny apartment. Three blocks from *my* office! A fresh start it would be. *Tomorrow I will be free, my father not able to ever touch me again. Tomorrow I will know what it is to be happy!*

As we sat around the supper table that evening, I announced it to everyone, my mother, brother and sister, my father. "I got my first paycheck today and rented an apartment close to my work! I'm so excited! You'll have to come see it!" I had planned this speech carefully, hoping to dodge the objections of my father. I made my voice cheerful.

Pausing only a moment before looking up from his plate of meatloaf and mashed potatoes, my father glared at me. "We'll talk about it later, not now, not at supper." Concentrating on our own plates of meatloaf, we each ate in silence. Fearful silence.

In my silence I understood why my father would try to stop me. The others did not, so they looked only at their own dinner plates. Once again, I was the bringer of tension into our home.

Much later, in the night, he came downstairs, into my room. Closing the door, he leaned against it, hand on the doorknob, looking powerful. Then, folding his arms across his chest he began, "I thought you might do this. You're over eighteen now, and you think you can decide whatever you want to do? But here's the thing.

"Remember when you wandered around the neighborhood so drunk the police picked you up? And the time you walked out of school one day, in the middle of class, and stupidly roamed around until the police found you again, remember that? That proves you're incompetent to live on your own and need supervision. See, I talked to a lawyer and a judge and they will declare me your legal guardian if I ask for it. You're not moving out, so don't try this again." He did not shut the door when he left my room.

Collapsing on my bed, I cried deep, angry sobs. My easy plan had failed! I didn't know he was lying. Believing he could really do that, I was only afraid.

And so I sat, every day, in my boring job. In the small dingy office. Hopeless.

∼

Until I saw the man at the desk over there, in the corner of the room. I knew he was looking at me, I could tell. He tried to look away whenever I caught him, but he was definitely watching me. His black hair magnificent as the sunlight reached across his desk. He'd run his fingers through his hair, pushing it back when having trouble making a sale, when nervous. I knew because I'd been watching him too. He wasn't the only one watching.

I tried not having a waking dream about him. It was hard.

One morning he brought me coffee from the diner downstairs. Just the way I liked it, cream and a little sugar. How did he know? Was he watching me at the diner, when I bought my own coffee? I'd skipped coffee this morning, running late for work. Did he know that, too?

But there he was, that crooked smile of his, only one corner of his mouth turned up a little, and that shiny black hair. Him, in a white shirt. I always did think men with shining coal black hair should wear white shirts. Always.

He stood at my desk, handing me the paper cup of my own favorite coffee. I smiled back because this, this moment felt really good. I was flattered.

Every day for the next few weeks he brought me coffee. I got used to the routine, to the attention. I liked the glances of the other phone salesmen, watching this dance at my desk. I began to feel important.

Then there was the day I saw him walking toward me, coffee cup in hand, no lid. I wondered at that. Walking across the street, riding the elevator, managing the office door, without a lid?

"There, try that," was all he said as he placed it in front of me. Whipped cream towered over my coffee! Mounds of it! It looked gorgeous, but nobody in 1962 ever put whipped cream on coffee! I didn't know what to say.

Walking to his own desk, he stopped, made a quick little turn, came back and flashed a spoon from his pocket. Laid it on my desk. Right next to the coffee. The coffee with all that whipped cream. There was a jauntiness to his steps as he went on to his own desk. To his own boring job. He paused before sitting down. "Want to have lunch with me today?" And that's how it started. How he became my new dream. His name was Smitty.

We spent many evenings together. Not too many evenings. Not for too long either. My father was possessive and counted the hours I spent with "boyfriends." And angry if I crossed the line. A line never clearly defined, to keep me wondering, to keep me afraid. I was afraid.

And Smitty knew. I don't know how he knew, but he did. He made sure the time we had together was spent well. Spent talking about us, our hopes and dreams and hurts and heartbreaks. Not about other things like what to eat or where to go. He decided all that before meeting me at the elevator after work. On the nights we could be together.

I trusted him and began to talk to him about my dad touching me and kissing me. Ever since I was a very little girl. I told him my real dream, the one nobody understood.

"All I've ever wanted is to get married and have children. To be a mommy. When I was in kindergarten, the teacher wanted us to say what we wanted to be when we grew up. I said I wanted to be a mommy and she kept trying to get me to say what I wanted to do first. But that was what I wanted to do first. I couldn't pick something else. I just want to be a mother...the greatest thing in the world to be. That's my real dream."

He was the first person to not try to talk me out of it. The first person to love my dream. And so I loved him.

I loved this man who shared his own pain. The pain of losing his first wife while hiking in Canadian mountains. Seven months pregnant, she fell at the edge of a trail. Down the hill. It took hours to get her out. Both wife and child lost in one careless moment. Tears pouring down his cheeks as he told the story, gasping for breath with each sentence. Taking a long time to say it all. I cried.

And so it was, we two wounded people came together, sharing pain and dreams. Slowly touching hands, and faces, and arms, and bodies.

Knowing if I got pregnant, he would marry me and I would then be rescued from my Dad. Knowing I could rescue him from his own remorse and aloneness. And I knew my father wouldn't object to this marriage if I was pregnant, good Catholics that we were.

And that's how I came to get myself pregnant and marry him. My Smitty.

I should have known better, but I didn't. It took a long time to know that my Smitty was a liar. That he had dreams to chase that did not include me. I didn't want to know and it took a long time for me to want to know. And then a long time to accept after knowing.

~

We started life together then, in a nice apartment, with a baby on the way. My baby! "Now I am the boss of me, and I can forget everything else that happened before." I said this to myself every night before I went to bed…and reminded myself every morning while brushing my teeth.

As my belly swelled, as I put my hand on it and felt a child move, as I sat each day in my chair at the window overlooking a lake, I was really, really happy. *I'm going to be a mommy, now. My days are filled with love, and I will make life perfect for this tiny creature. All my dreams have come true!*

I bought baby clothes, folded them gently and put them in drawers, in the little dresser next to the bassinette. Every night I got them out again, spread them on the bed just to look at them and touch them. Each tiny undershirt, each soft nightgown, those tiny, tiny baby socks. Picturing my tiny baby, here, on this bed, in these clothes, my baby to hold and to love forever.

Each night Smitty watched me from the doorway, saying nothing.

~

In three months I knew, *my Smitty is a liar*. He made up stories about where he worked so I wouldn't know he had no real job. Stories so detailed I never suspected they weren't true. Like the one of the man working next to him on the assembly line, who's little boy was in the hospital, the boy who wouldn't make it. Every night in bed, each of us on our own pillow, he talked about that poor little boy, about the frantic dad. Smitty could barely talk through his tears, tears streaming down his face. I loved this man who could care so much about a co-worker he'd only known a few months. My Smitty!

Six months pregnant, I learned there was no job, no assembly line, and no boy in the hospital. Lies were simply a cover. Smitty and his friend Bob were making phone calls each evening, scamming businessmen into paying for ads in a non-existent lodge magazine. I didn't know.

With a second shift job, Smitty was always home by midnight. Until the night he didn't come home. At two am I was worried. By four am I was afraid. At six am I panicked and threw up in the bathroom sink. Having only the factory name and street, I wandered twelve blocks, up and down that street, looking for the factory, looking for him, worried that he was injured. If he was alive. Until someone told me, "There's no factory by that name, not on this street! Not on any street!"

Walking back to the apartment was the only thing I could do. I walked slowly. *He lied to me! It was all a lie!*

~

But yet, I was still worried about Smitty, where was he? Why didn't he come home last night? And then, if there was no factory, what about the frantic dad whose little boy was dying in a hospital bed? Did he exist? Was he made up, too, just to make me believe?

Finally back in the apartment, I could only lay on my bed, afraid to think, afraid to feel. Afraid to hope. I needed Smitty to come back to this apartment, lay beside me, hold me and explain everything. To make me happy again.

~

At noon I heard his key in the lock and my fear became anger and I lunged at him as he walked through the door. Only as he held me, stroked my hair, did I cry. Only then.

He began to tell me how sorry he was, about overtime, about the little boy in the hospital.

Pulling away from him, I screamed, "Stop! Stop!"

"I went there, to look for you. At that factory place. I was worried and scared. I went there and looked for you."

Crumbling at my feet, this husband of mine cried, sobbing,

barely able to get the words out. "I'm so, so sorry! I couldn't find a regular job, I tried, and then I was too ashamed to tell you. I wanted you to be proud of me and feel safe knowing I wasn't just working on commissions again. I want you to be proud of me, please! Please, please forgive me! I did it for you."

"I don't want to talk to you!" I shouted and marched into the bedroom, slammed the door behind me. I tried running my hand over the carefully folded baby clothes to comfort myself. Thinking, *this is sad, so sad. And I don't want to be sad. I'm having a baby. I want to be happy.*

And there he was, Smitty, once again in that white shirt, glistening black hair pushed back carefully again as though he'd just run his fingers through it. There he stood, placing one hand on my swollen belly, the other holding out to me a cup of coffee. Take-out coffee piled high with a mountain of whipped cream. That slightly crooked smile. Running his own hand over the baby clothes, the teddy bear. Reminding me, "I made up that story because I love you. I only did it for you, Babe!"

In that moment I knew I had to look at him. *So he lies a lot. But he loves me and our baby and that counts for something. He only lies to protect me. And he loves me. I know that part is true. I know that part's not a lie. This will be ok. As long as he's here, he works and pays the rent. There is always food in the refrigerator and the cupboards are full. He gives me money to buy baby things. This will be ok. I know it will. I'll be ok.*

That's how I decided to believe him. Because it was easier. I did not feel the trap here because in this trap I could feel safe and loved.

This was the first time I sold myself for groceries in the cupboard.

Chapter 2 – Baby Girl!

I had always loved hearing Smitty tell stories! He had such a flair for them. Yet now I wondered what was real and what was pretend. I couldn't tell the difference. *But then, do I really want to know? What if I don't like the answer?* I tried to believe it didn't matter, now that my Smitty was back, now that he was warm and attentive.

Yet I was sad for him. He seemed withdrawn, and I wondered if he was lost without the pretending, without grand stories to tell. Now that he was only selling legal ads again, tedious, boring work. But he did it. Not well enough though, to keep us in our top floor apartment with the nice, big window I loved. The window overlooking the lake. We moved, then, to the second floor, window only overlooking a parking lot. He was embarrassed; I was just glad he was still there, with me, as I was about to have a baby for the first time and I was scared.

But each day, as I caressed and refolded the baby clothes, I made myself think about the baby, only the baby, my baby to hold and love and care for. My only dream coming true. Happiness and trust crept into my heart again, pushing anger and suspicion into hiding places.

I chased away fear with a daydream. Me and Smitty, together, holding hands. Ready to cherish and nurture this new creature of ours. These things I shared with him.

"I know, I understand, Babe! I do, and I will be right by your side, right there with you, making a life for this baby. You are my family."

In some dark moments, when I doubted him, I made myself remember that first babe, born in the mountains. A child he never held or hugged. In those moments, I knew he would not miss those moments with me. He would be here to hug our child, to hold me during labor. And happiness would shove our pain away. *Happiness is greater and bigger than pain. Happiness is so big it makes hurt go away. If I think only these things, I will be glad again.*

~

He left two weeks before my due date. "An important business trip," he announced. "I'll be back in plenty of time! It's only for a few days! You understand. I'm doing this for us, for the baby, we can use the money!"

But I didn't understand! I cried and pled as he packed his suitcase. Even as I unpacked it, frantic and screaming, throwing his clothes back in their drawers.

"Stop this!" he yelled. "Stop! I'll be back in time, I promise. You're being ridiculous, not even due for two weeks. There's plenty of time! I'll be here. It's not a problem." He threw his clothes back into the open suitcase.

I didn't believe him and was afraid, very afraid.

Watching him walk out the door, down the hall, I finally found my calm voice. "Some women die in childbirth, you know. Don't forget about that!" Forming each word slowly, gravely, to achieve maximum impact, the greatest hurt, I wanted to call up his most painful memories. *I guess he didn't hear me because he keeps walking.* Without turning, he called over his shoulder, "See you in two days." *I guess I'm right, he didn't hear me!*

Standing in the door of our apartment, I watched him walk away, down the hall, into the elevator. I waited there, by the door, knowing he would change his mind and come back, back to me. But he didn't. I waited an hour before I closed the door to our apartment.

I don't know how to do this, how to trust him now. Believe in him. And then it came to me. *I will pretend that I do. He's not the only one who can pretend! I will pretend till it's real.*

~

The next day I gave birth to a beautiful baby girl. Six pounds twelve ounces. I cried as I held her in my arms, snuggling her head beneath my chin. Taking in her wonderful baby smell. Wondering if Smitty would come back.

What will I do if he doesn't? Will I have to get a job? Will I have to find a baby sitter? What will I do? Snuggling my tiny daughter close to my chest, wondering how to protect her, how to keep her safe, I closed my eyes, and cried.

And then, there he was, brushing away my tears. I opened my eyes to see him. My Smitty! He was there! He was really there! *See*, I said to myself, not to him, just to my own self. *I pretended everything would be ok, and it is. He's come back, and he's here, holding our baby girl. Maybe pretending made this good thing happen.*

When the birth certificate lady came in, he was quick to say he wanted to pick the name. Having never discussed names, I was surprised.

"It will be Lucy!" he said.

A fleeting thought, as tiny as a speck of dust, crossed my mind. *Lucy! Why Lucy? Where did that come from?* But I didn't ask.

But I should have paid attention because it was a critical moment that I would later never be able to forgive.

I knew now that because he had lied, because he left me alone to give birth, I would need to remind myself often that he really loved us! But on this day, I didn't care. I had a beautiful baby girl and Smitty was here.

~

I was soon pregnant with our second baby, and busy mothering and homemaking. Too busy to notice they were doing it again, Smitty and Bob. They were selling ads in trade magazines, Again, there was no magazine, only another imaginary one. This time, however, complaints were made to the police. "We paid for those ads every month! Where's the magazine?" Avoiding arrest, they vacated their cheap office.

No income now, trying to keep a low-profile, we left our second floor apartment. Moved to the one room efficiency in the basement. No windows there, no windows to let in a fresh breeze every day. No windows. Only stuffy, hot, moldy air.

He didn't pay the rent there either, and I hid from the landlady and washed clothes in the bathtub.

Yet there was still a story he could tell. "It's not my fault, Babe. I sold all those ads for a new magazine Bob was opening. I believed in him. How was I supposed to know it was a fake! I did it in good faith! No one can blame me, it's not my fault! I was just trying to earn money for us, for you and Lucy, and this new baby. I only did it for you."

Climbing the basement stairs every day, I walked to the park, carrying my baby daughter, wishing I had a stroller. Needing to get away from that basement. I returned home in the afternoon, fixed spaghetti for supper, smiled. This I could do. It was all I knew how to do in that moment.

~

A week later, we heard the news, standing in the corner deli one day. Bob was arrested! I could taste fear in my throat. *Would the police be at our door next? Did they have Smitty's name?* We didn't know. He was frantic, ready to run away. I could tell.

And so this time, this one time, I found my strong voice and announced, "You are not leaving without me. Not this time."

Recalling my grandmother's note at the bottom of every Christmas card, her scribbled words, "Anybody want to come back to the Midwest again, I'll pay your way." Remembering that, I called her and rescued us. "We'll run away together," I told my Smitty. "This will be a new start for us, two thousand miles away." I believed it myself.

I pondered all these things in my heart as, day after day, the train made its way across the country, from West Coast to Midwest, and I was hopeful.

Chapter 3 – Indiana, 1963

And so it was, a true fresh start. In this new city he got a real job at a local hospital. I knew because I saw the real paychecks. Every week he gave them to me. And trust began to grow in my heart. Just a little. Like a seed that grows into a baby plant, soft and vulnerable, but there just the same. Fragile.

The little plant of trust grew as he came home from work each day, as he hugged and kissed each of us. As he sat on the back steps with the children, new infant Matthew on his lap, watching our Lucy pick bright yellow dandelion blooms while I cooked supper. I watched him settle in, be content. This summer I was happy. A sweet little girl, a new baby boy, a spacious, two bedroom apartment with lots of windows. And a husband who loved me.

After supper, when the babies were asleep, we sat on the front porch steps, shared a beer, watched traffic up and down Main Street. Tried to guess what the semis were carrying and where they were going. I didn't know it was dangerous to play this game with a man who was nurturing his own dreams! Dreams of taking off to explore new places. New challenges.

I busied myself making a home for us, hanging laundry to dry on the line in the little side yard. Proud to display my diapers, scrubbed to make white as new. Lines of long, blazingly white diapers blowing in the breeze, my cute, curly-haired Lucy in her pink sun suit climbing in and out of the clothes basket. My baby Matthew sleeping in the buggy. I loved this life!

Soon pregnant with my third child, I would give birth the same month my first was two years old! People were shocked. Three babies under two! But I was delighted!

~

Until Smitty brought home a huge roll-top desk. Placed it in the corner of our bedroom and spent hours there every evening. Instead of sitting on the porch steps with me. I didn't pay attention to what he was doing, hunched over that desk, studying all those papers. I didn't pay attention because I didn't want to know. I was busy protecting the now withering trust struggling to stay alive in my own fragile heart.

"Hey, babe," he called out one night, "Bring me another cup Java." His word for coffee. Lingering over his shoulder, on that night, I noticed the maps he was studying. Lots of them!

I pretended I didn't see because I wanted to believe he was still as happy and contented as I was, here in this apartment on Main Street. With me. With our babies.

It's ok, he can look at maps, anybody can look at maps, it doesn't mean a thing. I said this to myself every evening as I carried his mug of coffee down the hall, repeating it to make it real. Repeating it to push away fear.

But more maps arrived in the mail, maps I couldn't ignore.

And then he said it, the words I had been dreading. "Look here, Babe, on this map, there's a lost gold mine in the mountains outside of Vancouver, Canada. And I know where it is Babe! I've been studying this a long time. It's worth millions! It will do so much for us if I can get to it. And I've lived there before, remember? I know those mountains like the back of my hand!"

His excitement filled the room! His face animated, eyes lit up, his words electric. This was a part of him that I loved, his enthusiasm for life, for adventure.

But hearing these words now, the words he said, I was only

angry. *Why did he have to say this, why did he have to made it real! He's leaving, leaving again while I am pregnant! It's true! It's true and I can't stop it!* I walked away from him, out of the bedroom, out to the porch to sit by myself. Sitting on the top step, I said these words out loud for my own self to hear, to be sure I knew, *I am not the boss of even my own life.*

~

I began to dread getting the mail every day; it brought more maps and charts and land surveys. Piles on his desk, spilling over onto the floor beside his chair.

"I will give you everything, Babe," he promised every night as we lay in bed, tension between us like a scratchy old blanket. "A house of our own, a yard. Pets for the kids, even. A swing set!" I stopped listening. I didn't want everything. I only wanted him here, in our home, with our babies. I tried very hard to ignore the ache growing in my heart.

Thinking of these things, I grasped for hope, for a reason to believe, or a reason to pretend. *He can't go off searching the mountains for gold without a backer*, I thought. *He needs money. These things take equipment. And what about living expenses? How will he live? How will I live?*

And so I decided there was no danger after all. Planning can be a little like pretending, like playing with a dream. *Maybe he's really just a little boy with a few toys, pretending he's going on an adventure. Don't take his dream away,* I told myself. *After all, it's only a dream!*

Except on the days I remembered the charmer he was, that he could talk people into anything. If he found a backer, someone willing to invest, someone willing to believe his dream, he'd be gone. On those days I was most afraid.

On most days I did not think about this. I brought coffee to him as he worked at his desk each night. Some nights I even brought coffee piled high with whipped cream. Hoping to pull him back into our dream. Maybe.

~

In three weeks he found an investor. Now maps, geological data and charts began to cover every surface of our home. Equipment lists on the coffee table, gear and supply catalogues on the kitchen table. His dream was coming true and he was so excited! I was not.

"Listen, listen to me," his urgent words tumbling into my lap, proud of the deal he had negotiated, a deal that included a weekly check for me. "See," he said, "I'm not really leaving you. You'll be taken care of and I'll come back a rich, famous man."

"But I'm having a baby, alone, again," I was angry and argued. I cried and pouted. He promised to be back before the baby was born. I didn't believe him. Not this time. I didn't believe him.

Sitting in the rocker on the porch, alone each evening, I wanted to be peaceful. The scratchy blanket of discontent that lay between us in our bed at night now followed me each day, a cape that hung across my shoulders. It was heavy, and ugly, and I wanted to discard it.

And so I found I could be good at talking myself into things. He wanted me to be proud of him, believe in him. I could do that. I put away the words, "I am the boss of me" and replaced them with, "What do you want me to be? I will be that." And so I became very good at pretending to be what someone else needed me to be.

~

Until he left and I was alone in the big apartment with two children, under two, There was no reason now to pretend I believed in the long, lost gold mine!

Each day had too many hours, turning into weeks and months of isolation. No car. Winter months made taking a walk impossible. I was lonely beyond belief.

But I Can Learn

Then I discovered the connecting door in my bedroom closet. Where a retired couple lived on the other side. Nice friendly people. I wished they would invite me over. I wished anybody would invite me over. Or visit me.

No one did, so I began leaving the connecting door unlocked on my side. I put toys on the floor so Lucy would play there. I showed her how to knock on their door.

When retired man or retired lady opened their side of the door, my bold little girl walked right in. Of course she did, she was almost two. And so adorable, with her curly hair and eagerness to talk! They couldn't resist chatting with her. I followed, of course, pretending to be dismayed that she'd "bothered them".

"I'm so sorry, let me get her." Pretending to be embarrassed, I fidgeted, taking time to get us all back to our side of the door, taking time to let Matthew crawl after us. I hoped they'd say, "Oh, it's no problem, They're so cute. Please stay for supper, we'd love to have you." And they never did. They were nice, friendly people, but they never asked us to stay.

Eventually I "let" Lucy do it several times a day. I knew I was using an innocent two-year old to get myself a few moments of neighborly contact, hoping there would be more. I felt selfish and was embarrassed to do it, embarrassed in front of own myself. It gained me nothing, but still, again tomorrow, I would choose embarrassed over lonely. Over crushing loneliness, over loneliness that I didn't know how to pretend away.

~

Smitty called once a week. He was renting a room from a family living close to "his mountain." He was happy there. I could tell by his voice, the eagerness as he talked about the progress he was making, finding his gold mine, getting closer to his dream. I talked about the children, to pull him back to us, to make him be "My Smitty" again. But he wouldn't stop talking about the gold mine. I always hung up feeling angry. And lonelier than before he called. I started to wish he wouldn't call. Disappointment can be even harder to bear than loneliness.

~

Weeks later, my hands began to shake as I opened the mail, because the return address was a motel in Seattle, Washington. Ripping the envelope open, I was left holding a bill for "Mr. and Mrs." This was now something I couldn't pretend away, not a hotel bill that clearly did not include me! I phoned Smitty. I didn't plan ahead what to say because my heart was beating too fast and I was too angry. Too angry to be afraid right then.

A young-girl voice answered the phone, the daughter of the family he rented the room from. She passed the phone to Smitty.

"I can't talk now," he whispered.

Letting my anger show, I shouted, "If you don't call me in thirty minutes from a place you can talk, I'll call back and tell those people you live with that you're a married man." Ten minutes later, my phone rang!

He denied the bill was his. He denied having an affair. I didn't listen, I didn't plead or cry. I didn't shout. In a simple, firm voice, a voice I didn't know I had, I gave my second ultimatum. "Come home now or I will tell your investor what you are really doing with his money." He agreed. "Don't be upset. I can explain everything." He began to cry. I hung up.

~

Five days I waited. Eight months pregnant now, large with child, large with children, I kept busy. Anger had replaced loneliness.

From this day on I was never the same. It was the first time I could not pretend myself into believing and hoping.

I could only sit and wait for Smitty to come home.

Chapter 4 – A Surprise Visitor

Until my doorbell rang early one afternoon. There on the top step was a young woman I did not know, asking if I was Mrs. Byron. "No, I'm sorry, you must have the wrong address," I told her as I moved to shut the door.

Stepping back, she checked the house number, and I watched her study the photo she held in her hand. She seemed confused, lost, finally saying, "Well, then, do Lucy and Matthew live here?"

My heart stopped and I struggled to breathe. She'd just asked to see my children! My children! I grabbed the picture she held. Too stunned to speak, I could only stare at it, trying to get my brain to work! It was a picture of my children, my children with Smitty, on our front porch. My own children! Finally recovering, I said, "Oh… I think you'd better come in".

She was eager to talk, this young girl, sitting on my couch, hands folded in her lap. I was eager to listen as her story unfolded.

"My parents have a big house, we're on the road up into the mountains, you see, and we rent rooms to travelers. When this man, Smitty, moved in, I liked him right from the start! He was so sad, and had such a sad, sad story."

Of course he did. He's a Master Storyteller who never passes up an audience. I did not say it to her, only to myself.

"Tell me the story," I said instead. We moved to my kitchen table, hugged our steamy cups of coffee. I was glad the children were taking a long nap.

"See, he had a wife, 'cause he was married once. They had these two beautiful children," she began, touching the photo she'd held, standing on my porch earlier.

"But she, the wife, was a dreadful drug addict! Still is, really. So he had to divorce her and take custody of the babies in order to protect them from her. In case she'd hurt them, you see. But you know all that part, Mrs. Byron. That's why he hired you. To care for them."

She stopped to wipe her eyes and blow her nose.

I sat up straighter, at full attention now, shocked. *Did she just call me Mrs. Byron? Does she think I'm only here to "watch the children! That I'm only a hired housekeeper!"*

Taking a sip of coffee, she continued. "It's so hard for him, taking care of two babies all alone."

"He hates being away, but if he can just find this gold mine he can do better for them. They don't even have a real mother. Every time he talks about them, he cries, he misses them so much! When he finds this mine, he'll be rich and won't have to work, and he'll be home and take care of them himself. "

Watching her face, I could see she believed him, and loved him. As this sweet young girl sat at my table, she continued. Telling me how they fell in love and got married.

Wait! Married! He married her!

"I'm going to be mommy to these poor abandoned babies," she said. Laying a hand on mine, she added in a comforting voice, "Mrs. Byron, I'm sorry, but I'm sure you won't be needed, now that I'm here to be their mother."

Appalled, I excused myself, went to the bathroom and threw up in the toilet. How could this be! Fear gripped my stomach and I threw up again. Looking at myself in the mirror, I knew I had to splash cold water on my face and be brave. Not afraid. Protect my children.

Returning to the table, I encouraged her to continue. I wanted all of the story! How had this moved from the hotel bill, my phone call to Smitty, and now they're here to take my babies away from me?

~

Once married, she started pushing him to come for the children and insisting they rent a car and start the four day trip. He argued, but there was no story he could tell that would overcome her eagerness to be their mommy. He rented the car.

As they drove, *she* sang nursery rhymes, hugged imaginary children, and bought teddy bears at every stop.

As they drove, *he* talked about the work he was missing in Canada, about his need to get back there. Urging her to forget this until he was settled, when he had made his fortune. It would be better for the children then.

Sure, because he knew the end of the trip would be a disaster when she met me! I didn't say it, I only reached across the table to touch her hand, to encourage her to continue.

"He wanted to wait to come here, but I just couldn't, Mrs. Byron! I was too excited to wait! I wanted to see the children!'

He couldn't change her mind, and so they trekked across the country and finally checked into a motel here, in my city.

"After he carried the suitcases into the room, and set them on the bed, he walked out. He just said, 'I need some air, I'm going for a drive.'

Yes, he's trapped now, wondering what his next move can be. I didn't say that either. Only to myself I said it in my sarcastic voice.

She drank the rest of her coffee, set the mug down, and stared at me, eager to tell the rest of the story. Me eager to hear. I gripped my coffee mug tighter so she couldn't see my hands shaking.

"What was I supposed to do then? Just sit on the bed? When he didn't come back after a few hours, I got worried. What if something had happened to him? I know I shouldn't have, it's not right to snoop through people's stuff, but I searched his suitcase. That's when I found this photo of the children sitting on the porch. See here, on the back is this address! So I called a taxi and came here! Oh, and I brought a teddy bear for each of the children! Do you think they'll like them?" She drew several beautiful and soft bears from the large bag sitting at her feet.

And that's how she came to be standing on my front porch, asking if I was Mrs. Byron, that "pregnant housekeeper".

Then, I could be silent no longer and I told her the truth. The blunt truth.

"There is no pregnant Mrs. Byron. There is no drug addict ex-wife. I am the wife, the mother of Lucy and Matthew. I have been married to Smitty for several years. I have never used drugs and these are our children together. These are my children."

Waiting for her response, waiting for her words, I only saw her staring at me. Then not staring at me, staring past me. She was staring at Smitty, standing at the kitchen door!

She did not look at me, and she did not say a word. She walked out onto the porch with him, "Go back to the motel! I don't want to see you!" I could hear her words because she spoke angrily, yelling. He spoke quietly and I did not hear his.

Minutes later she came back into my kitchen, closed the screen door, closed the big door, turned the lock. and came back to the table with me. "Can I spend the night here, would you mind? I don't know where else to go."

"Of course I don't mind, I'm sorry this is happening to you." It was the truth, not a pretend part. I really was sorry for her. I waited for her to cry, to be angry, or to yell, but she didn't. She was only quiet. Strangely calm and quiet.

I watched this young Catholic girl, so in love, so hopeful for the future, so ready to mother someone else's children. I listened as she called her father, he would send her a plane ticket home.

Smitty stole her innocence, yet still I envied her. That she had innocence to steal, that she had a dad to rescue her. I had Smitty and a dad who stole my innocence when I was a toddler. There was no one to rescue me, ever. So I did envy her.

Afternoon wore into evening. She played with the children. Held them close as she read the story to them at bedtime. Giving the teddy bears she had so lovingly bought. Passing time until her plane in the morning. I could only smile, hand her an extra nightie and toothbrush. This sad girl. She didn't talk much after that, there was nothing left to say. My heart ached for her.

~

Smitty came the next day, after she left.

"I miss you and the children so much. I'm so, so sorry. This whole thing was a mistake, I never should have gone. I should have never left you here alone. Please, please forgive me! I have missed you so much!"

I listened once again to those gut-wrenching sobs that shook his whole body. As he knelt before me, head in my lap, holding my hands, I saw the sweat on his neck, on his temples. I listened to him promising he would never leave again. I wanted to reach out, stroke his hair, comfort him, but I made myself not do it.

I couldn't answer. Not this time. I stared at him, making myself be cold and strong.

If I decide to believe him, to let him stay here with us, maybe he will get a job again, pay the rent and buy groceries. He would be with me when I have this baby. I won't be alone. It might be ok for a while. Maybe it will be ok.

I did not get a chance to decide because the doorbell rang and two detectives were there, on my porch, then in my house.

They arrested him for a stolen car, because the rental was only for two days and hadn't been returned a week later. And for bad checks he'd written on their trip across the country.

"How long will he be in jail," I asked, worried about myself, about my babies. Not about him.

Clair

"It'll be at least ninety days, mam." I watched them put him in the car and drive away.

"There will be only a few more checks for me from the investor." I said the words out loud, for myself, to be sure I heard. "I am alone again, soon to go into labor, soon to have three babies. I have to buy groceries and pay rent, and I have no idea how to do this. No idea!"

So I just sat on the porch steps and watched the trucks go by. I didn't know what else to do.

Chapter 5 – Everything Is Wrong

Indeed the day did come when Smitty's Mr. Investor Person sat on my couch, briefcase at his feet. Shoulders slouched, fists clenched. He looked defeated and I felt sorry for him. But more scared for me.

"I know this isn't your fault," he began. "And I feel sorry for you, really I do. But I can't keep sending you a check every month, you understand! I've lost a lot of money here, really a lot of money on Smitty! I can do, maybe two more, that'll give you some time after your baby's born. I'm sorry, but I'm not to blame here. This isn't my fault and I can't be responsible for this." Knowing he was being generous to me, I was grateful and tried to show that.

"Can I get you a cup of coffee, glass of ice tea? I just made some, it's really cold. I could get you a glass of that!" I threw words out into the room, random words, hoping to dispel the awkwardness between us.

"No, I have other appointments, I have to get going right away now." I knew he just wanted to be away from me.

Grabbing his jacket, his briefcase, he left. No use trying to act normal when doom stood in the room for both of us. His business now almost bankrupt, I knew he could not care about the poverty waiting on my doorstep, only the bankruptcy on his.

~

Thrilled when spring came early, I took my children for long, slow walks around the block. To watch trees bud, birds sing, to feel a fresh breeze on my skin. To get out of the apartment, to walk to the grocery, to try to forget the questions hanging over me.

Each movement of my soon-to-be-born baby reminded me this peace would not last. Avoiding the landlady, washing clothes in the bathtub again, saving quarters by not using the washing machine in the basement, doing these things, I tucked money away.

Knowing I could do those things only for the next month, maybe. Eventually I would have to face the truth. I would have to stop pretending I was still a woman whose husband was only away on a business trip.

I would have to stop pretending I wasn't terrified.

∼

But I found friends, on those walks around the block. A nice couple with a little girl about the same age as my Lucy, living in the house in back of us. Sharing a driveway, it was easy to visit with them, to let our little girls play together.

When I was out with my children, she joined me with her daughter, walking over to me on her own. I hadn't tried to make it happen this time and I was delighted to maybe have a friend! Her name was Jenni, married to Brad, and she talked and chatted with me like mom's do. "So, what are you fixing for supper tonight"? "I'm just fixing spaghetti, what about you"? "Oh, how do you get your diapers so white?" Just two moms, talking, normal. I cherished these moments. Moments when I could still pretend everything was all right.

Coming home from work every night, Brad played with the children on the lawn. Being with this family, liked by them, fed my lonely soul and I relaxed. A little. I didn't tell them my husband was in jail, I told the lie that he was away on business. But as we sat on their porch every evening, sipping coffee, I couldn't chase away the guilt, knowing I was a fraud, leading them to believe a lie. Just as Smitty had led me to believe his stories.

Am I doing the same thing? I asked myself. *Have I become Smitty? Am I now also a Master Storyteller, able to weave words and sentences into a lie in a way that others easily, happily believe?* Awkwardness began to replace joy and every evening guilt ate away parts of my soul.

In the afternoons, I swore I would tell the truth. *Tonight! I'll tell them tonight. It won't matter, because they really like me, but I have to tell the truth.* Yet each evening, as I sat in their porch rocker, safe there, trying to begin, I couldn't do it. I was afraid and embarrassed.

Until one evening, unable stand it a moment longer, I just blurted it out, "I'm such a liar! My husband isn't away on business...he's in jail because he stole a car and wrote bad checks! And he married another girl, not me, another girl." Shock written on their faces, they stared at me, eyes locking onto mine, only waiting. "I have no income now and no idea what I will do or where I will go, after this baby is born."

Silence. There was still only silence as I sat, waiting. Waiting for them to say something, waiting for the words I'd thrown at them to have meaning. Waiting for them to tell me to leave. To no longer be friends, watching them stare at each other until finally they spoke.

"Oh, my gosh! How awful! That's terrible! We're so sorry! What are you going to do? Is he coming back? How long will he be in jail? What are you going to do?" Flooding me with questions, the same questions I asked myself every day yet had no answer to.

So grateful they didn't say, "Why did you lie to us?" I finally let tears flow and launched into the story of Smitty and me. The whole story. Of pain and deceit, of lying and forgiving, and hopes destroyed. Relieved to tell it all.

But not about why I married him, not about that. I couldn't tell about that. I didn't know the words. I couldn't tell them about that part, the part about my dad.

Their voices were sympathetic. "Oh, you won't be alone. We'll help and do whatever it takes, whatever you need. We're here to help."

~

And so it was, when my labor started, it was Brad who took me to the hospital, Brad who sat with me. "Today," I thought. "I have good people in my life and I will be ok."

The next day my second son was born. I named him Michael, and again Smitty was not there. Yet I held a precious babe to my chest, tucked his soft head under my chin and smelled the preciousness of him.

~

As we sat on their porch again, every evening after supper, in the rockers, we took turns holding, and cuddling Michael. We held him close, as we sat on that porch, drinking coffee, watching the other children play on the driveway. Talking about the future. My future was a bomb waiting to explode, and I didn't want to talk about it. They thought it was a problem they could solve by exchanging ideas, looking for answers, talking to each other. Having no ideas of my own, I listened to theirs. Every night, silently listening to these good people try to solve my future. I grew tired of hearing them talk.

Finally, frustrated, I had to say it. "We can't think of anything that will keep me home with my children. Or that will even give me a job paying enough to pay rent, groceries, and a babysitter. There is no answer to this!"

"No, you're wrong. Don't give up hope. We'll find something. I can ask at my work, if there's something there" That was Brad's idea. "I can watch your children while you work." That was Jenni's.

At night, alone in my own apartment, I lay in bed, staring at the ceiling. Every night, going over everything.

What are they thinking! I probably can only type thirty words a minute now, being so out of practice. Eighty words are gone forever! He won't find me a job in his office! What if I can only type twenty words per minute? What then?

And Jenni? Watch my three babies every day, all day! They are a lot of work and she'll get tired of it. She'll get tired of not having enough time for her own little girl, for herself, for Brad. I know she means well, but I also know it won't work for long. I believed they meant what they were saying. I also believed they wouldn't mean it a few months from now.

∼

And so it was that six little words crept into my thinking, and into our conversations on the porch at night. Six little words to change my life. "When Smitty gets out of jail."

"You're not thinking of taking him back, are you?" Brad asked, his voice angry. Jenni folded her arms across her chest, crossed her legs, leaned back in her chair, her whole body alive with indignation. "After all he's done to you!" was all she could manage to say. And, "It won't last, you know, he'll just take off again and leave you pregnant. Don't you dare take him back!" they threatened. "Don't you dare!"

To myself, I knew I might take him back. I wouldn't have to move, or get a job and leave my children. I could be a wife and mommy, even if it was only for a few months. Maybe a year. I didn't want to leave my babies with someone else every day! That wasn't the dream. It wasn't!

As that truth seeped into our conversations, long moments of silence replaced our friendly chatter on their porch each evening. Jennie stopped walking into my kitchen after lunch. Soon their car pulled out of the driveway after supper, returned late. So they wouldn't have to tell me to stop coming over. Slowly drifting apart, I didn't make them say why. I was embarrassed and so I just let it happen.

I knew they didn't want to rescue a girl who kept herself in danger. A stupid girl who let the same thing happen again and again. They didn't want that.

I didn't tell them I understood. I didn't tell them anything. I only smiled, waved when I saw them across the driveway, kept my own children in my yard and kept us to our own apartment. I let them drift away because I couldn't bear to hear their words, afraid they would remind me I was just a "stupid girl."

I put Lucy and Matthew to bed each night. Made oatmeal in the morning, played with them each day, fixed their lunches. Washed their hands and faces, read the usual stories, kissed and hugged them. Savoring their sweet smell as I tucked them in each night. I thought it would make me feel better, but it didn't. I was only a robot, doing those right things. Just doing them.

Gathering up my new baby boy, a little dark-haired fellow, swaddled in a light blanket, I sat on my own front porch each evening. My front porch that faced Main Street, and I watched the semis for a while. The porch that faced away from my neighbors, my friends.

No, not my friends anymore, I thought. *Not now. Now I am alone again.* I wanted to cry, but I couldn't. This was familiar. Here alone, holding a baby, this I was used to. Looking at his little face, peaceful and sweet. Holding him close to my chest, my cheek, my mouth resting against his soft baby hair, I wondered what kind of world I had brought him home to.

∼

Mr. Investor Person came again, looking worried, bringing the last check he would give to me. I put on my own saddest face, wore my oldest clothes, allowed tears to gather in the corners of my eyes, and hoped. Hoped he would say, "I can't just leave you like this! I guess I could continue supporting you until Smitty gets out of jail." I wanted to make him to feel guilty.

He has lots of money and can afford to help me. I know he lost a lot of money on Smitty, but that's not my fault! It's his own fault he didn't know it was a scam! If he's so smart, he should have known! So now he should take care of me!

I tried very hard not to be angry because I knew my anger would not make him decide to keep supporting me. But maybe tears, my sad face, old clothes would. They didn't. Handing me that one last check, he left without saying a word, without looking at my sad eyes.

~

Each day now there was only loneliness, again painful loneliness as I waded through each hour, talking to no one, only children. Waiting for the hours to pass, for days to be over.

Until I was willing to be friends with anyone, anyone willing to be friends with me. That person became the seventeen year old boy across the street. He'd come occasionally to babysit while I went to the grocery. A sweet boy, lonely himself, sad, confused. His mom was dying of cancer. He was the oldest of seven, taking care of the younger children. Almost a man, but still a boy, he was.

He lingered one evening, staying to visit, to watch as I put groceries away, to help with the children's baths and bedtime stories. I made coffee and we sat on the couch, talking about our lives.

He cried a little, sharing the pain, knowing he was losing his mom. I held his hand, touched his cheek, as his eyes searched my face. I knew he would kiss me, this boy. *Why should I push him away? This eager, kind, frustrated, lonely boy who likes me? Who needs the comfort I can give him?* And I liked his hand on my face, on my shoulder, the hand, of a man, not of a child. I didn't know how to say no to sex, or no to anything that would give me a few moments of un-loneliness. I should have known. I should have learned!

Because it felt wrong. I knew it was wrong. When he was there I didn't care.

When he left I felt too guilty to think about it. But a little voice in my heart kept telling me I was being a very bad person.

Chapter 6 – The Welfare Office

Surprised to find an envelope in my mailbox one morning, I carried it to the living room so I could read it while watching the children play. Settling back on a chair, I carefully tore it open to find the treasure inside. Somebody sent me a letter!

Carefully unfolding the paper, I found only an eviction notice in my hand. In thirty days I had to move! Pitifulness had not worked on Mr. Investor Person. It had not worked on the landlady. "I have to do something, but I don't know what!" Saying this out loud made it real. I could not wait for a rescuer. No one was coming to rescue me! No one knew I was here, I was invisible to the world!

~

In the morning, I scoured the ads in the newspaper, circling everything close by, then packed my three children in the wagon and went to look for cheaper places to live. And to other places to look for jobs. *Surely someone will take pity and help me*! Give me a place to stay or give me a job!

But my children could not sit quietly during interviews. They had to touch everything, talk non-stop, and chase each other around! As the adults shifted their eyes from me to the rowdy children, back and forth, me to them, I could tell they didn't see the pitiful me. They saw only a ragged woman busy corralling her children. They couldn't interview me, not for a job and not for an apartment. I felt stupid standing there. The next day, I asked the boy across the street to watch them again.

~

Getting off the bus at the Welfare Office the next day, I stared at the door. I didn't want to go in. I didn't want to be on welfare, and was ashamed to be there. I had not one idea how to put life together, but I did know this was the place to come, the place to start when a person needed help. And I needed help.

Waiting two hours before my name was called, looking around the shabby, dirty waiting room, I became embarrassed that my blue sweater was not as raggedy as the ones the other women wore, the other waiting women. *I should not have ironed my skirt, my blouse, or polished my shoes.* I looked around the room and knew that I stood out, didn't fit here, didn't look desperate enough. Finally somebody called my name, and it was my turn to be helped.

Coming here I hoped to find the sympathy I needed, yet as I looked at the woman across the desk, the woman who didn't look at me, I feared she might have none to give. She took my information, hurrying through each question without looking up, pages and pages of questions. Answers she wrote with her shiny pen, filling the blank lines, eyes never leaving the paper, eyes not seeing me. Invisible again.

"Okay, you are entitled to $235 a month," she announced, finally looking at me, at my face. "That's the allowance for "single mother, three children." Leaning forward, grasping the arms of my chair, I feared I would faint!

"I can't even rent an apartment for that!" I cried. "What can I do?" Determined to not cry in front of her. "How will I feed them? How will I pay a babysitter?" I was standing now, almost shouting the words at her!

"I'm sorry" was all she could say, and then I knew. "She listens to this a hundred times a day. This is old stuff to her. There's no sympathy, and now I know, no help here either."

Swallowing my fear, I forced myself to listen to her words, telling me to sit down, to concentrate on what she was saying to me.

"You could, you know, place the children in foster care until you sort things out," she continued in a flat voice. My anger turned to fear! "Foster care?" I whispered! I couldn't look at her, only at my hands in my lap, my fingers twisting into odd, hurtful shapes. "No, no! I will never do that! I'll find another way. I can't send my babies to foster care!" I said these words out loud as I left her office, running out of the building. Trying to run away from the nightmare.

Walking up and down the street, waiting for the bus, I forced myself to focus. *Okay now, I have to have an apartment close to my job or a bus line. If I do find a job, how do I know I can find a cheap apartment close by? And how can I hire a babysitter until I have a job, and how can I get a job until I know I will have a babysitter? Where should I start, what do I do first?* Over and over the questions repeated in my mind as the bus took me closer to home and three children and the boy-babysitter wondering what good news I would have.

Eviction looming over me, with no income, no job, no prospects, I was overwhelmed and I did the first thing I could think of. Call my relatives.

I called my grandmother and I called several aunts and uncles. "Well, I guess we could take one, not all three, but maybe one, just for a while, we could watch one for a few days." So my three babies were parceled out to three different homes. Separated from each other. Separated from me. The pain sat in my heart, in my throat, unbearable. *But at least it isn't foster care. At least it isn't that!* I waited for those words to comfort me. They didn't. Nothing did. Without my children beside me, nothing would.

~

The next day, I found a one room apartment on East Wayne Street, and a job as a waitress in a diner, a diner I could walk to, and I was relieved.

Maybe I can do this, maybe we will be all right! Without the children here, I can work two shifts. A double paycheck and all those tips! I didn't let myself think about the future, that this happiness, the double shifts, the tiny apartment, this could only work as long as I was alone. As long as I didn't need a babysitter, or a bigger apartment. I didn't want to think about that, though. I wanted to feel hopeful just for one moment.

Calling every day to check on my children, as I heard my relatives complain, the one moment of hope drifted away.

Don't cry now, don't think now! Just go to work! Sometimes I said this out loud to be sure I heard. *Don't think. Just go to work!*

It was a bad thing for me and for my children, but a good thing for the boy across the street. It was good for him to be away from me.

Chapter 7 – The Man On The Porch

The first night in my new apartment, I woke as usual, in the middle of the night to go to the bathroom. Reaching for the bedside lamp, turning it on, I saw the floor and walls covered with bugs, a million brown bugs that ran to hide from the light.

I didn't know what they were! Bigger than ants, bigger than flies, I'd never seen anything like them! I huddled on the bed, curling my bare feet under me, waiting for them to disappear into wherever they could hide. Before I could walk across the floor to the bathroom. I wished I had brought my shoes into bed with me. Slowly walking across the floor, avoiding the bugs that hadn't run off, I finally made it to the bathroom. Brushed a few off the toilet seat!

The next day I asked the lady living in the basement apartment. "Oh, they're just cockroaches," she told me. "But that's nothing! I take my baby to sleep in bed with me so the rats don't chew on his toes," she added, as though she was simply telling me what she had for breakfast. I was disgusted! She was not. I went back to my room.

When I reached in the drawer for a spoon, the roaches were there. When I opened the fridge, they were there also because the door seal was missing in places. When I took a bath, they filtered in and out of the overflow drain and explored the edges of the tub. Over the next few days, I learned to shake out my shoes and clothes before putting them on to be sure nobody was there. I learned to sleep with a light on. I learned to not take out the trash at night so that I would have less chance of seeing the rats lurking there, as big as cats. Sometimes the rats were there in the daytime too, but at night their beady eyes shined in the dark in a scary way and they were more likely to bare their teeth at me.

It's a good thing my babies are not here. I wished I wasn't there. This was the first time in my life I was glad to be alone.

~

Dark, puffy bags came to rest under each of my eyes. My hair was limp. I didn't care. I was too exhausted to care. The diner wasn't as close as I thought. A thirty minute walk, not ten minutes. Five hour shifts at work, five on-five off, round the clock. Serving coffee, and pie, and hamburgers to truckers. Or eggs and toast and sausage. More coffee. Rushing to fill each empty cup before that driver had to pull his semi out of the parking lot. Emptying ashtrays with leftover Old Gold and Marlboro cigarette stubs. Smile. Always be sure to smile.

Hurrying home to scrub the greasy food smell from my skin, the cigarette smoke from my hair, I watched the roaches on their own ventures, their own challenge to navigate their lives without falling into my bathwater. Every day I panicked. *I have to be back at the diner in a few hours.* Only a few hours until the next shift. Grabbing a few hours sleep seemed impossible. Until it wasn't. Until I was too exhausted to not sleep. On those day and nights I fell asleep sprawled across the bed in my uniform. Shoes still on. Back to work in five hours.

~

It was those truck drivers who taught me how to keep an impossible schedule and stay alert and cheerful. Little blue pills to stay awake, and little red ones to sleep quickly. I hoped these busy hours would give me the best tips. I wanted the money, wanted it badly.

I have to get out of here! And I want my children back! I recited it to myself over and over. Putting a jar on the cupboard for extra dollar tips gave me hope. I could watch it fill, money to save for getting my kids back. But only quarters went in, every night. Only a rare, occasional dollar. It was a small diner, after all, on a side street, frequented by working men and truckers, men with few dollars to spare. I threw the jar away because it was depressing to look at it empty.

~

It was by chance the first time a trucker gave me a ride home. He liked me, I could tell. His name was Joe, his rig was emerald green, with gold lettering. He smiled at me a lot.

I invited him into my apartment, offered him a beer, as a way to say thanks for the ride. Bottle half empty, he began taking his shirt off, proceeding to undress. Taking my hand, he led me to the bed. I could have stopped this, could have said no, but I didn't know that I could. Later, gathering up his clothes, he placed a twenty dollar bill on the table, nodded, smiled, and left.

I was stunned, and ashamed, yet I kissed the bill and hid it in an envelope in the fridge.

Maybe I can make other truckers like me enough to help out! It's not like they're paying me for sex, not like I'm charging them! I'm not charging them! I can't help it if they offer. We're just friends helping each other out. I'm not charging!

I got a new jar and began putting twenty dollar bills into it! *One step closer to bringing my children home to me.* I kept that jar in the fridge, out of sight.

~

Looking in a mirror, at myself one day, I said out loud, *You look too young! You need some make up.* I tried the blue mascara, a bit of red lipstick, put some color on my cheeks. Standing back, surveying myself, I said to the girl in mirror, *Wow! You look gorgeous!*

Yet I knew it wouldn't work. Scrubbing my face with hot soapy water, looking in the mirror again, I knew, *These men like me exactly because I do look young and innocent, it appeals to rough men leading lonely lives out on the road.*

And so I became the 'innocent and needy girl' for them, playing the part. I could do this because I had decided I could be whatever someone wanted me to be. Decided before Smitty left for Canada. I remembered that.

∼

Until there was Kurt, a clean, young man, on his first trucking job, who didn't know he was not the only one giving a girl a ride home, having a beer, being admired and appreciated and leaving a little cash to help her out. I didn't know how much he liked me, that he was serious, that he hoped to take me out of a tiny apartment and give my kids a real home.

I wished I'd known, before the night he knocked on my door, late, after midnight. Unexpected. I didn't answer. Because Green-Moving-Van Joe was there. I whispered, "Don't move, just wait." In my bed, with this man, we lay motionless.

"Who is that," Joe whispered back. "I don't know! Who would come to my door in the middle of the night?" On the other side of the door, the other man stood, maybe listening. We didn't move until we heard him walk away, heard a car move down the street.

I breathed again, a sigh of relief. And I felt embarrassed. And ashamed. And guilty.

He came back, Kurt who had pounded on my door, he came back an hour later, when I was alone, asleep. I answered the door. Charging into my room, his anger and disgust exploded. He pushed me to the floor. *He knows*, I said to myself, as I crawled away from his boot, the boot that chased me, kicking and kicking. *I don't know how he knows what I was doing, behind my own closed door, but he knows!*

With each kick of his boot, each pound with his fist, he vented his anger, shouting, "I thought you were different! I was going to take you out of here, take care of you, of your children! I thought you were different!"

"Stop, wait, let me explain," I pled, crawling away, my hands reaching out to pick myself up from the floor. Sobbing, afraid.

His disgust great, my words only fueled his rage. I stopped talking, and pleading. Waited for the hitting to stop. He turned, calm now, slowly locked eyes with mine, tilted my head up, and spit in my face.

That was the first night guilt and shame were visible on my body. Turning to leave my apartment, he did not bother to shut the door. Too stunned to move, I sat on the floor for a long time before I got up, shut the door, and took a bath. *How appropriate that I watch dirty little cockroaches walk around my tub.* Their company seemed deserved. "This will never end," I said, out loud, even though only I could hear.

~

One by one my aunts and uncles called the diner. "You have to come get this baby! He wakes up in the middle of the night! I can't have this! You have to come get him. Today!"

Or another, "I can't keep this boy any longer, he gets into everything!"

I called the Welfare Department Lady and asked for foster care only because I couldn't bring my babies to that apartment, not there. Not there with the roaches. Not ever there.

I couldn't let the lady in the basement apartment with rats watch them. *I don't see any choice. And don't cry! I have to serve pie and coffee to those four men waiting at the end of the counter.*

Arriving home from work, on this day, the day my children went to foster care, I did not ignore the man who always sat on the porch across the street. The man who had smiled and waved at me every day as I passed him. The man who did not sell little red and blue pills to help a person keep working. He held peace and comfort, heroin in a warm syringe. I walked up to his porch instead of mine, and said "Hi". Just "Hi" because I didn't know what else to do.

I didn't need to know because he took my hand, and led me into his apartment, and taught me how to enter a new and peaceful world. I slept well that night.

~

Letters came from Smitty in jail, letters forwarded from our old address. I didn't answer him because I wanted him to worry, to feel bad for us. To be frantic, like me.

But week after week he only wrote about God, and a preacher who came to the jail. Every letter the same, "I'm a changed person." I didn't believe him, crumpled the letters and threw them in the trash.

When he got out of jail, he waited a few weeks before he came to see me. I know because I saw him standing across the street, watching me leave to walk to work. I looked for him at the diner, but was too busy to see if he stood across the street, watching me there.

And then he was gone. I didn't see him for two weeks. Until he suddenly knocked on my door, late one night. Letting him in, I did not talk or look at his face, or his eyes. Only crossed the room and sat on the bed, waiting, staring at my knees. He knelt before me, took my hands in his, his touch soft. He wore a white shirt.

"I have a good job," he said, in a voice soft and gentle, holding my hand. "And a nice new apartment, three bedrooms. Ready for you and the children. Come with me! "

I don't want to be with him! But I don't want to be in this apartment either! And I want my children!

"Right now," he said, again. "Come with me and we can get the children tomorrow. You can quit that job, and stay home and be their mother again. I know that's what you want. I can give it to you right now, tonight."

Regardless of how I felt, regardless of how long I thought it might last, I could not pass up this chance to be with my children, to leave roaches behind, to leave the grueling shifts at the diner.

I was a drowning person who could not say no to the life preserver just because the wrong person held the other end of the rope. I looked at Smitty, him with his coal black hair combed nice. His white shirt and soft eyes, and I said, "yes."

When he was asleep, in the middle of the night, I walked across the street in my jammies and knocked on the door of the man with the tiny silver packets of confidence and comfort.

Chapter 8 – A Puffy Envelope

I walked through the new, large apartment. An older home with large rooms, high ceilings and tall windows! I loved this place. I loved it the moment I walked through it! From the three bedrooms, to the living room, the kitchen, out to the front and back porches, and the small back yard. It was my dream home!

Smitty walked with me from room to room. "Look, I painted all the walls so it would be fresh and new for you! And see the new white linoleum on the floors. See what I did? I did all this just for you! To make up for everything. Because I just love you so much." Listening to him brag, I nodded in all the right places. *I bet a landlord did this! You want me to look at you, admire you, pretend all that other stuff never happened! Hug you and be grateful like you're a hero who rescued me.* But I couldn't. I just couldn't because I knew, *This is only a game to him, a game. And he's won.*

I wanted to yell, *This is not a game! This is my lif*e! because I was still so angry! Until I looked at the floor with no cockroaches, ran my hand over the clean walls. *My children can be snuggled in their own beds, my boys in one room, Lucy in another, right down the hall from where I am standing now. I can watch them sleep and I won't have to work at the diner tomorrow. I can stay here with them.*

And so, I walked across the room and put my arms around his waist in a hug, and said "Thank you, thank you for doing all this for us!" I could play the game too.

~

We went to the grocery store and bought lots of food and I wondered if the check was good. We went to Marley's to buy sheets and towels and dishes and pots and pans and clothes – lots of clothes. I wondered about that check, too, but I didn't really care.

For now, tonight, for this week, and probably for this month, I am safe!

~

Smitty's job was in a hospital. He'd been trained as a commercial heating-air conditioning mechanic, so it was easy for him to find a job that paid well. When he wanted to work. We settled into a comfortable routine because I loved making a home for us. Staring at him over coffee each morning, I wondered. *What does he love? I love making a home, but I don't know what he loves, besides lying and running away.* While he read the newspaper, I took time to really look at him. *I don't know this man. He talks about some religious experience he had in jail. Says he's a changed person. Talks about it every night when we sit on the porch steps. I want to believe him, but I don't. I wish I could, but I don't believe him.*

With all my heart I wanted to love him and believe in him, but I couldn't. I could not find the Smitty with the gorgeous black hair, white shirt. The Smitty who surprised me with whipped cream coffee. The Smitty who shared my dreams of home and family.

Where is he? Where can I find that Smitty again, to love?

~

One morning, I was surprised by a knock at my front door. There stood a strange man in a grey suit, a black tie, a stiff white shirt. "Hello,

I'm Pastor Hedstrom. I talked with your husband when he was in jail."

I stepped out onto the porch with him, not letting him into my house because I did not want him to tell me the same things Smitty did, about how changed he was. I didn't want to hear it!

"Your husband asked me to visit you," he explained. "To talk about meeting Jesus and the changes he's had in his life. Jesus can change your life, too. Smitty wanted me to tell you about this." He held out some little papers, trying to give them to me. I looked away.

I did not want him here, I did not want to listen to him, I did not want his little papers. Leaving him there, on the porch, I went into the house and closed the door. *I don't believe it, I don't believe a word of it!*

And then I changed a baby's diaper to distract myself.

~

Smitty said the same things! I didn't understand him either, and grew irritable at his words. He had so many words! Sitting at the kitchen table with his coffee, he talked while I washed load after load of clothes in my wringer washer. He refilled his cup and followed me outside, sat on the porch and talked while I hung clean, wet clothes on the line. He sat, bible on his lap, talking about change, about hearts, and other stuff I didn't understand.

How can you talk about change while you sit there, all comfortable! If you're so changed, how come you don't come over here and hand me diapers so I don't have to bend over this basket so much? If you're so changed, how come you don't stop talking and start asking me how I feel? Again, these things I wanted to say but didn't because I was afraid.

On other days, I listened intently and wondered, *If I could believe his change was real, forever real, could I love him again?* Watching him every night over dinner, watching him read the newspaper, watching him play with the children in the yard, I thought that if I could just find the soft heart that was my Smitty, the Smitty I had been drawn to, the

Smitty I loved, if I could find that, then I think I would believe him. I would love him again. I tried, really tried. But I couldn't find his soft heart. Couldn't find my soft heart. *Were they simply lost, or had they never been?*

And then, because I couldn't love him, I began to believe, *Yup, what my dad said was right. I am a very selfish person who doesn't care about anyone else, only myself.*

But I could act unselfish, I could do that. It was like pretending. For my family, I could do that. I could pretend to hope. I could pretend to love Smitty. I had become good at pretending when I had to.

∼

"You just have to trust me and trust God," he'd say every day. And every day I thought, *Well, I trusted you and you threw it in the trash! Even if I get it back, it won't be the same. You just can't throw a person in the trash and think you can pull them out like nothing happened!* But I didn't say it, because I was trying very hard to not be an angry, selfish person.

∼

When I was a little girl, I had watched Gunsmoke, and The Rifleman, on TV. Shows about men who swooped in and rescued the helpless and killed the bad guys, or locked them up. I'd dream that James Arness would ride into town and rescue me from my dad. He didn't. I thought Smitty had, that first year we were married, but he hadn't. *And this rescue now,* I told myself, *It's only for a little while. He'll get tired, or restless, or bored and leave. But for now he's here, paying the rent and buying groceries.* And I was thankful for that.

In two weeks he stopped talking about change and trust and love, and we became two broken people with nothing important to say to each other. Two nice-looking people, sitting on the porch steps. Silent.

But I had my children, Lucy and Matthew and Michael. Under age three. I became too busy to ponder trust or to seek love with a grown man. Matthew, now almost two, often woke at five am, and couldn't stay in bed and read books and be quiet in the morning! I'd like it if he'd come and crawl in bed with me and wake me up. He didn't. He roamed the house.

Once he entertained himself by crawling in the crib with baby Michael, rubbing him with the Vaseline he found on the dresser! Adding baby powder, creating a sticky mess. When the baby cried, Matthew soothed him with a package of crackers!

Walking into the room, I saw a sticky baby covered in gooey powder, surrounded by cracker crumbs. As I ran plenty of warm water in the tub, I could only smile. I didn't care about the mess or that it would take all morning to clean up. I was happy little Matthew was with me. I was just happy I had a baby boy to wash up in a tub of soapy water. I was just happy I even had a tub of hot, soapy water! I was just happy there were no roaches in that bathroom.

~

I kept my wringer washer in the kitchen, handy, as I washed clothes every day. I loved that washer because it let diapers wash as long as I wanted!

Coming into the kitchen one morning, finding the washer filled with a goopy mess, I saw a little boy standing on a chair, proud that he'd 'helped Mom.' Mistaking large boxes of baby cereal for laundry soap, the boxes looking the same to him, he'd added them to the wash! Again, I couldn't scold him. I should have, but I couldn't. I was just happy he was here with me.

Those were good days, with milk delivered to my front porch and a sweet girl who came once a week from the State School to learn a skill by helping to clean my house. I hung diapers outdoors on the line again, as my children played in the yard. I gave them paper sacks and told them to pick all the bright, yellow dandelion blooms they could find! I loved being this person, having birthday parties for the children and walking around the neighborhood every evening.

But I could not fool myself every day, hoping this would last. I knew it wouldn't. I couldn't know how to protect myself from poverty lurking in the background.

But now I found I could protect myself from another pregnancy! There were new little pills on the market, pills for women, one little pill every day, and no baby. Birth Control pills! I wanted lots of babies, but knew I shouldn't have them. Knowing Smitty would leave when I was pregnant again, when I was pregnant and vulnerable, I took The Pill and hid the packet without thinking why. Some instinct told me to.

~

It took about three months for him to become alarmed. One evening he began pulling out drawers and turning them upside down. He put his hand in every sleeve and every pocket. I sat on the bed and watched.

"What are you looking for?" I asked in my most gentle, non-threatening voice. The first night he growled, "Never mind! I'm just looking for something, none of your business what!" The second night he attacked the closet, leaving a pile of crumpled clothes on the floor, finding nothing.

This time my questions were met with silence, so I stopped asking. I didn't need to ask. I knew. *He's looking for my birth control.*

Room by room, each night a different room before he wore himself out and went to bed. I watched, sometimes afraid, sometimes confident. Hiding them back in a room he'd already searched. Only to find him searching it again. It was random and unpredictable. I became afraid every night.

When he found the pills, he didn't tell me. They were simply gone in the morning. I was afraid to ask for them, I was afraid to tell the pharmacist I lost them. My free sample was gone, and I had not yet been able to sneak enough out of my grocery budget to pay for them. I was afraid to ask for extra spending money because I knew he wouldn't give me any.

And so now each night when I put my children to bed, I hugged them close and cried silently. I knew the end was soon to come, and the days of hoping were over, and I was trapped.

The following month I was pregnant and this was the first time I was not happy to be. *I am a terrible person, a terrible person to not want a baby! Who doesn't want a baby?* I didn't tell him I was pregnant. I kept the secret because I wanted to hang on to as much time here in this home, with my children, as I could.

But my secret could not be kept for long. He was thrilled to learn the truth. <u>He</u> had a bigger secret! It came to light the following month and I was not thrilled.

A puffy envelope came in the mail one day. The New Jersey postmark caught my attention. It was addressed to him, not to us. My curiosity aroused, I opened it.

With one glance at the first page, it was obvious what they were.

"These are divorce papers!" I said, blurting the words out loud, in shock! I read each paragraph carefully, page one, holding my breath. I could not run away from the words, sharp black letters on crisp white paper.

"He has a wife in New Jersey!" I had to say the words out loud or they wouldn't be real. "She has a name, her name is Joan and she wants a divorce because he's deserted her and…and". I stopped to read this sentence again, carefully. "Because he's committed adultery with… with me!" "That's my name! I am 'the other woman' named in her divorce." Afraid of what more there was, I quickly turned the page.

There were five children, <u>their</u> five children together! She wanted child support, and listed the name of each child. I carefully read that paragraph, there on page three.

"Fred age 15, Lucy age 14, James age 12, Allan…wait…wait…go back!" I slowly read the names again, willing my hands to stop shaking. The second name is Lucy. Lucy?! my mind screamed. No longer able to stand, I slid to the floor.

He has already had a daughter named Lucy and she's fourteen years old? But, but that's the name he picked for our daughter, my first baby! I stopped reading, trying hard to catch my breath. "Breathe!" I told myself. I had to say it out loud, hoping that would help, because I couldn't breathe!

There was so much there, in those pages, to scare me, to anger me, but Lucy's name broke me. I don't know why, but it did. How could he choose to name my first child after a daughter he already had! With his real wife! I stood up, papers in hand, and said, out loud, for myself to hear, "I'm glad I didn't learn to trust him."

I was broken in a place of my heart I hadn't known existed. A place now forever broken.

∼

There was so much I needed to say when he came home. So much I was afraid to say. I was afraid for myself and my children. What did this mean? What was going to happen to us? Was I even really married?

Mostly I was afraid of my own anger. Afraid it would erupt like it almost did on those days in the attic with my Dad. I decided to wait, wait for his reactions, what he would say to me. What would he say to help me feel better, to not be so afraid?

I placed the papers on the kitchen table, telling him he had mail there, placing a cup of coffee in front of him as he read them. And waited. Waited for him to react.

It was not what I expected.

Pounding his fist on the table, his words burst forth like a volcano! "How can she do this to me! Her parents have money, they don't need anything from me. It's been over for years! She has no right to do this!" More and more angry words, words tumbling over words.

His first response was of "the unfairly persecuted Smitty," and I was not in his picture.

Leaning against the counter, I watched his face. Watched him sit, gripping the coffee cup. Watched the lines on his face relax. Watched his eyes move from the papers to me.

Watched his face soften as he stared at me for long moments. Watched anger take a back seat as he struggled to bring me back into the picture.

"Don't worry babe, I can make this work. Don't you worry about it."

I wondered how, how he could make it work, how he could pay huge child support and take care of us. But I didn't ask questions or even talk about the letter. What words could I find? I had none because I was too numb.

In that moment I did the only thing I knew to do – I turned and made spaghetti for supper.

~

In the next few weeks, our days continued as though nothing had happened. Expert at pretending, I pretended we could afford child support for those five children in New Jersey. I pretended my life would not fall apart. I pretended that cramps and bleeding were not important. I pretended I was not losing that baby.

I carried heavy baskets of wet clothes out to the line. I played with my children, lifting them up high into the air until they squealed with delight. I scrubbed floors until my back ached.

When I lost the baby, I was relieved, but guilt soon pushed away relief. *What kind of person causes themselves to lose a baby and then is glad?* One more time to prove my dad was right, I was a very selfish person. And a very bad person.

~

A few nights later, Smitty poured a cup of coffee for each of us and invited me to sit with him on the back porch. We watched the children scatter sand out of the sandbox for a while, as he slowly savored his coffee. I held my cup, but could not drink it. My throat choked with fear because I knew what he was getting ready to tell me.

"We must move to a smaller apartment. It's not my fault my paycheck is so drastically cut with that child support taken out."

I heard him say he would find a place tomorrow, but I stopped listening when he began to talk about his 'unfair wife'. I was distracted, searching, wondering what I could do. *Did I have any options of my own? Did I have any control of what happened to me?*

No, you can only smile and love your children. Smile while you do laundry and while you cook supper every night. You have no choices. Just smile! Because you are most certainly not the boss of your own life now!

~

In six days we moved to a small, two bedroom duplex on Packard Avenue. I was lost there, unable to pick up the familiar routine of my life. The wringer washer was in the basement, the children were stuffed into one small room, there was no kitchen table for meals. No kitchen table until I rescued one from the neighbor's trash.

I sat up alone at night, waiting to see if this place had roaches. If it did, I wanted to see them first! I held my flashlight, shining it around the room every half hour.

If they're here at least they won't surprise me! This I could control…when I saw the roaches. I didn't see any for two nights, and slept a little better after that.

Each night, as I lay beside Smitty, as he slept soundly, I wondered what was next. I grew tired of wondering, every day wondering.

Am I doomed to be always swept along, like a ship in a storm, at the mercy of waves powerful enough to crack my boat apart? To crack me apart?

Some nights I was afraid to think, other nights I was afraid not to think. Until one night, suddenly I knew! *I do have a choice. If he's going to leave, I can choose when! Now, while I'm not pregnant. I can be the boss of me after all! If I am going to be alone, I want to have only three babies. Not four. Not five"*

I lay very still, afraid to move for fear I would break. Instead of waiting for him to leave, I could tell him to leave now! I was afraid to think it, but once I had, I couldn't stop! I didn't move for an hour, hoping the thought would go away but it didn't. *I can tell him to leave now while I'm not pregnant.*

As I relaxed a little, getting used to the idea, over the next few days, another, more familiar, more comfortable thought came to me. *Maybe he'll want to stay, maybe he'll keep his job and help support us. Maybe he'll even try to win me back*!

And so, that morning, before he left for work, I told Smitty I wanted him to move out. "I don't want any more surprises!" I explained. "I want you to find your own place, and you can come visit the kids whenever you want." I did not sit down while he ate his breakfast. I stayed standing at the stove. I felt stronger standing up. I did not want to feel friendly, sitting across the table from him. I did not want to change my mind. I stayed standing, shoulders straight, hands in my apron pockets so he wouldn't see them shaking. I needed to look strong.

I wanted to know if he loved me, if he could stay and be husband and father here.

I told him to leave, but I wanted him to win me back.

He didn't try. In three days, he was on a bus to New Jersey, promising to send money to me. I didn't think he would.

~

Sitting on the couch, staring at the floor when he was gone, I didn't know what to do. I had made a decision, hoping it would turn out well, hoping I could be in control. That I could be the boss of me, of my own life. It hadn't turned out well, and I was not in control. Smitty was gone and I was surprised he hadn't tried to change my mind, hadn't tried to keep us together. "Your Mom is a foolish, foolish girl!" I said to my children.

The next day, as the children napped, I took inventory. In my purse, ten dollars tucked away. I looked in the kitchen drawer. I found only an envelope of receipts. Rent was due in one week. I went to the cupboards. One box of oatmeal, three boxes of macaroni and cheese, a few cans of soup, a little peanut butter. In the fridge, a few slices of cheese, half a loaf of bread. I shook the milk carton, only a little left.

I started a list, on paper, hoping a solution would appear.

"This time there is no boy across the street to babysit for free"

"I have no job."

"I have no money to pay a sitter while I look for a job."

"I have no money to pay the rent next month."

"I have no money to buy groceries for next week."

"I have exhausted what little help my relatives would give."

"My children will be hungry tomorrow."

I sat on the couch and looked at the list for a long time before I could let myself see, *Foster care is the only way. I can't let my children be hungry. I can't let them get thrown out of their beds when I don't pay the rent! Just for now, until I find a job and a babysitter. Don't think about it! Don't feel it! You have to do this! You have no choice!*

In the morning I called the foster care lady, and this time I did not cry when I hung up the phone. I did not cry when she picked up the children because I could not look at their little faces.

In my then empty house, I sat alone on my couch, sad and broken.

Then I turned to the mirror on the wall behind me, and spoke to myself out loud to be sure I heard. "I will do it right this time because I don't want to repeat last year. This time I will look for a good job and I will avoid roaches and rats and men who spit in my face. This time I will avoid little blue pills and little red pills and comfort in a syringe."

I sat on the couch, stared at my hands in my lap.

I hope I can. I don't know how, but maybe I can. Maybe.

Chapter 9 – I Need A Job!

I struggled through the night, awake every hour, afraid of my decision to have Smitty leave. *Have I been foolish? Here I am again, with no job skills, no money, no car, alone. What made me think this was a good idea?!* Tossing and turning, sleeping fitfully, I finally went into the children's room and slept in their beds, hoping to feel close to them. That didn't help.

I made myself remember good things: how hopeful I'd been. How happy I was when pregnant with Lucy, laying out all the baby clothes on the bed, anxious to hold her. Remembering that didn't help me to feel better either.

How did I get to this place? What has happened to me? I asked every time I woke. There was no answer.

As morning came, I drug myself out of bed, relieved the night was over, the first night without my children. Sitting on my tiny porch, on the chair I'd drug from the kitchen, coffee cup in hand, I watched the neighborhood wake up. The children pushing each other around as they waited for the bus, mom's waving good-by as husbands went off to work. I wanted to be in those pictures and wondered if that could ever be my life.

I quickly gulped the rest of my coffee to stop the pain in my throat that always came before I cried. Because I could not let myself cry, not now. I pushed away useless wishing, watching those other families.

I have to get a job! Stop this silly, useless wishing! Get a job!

I told myself, pulling my chair back into the kitchen.

I said it again as I stood in front of the bathroom mirror. *I have to get a job!* I rolled my hair, and applied make up just like in the picture I had taped on the wall, cut from a magazine. *You need to look sharp. Not pitiful. Not desperate! A little more blue eye shadow should do... there, that's better.* I had learned, at least, that being pitiful didn't work.

I kept a conversation going with myself to chase away the fear, to chase away loneliness.

Dressed in a plain skirt and white blouse, sitting on the bed with my second cup of coffee, I was unsure what to do next.

"Well, I'm all ready to go, so now what?" I said it out loud, to make it more real, to keep the wishing away. Saying things out loud, hearing my voice in the empty rooms, made me feel tougher. And I needed to be tough today.

~

I took a bus downtown. Downtown had offices and stores, men in business suits and women in high-heels and nice dresses. People who drove cars and not semi-trucks. A good place to start.

The bus dropped me off at Marley's Department Store, the center of town. It was a crowded corner, people getting on and off buses, some just standing around hypnotized by the smell of Marley's Donuts. The newsstand on the corner headlined the Beatles coming to America again. *Again?* I wondered. *Again?* I studied the picture of four young men with long hair as they stared out from the newspaper's front page, but I still did not know who the Beatles were. I guessed I'd been too busy to read newspapers or watch television.

Walking to the next corner, away from the crowd, I decided. *I guess I'll just go door to door until somebody hires me.*

The courthouse on my right was too scary and formal looking. So were the shiny office buildings just behind me. *Forget those*, I told myself. *Nobody there will hire you. Start with restaurants, that's the only experience you have.* But I didn't say it out loud this time because I didn't want people to notice me and stare.

The street on the left had three restaurants, all in a row. I started with the first, there on the corner, Azie's Coffee Shop. They hired me. "You start tomorrow."

Walking home, I almost shouted, *I've got a job! I've got a job! Businessmen and secretaries and bank tellers come there for lunches and coffee breaks! Nice people. Good people.* Later I told myself in the mirror, *I'll make good money, have the kids back in no time!*

I enjoyed those customers. Mr. Grey Suit always came for lunch, egg salad sandwich and chicken soup, coffee with cream. He was friendly and talked to me every time I walked by. And every day he tipped me twenty-five cents. All the Mr. Suits did, twenty-five cents. Sometimes only two dimes, twenty cents, never a dollar. And I needed dollars.

For their afternoon pie and coffee they left me five cents. I tried being friendlier, remembering something they said from the day before, something I could ask them about to show I had been listening and cared about them. I tried being faster, bringing coffee right when they sat down. But every day it was the same, twenty five cents for lunch, five cents for afternoon break.

After three days my tips came to about five dollars and my hourly pay not much more than that. My heart sank and I realized, *I can't even pay a babysitter with this!*

I walked to the next place down the street, Johnny's Piano Bar, a tiny place. I liked how it looked, classy, all dark and cozy inside. "We're not hiring!" The bartender was quick to usher me out the door. I didn't know why.

Next was the Van Clyde Hotel. Just walking into the lobby required one to be bold. It was elaborate and gold and grand in its hugeness. From the center of the towering ceiling hung an elegant chandelier, sparkling as though it were made of diamonds. I was awestruck but pretended I was not. Walking in, my footsteps echoed off the walls and I was embarrassed. The man in a uniform watched me. He did not make me leave.

Not sure of where to go, I spotted the coffee shop on the left. That seemed safe. I went there. Booths with orange leather seats lined the street wall so customers had a view. I liked that. Plastic yellow flowers sat between the salt and pepper shakers. Ketchup and mustard containers in back. I sat at the counter and ordered lemonade so I could look the place over. It was much nicer than the diner, but still smelled like fried eggs. I was about to ask if they were hiring, but noticed the quarters and dimes left on the tables, the tips.

Knowing this was not what I needed, I paid for my lemonade and walked into the huge lobby again, walking softly so I wasn't so noisy, calling attention to myself. Uniform Man watched me carefully but did not leave his post.

Across the lobby I saw a restaurant with elegant long white tablecloths and napkins. Candles on the tables, tiny vases with real flowers. No ketchup bottles! I was awed!

You have to try here, I told myself. *This is a really nice place, the tips are probably good. Stop being scared! You have to try here.*

I put on my most confident walk, held my head high, and pretended I came here every day.

Barbara the Hostess looked me over, head to toe, and said, "I'll hire you, never mind experience. You have a nice look, that innocent little girl thing. Customers like that, it's different. And I can teach you everything else you need to know. Be here at 3:30 tomorrow, wear a fitted black silk uniform skirt, white blouse. And make sure your skirt fits well!"

I bought the tightest skirt I could find, and went home to wash and iron my only white blouse. Looking at myself in the mirror, wearing those new clothes, I wondered why she thought I had a nice look.

Look at you. You barely weigh ninety pounds. I pointed at the girl I saw in front of me, *Look, ordinary brown hair, curls out of control. Nope, you're sure no Marilyn Monroe!*

The next day, I taped new pictures on my bathroom wall, pictures of elegant looking ladies. I pinned my hair up, leaving a few loose curls, so that I would look sophisticated for my new job.

∼

From four pm to eight, this restaurant was a chandeliered, elegant room, serving men staying at the hotel, here on business trips...but at eight-thirty the kitchen closed, the tablecloths came off, candles in red globes replaced the flowers. The band came in and the previously unnoticed dance floor was soon full. Donnie Parks was an Elvis-type singer...his group entertained the customers, flirted with the waitresses, and slept with most of them. This was one stop in a string of popular downtown nightclubs, busy till two am when the last drink could be legally served. I was in a new world, and I liked it!

But I acclimated easily because I was made to travel with my dad on business trips when I was a kid. We ate at fancy hotel dining rooms.

Soon I learned the drill of working here. The hostess is the manager of the waitresses. She decides where customers are seated. If you're good at the job and she likes you, you get good tables with high-tipping customers. Girls she doesn't like get the unknowns. When she sits the owner of Paris Women's Clothing, a big spender, in your section, you know you've made it!

She gave me a small section of tables to work. I was new, so she didn't put favored, high tipping customers in my section. She taught well, I listened intently. I learned to fillet a fish and serve chateaubriand at the table with a flair.

Woody the Bartender was a patient man who looked after the girls even as he flirted with them. He told me how to serve the drinks...bourbon and soda, rum and coke, all mixed at the tables. I learned the language of a bar...scotch neat...or on the rocks, martini straight up.

Jimmy was the head cook and ran a tight ship in the kitchen, from the salad girl to the pastry chef. He was an artist who wanted his creations served immediately...hot! He yelled a lot.

Busboys cleared the tables. If they didn't like you, your cash tips disappeared, dirty dishes sat on your tables and the hostess couldn't seat new people in your section.

Before leaving the hotel the first night, I stopped in the Ladies' Room to count my tips. I had stuffed cash in my pockets all night, too busy to keep track of it. As I pulled five and ten dollar bills out, I knew I had made enough money to pay a babysitter for a week. I carefully folded each bill to fit in my shoes before starting the long walk home. It was three am.

∼

By the third week I had an apartment on a bus line and several babysitters in the neighborhood. I was making enough to pay for everything. None left over, but added to my $235 welfare check, it would be enough! I was very proud of myself.

I called my caseworker. "You can bring my babies home," I said, full of success, proud of myself. "I have an apartment, a babysitter, and a job!"

"Not so fast this time," she answered. "I need to schedule a home visit, look at your finances, be certain you're ready to really provide for the children this time."

My confidence faded, but I only answered, "Great! Can you come today?"

I could tell, even over the phone, she was stalling. "I can fit you in Thursday, two weeks from now. How's ten am?" My heart sank, "Two weeks!?" I forced myself to keep a steady, happy voice, to impress her.

"Ok, that's fine." I said it was fine because I wanted to seem mature and I needed her to like me, but it wasn't fine! Not with me. I had more than two weeks to wait. Two weeks. Fourteen days, maybe more. And what if I didn't pass? I sat on the bench in the phone booth and cried. I cried for a long time. Then I walked home to put on my black silk skirt, to pin my hair up, to apply blue eye shadow. Put on my most smiling face and go to work!

~

By the time the caseworker came, I had cleaned the apartment, washed all the curtains, and put flowers on the table. Teddy bears on the kids' beds. New towels in the bathroom. A fresh bar of soap out. Food in the fridge.

As I walked Caseworker Lady from room to room, she checked things off on her clipboard. I could see I was passing everything. She smiled, surprised, pleased, and said, "Your children can come home, I'll bring them in the morning." I couldn't help it...I hugged her. I was so excited! I had done it! I had really done it! No blue or red pills. No truck drivers helping me out. I had done it on my very own!

~

As the children, my own children, walked up the steps to our apartment, I could see a little panic on their tiny faces. I watched them take each step carefully, unsure of where they were going. I saw they had lost the joyful bounce children have, children who charge into each new room, eager to see what's there. My children walked with caution. In my heart, only in my heart where they wouldn't see, I cried, because I knew this was my fault.

We were awkward together, that first morning. They met the babysitter but pretended they didn't see her. I was so happy to have them, to curl up on the couch with blankets and books. I held them tightly, I could smell their baby shampoo smell, I could kiss the tops of their heads. It would have been impossible to hold them any closer yet they seemed very far away. In another place.

Clair

The next day I left them with the babysitter, waved good-by as I walked down the stairs to catch the bus to work. They watched me leave, but did not wave back. On the bus ride, I fought hard to push away the thought, "I have lost something and I will never get it back."

Chapter 10 – Just Work Harder!

I wanted to leave my sadness on the bus, but it followed me into the hotel. Crushing sadness. *Stop pouting, you have to go to work, you have to make money, you have to smile.*

I went to the bar and motioned for Woody to pour me a shot of bourbon so I could put on my happy face for the customers.

At the end of a few weeks, working 3pm to 3am, both the dinner hours and the nightclub hours, exhaustion never went away. Walking up the stairs to my apartment at the end of a shift, my feet hurt too much to leave my shoes on. I fell asleep on the couch, too tired to undress and get into bed. At eight am, I woke to three sweet little faces looking at me, needing to be fed. There were dirty clothes and diapers to carry to the laundromat and back. Food to shop for, cook, and clean up after. And children needing hugs and stories read. Hugs my heart ached to give. Books I wanted to read to them, cuddled on the couch. If I could.

The morning I fell on the bottom two steps, trying to balance a laundry basket while holding Michael's hand, I knew I was failing.

I have to find a live-in babysitter to help because I have to sleep. I cried because I did not want to give up the homemaking things, the laundry and cooking and cleaning, things I loved to do. I did not want someone else doing them while I went to work. I wanted me to be the mother, the woman of the house. I did not want to be the man who just went to work and paid for everything. But these were thoughts I could not allow, not now, maybe not ever. *"Stop it!"* I scolded myself again. *"If you don't go to work and pay for things, there won't be any home to take care of.*

There won't be any children to look after. Get cleaned up and go to work!"

Scouring the newspaper the next day, under 'jobs wanted', I found Gertie, an elderly lady needing a place to stay. Perfect! I moved her in the same day, after a short interview. A very short interview so that I had time for a nap before catching the bus to the hotel.

Gertie was wonderful! An eighty-something, grey-haired, big busted, cheerful-beyond-belief, gramma, just round enough all over to be cuddly. She and the children were instant friends and loved each other.

But she became a substitute mommy and I didn't feel good about that. I became the seldom-at-home-awake breadwinner. I didn't feel good about that either.

After six months, I was well established with a good section of tables, and customers who asked for me. Most were traveling businessmen staying at the hotel. I memorized their names and favored cocktail and had it waiting when they got to their table. I knew how they liked their steaks, and if they wanted coffee after dinner. I kept a file card on each person to remember their wedding anniversaries and wife and children's birthdays to remind them they needed to shop before going home. I perfected a smile, an intent gaze that said "I think you are important." They tipped me well.

And finally, Mr. Paris Women's Clothing was seated at my table.

Now I yelled at Jimmy The Cook if he didn't get my steak out fast enough or if it wasn't done right, but I also shared my big tips with him. I slipped the busboy five dollars so he'd get my tables cleaned quickly and I could get another customer. Woody The Bartender poured extra shots of whiskey...one for the customer...one for me. He didn't ask, just poured.

We moved to a bigger apartment, because I wanted Gertie to have her own room. I wanted a place on the first floor, with a big kitchen and a small yard for a sand box.

"Just work harder to pay for it," I told myself in the mirror, during one of those early morning chats when everyone was asleep and I could talk out loud to myself. To make me strong.

I hugged my children sometimes, and let them crawl in bed with me to cuddle and I felt guilty for being away so much, and sad that I didn't know what else to do. Sad that I couldn't find a way to stay home, to take care of them myself.

I remembered that little girl in kindergarten, when the teacher asked all of us what we wanted to be when we grew up. I wanted to be a mommy. Just a mommy. She couldn't get me to pick something else because that's all I wanted...to be a mommy.

I was a mommy now, but so numb with guilt that I could hardly stand to be there with my children. They'd cling to me when I was home, when I was not asleep, and I felt guilty hugging them back, knowing in a few hours I'd leave, again. I was failing to be a good mom!

I couldn't bring my two worlds together. I didn't know how to do that!

In one world I wore my shiny, tight silk skirt and wooed men. I closed my heart and kept sadness and guilt hidden from others to see. I performed without real feeling, only pretend emotion. Pretended to be happy, pretended to like everybody, pretended to not be tired, pretended this is the life I've chosen. "I can be whatever you want me to be. What would you like?" I was successful in this world.

In my other world, at home, I wore my jammies and no make-up. I let my curly hair hang loose. Here I kept men out. At home, in this world, I needed to have an open heart with my children. To love them and play with them without reserve, without pretending. It was hard to do in the too few hours I had before it was time to put on the black skirt again, pin my hair up and leave for the hotel.

I didn't know how to be both people. For the first hour, as I re-entered each world, I carried a little of the old with me. When I first got to work, I had the right clothes on, but a part of me was still in jammies and slippers, sitting on the couch holding my children. *"Stop thinking of them! This is party girl time.*

I recited it over and over, but sometimes it didn't work, I couldn't leave the mommy-me on the bus. On those days, my first stop was the bar window. Woody sighed and poured me a shot of bourbon. I gulped it down. He looked at me, then nodded at my empty glass. Some days I nodded also and he poured another. This became the ritual to throw me into party-world before setting my tables, before welcoming the gentlemen of the evening..

Some nights, hard nights, after my shift, before walking home, I went to the hotel Ladies' Room, retrieved the needle and syringe carefully taped behind the cold water pipe under the sink, pulled the little foil packet of heroin from my pocket. This became the ritual that erased the party girl and eased me back into mommy-world before going home.

∼

I don't remember the first time a customer asked to meet me for a drink after work. In his hotel room. But I went. I knew what I was doing. I felt a little shy and awkward, but I did it anyway. He was slim, wore an expensive suit and watch, and he chose me.

He talked about his family and I made mental notes of more things to remember for him. He left $50 on the dresser, then he showered and took me home. I added more information on his file card, the things to remember for next time, because I knew there would be many more "next times."

I knew it was wrong and I knew I'd do it again and I wondered what my dad would think if he knew. I wondered if he'd be sorry for the times he offered me $50 to willingly have sex with him. I decided to charge men $100 so that I could be more valuable than my dad thought I was.

Chapter 11 – Number One Girl

I had good tables and great customers every night and my stack of blue file cards grew. When I added a name, I made one up. I knew I couldn't write their real name. I don't know how I knew, but I did. Mr. Robert Smeltz always ordered a Bloody Mary, so his card read, "Mr. Blood Mary". Mr. Alabama was the only southerner, and Mr. Dodge worked in the auto industry. I was delighted with myself for being so smart and creative.

Mr. Blue Suit (he always came to dinner in a navy blue blazer) liked his martini straight up with an olive *and* a twist, read the newspaper while he ate his salad, baked potato, and rare steak. He stayed at the hotel the second Wednesday of every month. When I saw him waiting for the hostess to seat him with me, I met him at his table, ready with his martini, and the newspaper folded to the financial page, just as he like it. I did the same for all my traveling business customers. "Sir, may I remind you, your wedding anniversary is next week." Or "How was your daughter's piano recital?" Each person an individual, the most important person in the room! It felt good to be in control, to be the boss of my life now.

These were the things that brought me large tips, tips I no longer only hoped for. In this, my hotel world, I was successful and glamorous. The pictures of pretty girls taped next to my mirror, pictures I had been driven to copy, were no longer there. I looked at my own self, in my new expensive black silk skirt and salon-styled hair. *You are a very glamourous girl and you work in a swanky place! You are a very important person!* I recited to myself in the mirror, every afternoon before going to work. In this hotel world, I knew how to shine.

But in my home world, as I stood in the kitchen each morning, fixing oatmeal for my children, I watched as Gertie buttered their toast. I noticed the way they looked at her as she brought it to the table, and I knew it wasn't the same way they looked at me, scooping oatmeal into their bowls, topping it with brown sugar. It wasn't the same. It wasn't tender. It didn't linger. I fed them, but they loved Gertie. I retreated to the bathroom and cried, then I went to work early so I wouldn't have to see them together. I didn't know how to compete with Gertie and I didn't want to be where I was a failure. I wanted to be where I was glamorous. I was ashamed as I left the house, but knew if I stayed there, watching, listening, I knew a tornado would gobble me up.

~

In the restaurant, in the nightclub, in these rooms in the hotel, I knew how to compete. Compete hard for tables and customers, for the eye of the bartender and musicians. As Woody The Bartender poured our drinks, grinned his crooked little smile, flashed sparkling eyes, he looked at me as though I was his favorite. I knew he was deciding which one of us to take to the back room on his break. I wanted him to choose me, so that I could be important. Important to someone. Musicians had keys to rooms upstairs and flirted with waitresses and customers. I wanted them to pick me.

I loved being noticed. I loved when they chose me. *Hey, dad! You should see me now! You said you had to teach me about sex because I was a cold, frigid girl? No one would ever want me? Well look at me now! The drummer wants me, the band leader wants me, the bartender wants me, even the rich businessmen want me! You were wrong! Everybody wants me!* I proved him wrong, and I liked that.

~

Until Sally The New Waitress came. Armed with "experience", she didn't have to earn the favored tables or customers. Her long blond hair was sleek and shiny, pulled back with a red ribbon. Her pony tail swished from side to side when she walked through the room. It matched the movement of her hips. Her dark brown eyes were a sharp contrast to her porcelain skin and yellow hair. She was now "the new girl" and everyone wanted her.

I was still a great waitress, I still had drinks waiting as gentlemen came to their tables, I still served steaks sizzling hot, and all my notecards were up to date. There was still a charm to the wispy curls that framed my face, escaping from my hairpins. I had my own swagger as I walked through the room, that made people look at me. But I was not new, mysterious and fresh, Sally was.

And she became shinier week after week. I watched it happen. No matter what I said to myself, to that girl in the mirror getting ready for work, no matter how I fixed my hair or how I changed my makeup, I became duller. If I was not the star of the room, then what was I? Nothing. Invisible.

Now when Woody poured my drinks and said, "Hey kid, you and me, about ten minutes?" with that shy grin of his, nodding towards the small private dining room to the right, his break room, I knew he had picked Janice twice last week, and Sally the past three nights. I was not first. Now, laying on the floor in that room, I did not look at him, or see his face or hear his voice. Now I saw only the peeling paint on the walls. My eyes were riveted to the stains on the carpet. I wondered if they had always been there.

Now the upstairs rooms looked old and worn. The bottle of champagne the drummer brought with him didn't restore the room's elegance. My shiny world had become dull.

Clair

~

I watched Sally take the shine from the entire hotel. She gave shiny-ness back every time she smiled, and she smiled often. Shiny-ness is magnetic, and people were drawn to her. Not me, though. I wasn't drawn to it, so she never smiled at me. Mr. Paris Women's Clothing was seated at her table now, and I didn't like her.

Night after night I was in a silent contest with Sally. I wanted to be the special girl again, yet I did not know how to make that happen. Here, for the first time in my life, I had not been the invisible person, no longer the girl not figured into anybody's plans. No longer the girl no one noticed. I was afraid to be invisible again.

If I was not the number one girl, what would I be? And if I was not number one, shiny girl, would my big tips go away? Would I lose my children again?

~

I no longer looked forward to going to work. And I no longer left the failure-mom at home when I walked into the restaurant. I carried her with me. The failure-person.

And now I stopped in the hotel ladies' room every night to give myself the warm, welcome shot, a ritual to keep the tornado of failure away.

~

Many weeks later, I bolted as I caught sight of myself in that ladies' room mirror. I touched the girl, staring out at me. She was a sharp contrast to how I felt. My heroin made me warm and cozy and lovable, but this girl, looking back at me, was not. I slid my fingers over the mirror,

How thin and pale you are! Curls that had escaped their pins were not really curls at all, but now only dull strands of messy hair. My lips were thin and grey, my blue eyes were flat. They seemed to have sunk deeper into my face.

This night I did not tape my needle and syringe back to the cold water pipe under the sink. I put them in my purse. "to keep close by."

On this night, I knew it was not Sally who stole my shiny-ness, my sparkle. I sat on the floor, my back against the cool tile wall, and I cried for more things I had lost and would never get back.

Knowing I would never again be number one girl at the VanClyde Hotel, I didn't rush to be early, to be the first girl there. I stayed home, helped with lunch, watched Gertie and the children laugh over silly things. I stayed home to tuck the children in for their naps. I looked at them, peaceful in their beds. I watched from the doorway until they drifted off. Every day I watched, and I yearned to be part of their world, a world I knew I had left.

∼

Why didn't I see this is where I belong, where I've always belonged, where I am important and where I am loved! I felt hopeful! Only for a moment. Until I remembered that I had to make money to pay for this home, these beds, this substitute mommy, and even the food in the fridge.

Wanting to be a good mom, to make up for leaving them, I watched Gertie, to learn. "Come here, Matthew, you've got peanut butter all over your face and hands. No! Don't touch the couch, get over here."

She could scold them and love them at the same time! Her old, wrinkled face sparkled as her arthritic fingers reached out for him with a warm, wet washcloth. She laughed as he tried to get away from her. It was their game together. She never left her chair, yet they laughed and pushed each other around until she caught him. He loved her enough to be caught and to stand still and let her wash him up. Watching them, I was delighted. I wanted that!

In the morning, after oatmeal, toast, and jam, I tried it. I looked at my three children, with faces and fingers sticky with strawberry jam. I mimicked Gertie, as I sat in my chair, holding a warm washcloth, saying the same words she had. They didn't squirm around close enough to let me catch them. One ran under the table, another into the bedroom. They laughed and giggled as I ran from room to room. When I caught them, one by one washing their hands and cheeks, it was not the same. They didn't melt into my touch. The fun with Gertie was letting her catch them. The fun with me was running away, was not being caught. I was not their mommy and I was devastated, and the tornado in my heart grew bigger.

This was the day I stopped trying to balance my two worlds. It was easier to let the bar engulf me.

∼

But decline is ugly. As an elegant girl I was paid one-hundred dollars. But I was losing weight, becoming skinny. There were dark circles under my eyes. I had to keep my arms covered to hide bruises and needle marks. I let two men take me to their room together. I woke up in a strange place and bought a newspaper to find what city I was in. A girl who has to shoot up in the bathroom sometimes is not worth $100. Neither is the girl who throws up.

I was not surprised when they began leaving seventy-five dollars. Fifty was condemning. At twenty I stopped noticing. Numbness does not hurt like defeat does. I did not challenge the verdict this time. My dad was right.

∼

Craving the attention that had helped me to not be afraid, to feel important, I cut my hair, and bought an elegant, slinky black cocktail dress and went to another hotel lounge on my nights off. In this new place, sitting at the bar, slowly crossing my legs just so, I was the new girl again! I sat up straight and struck coy poses and engaged in conversations, let men buy me drinks. I assessed what they wanted, what they wanted me to be.

For some, my eyes said, "I'm not sure I want to go upstairs with you. Maybe you need to convince me." For others my pose said, "Let's skip the small talk and take our drinks upstairs." *I can be anything you want me to be, and I can find what you like if you don't know.* Here I was important, here I was wanted again and it felt very good. I looked forward to my nights off.

I liked the lawyer in the black suit, gold watch, and expertly groomed gray hair . He never wore a tie, left the top two buttons of his crisp white shirt open, casual. He liked me. He paid well and we had fun together. He didn't mind the needle marks on my arms, the bruises from careless injections. "Baby, everybody does what they have to do. You're ok, you're just getting along." I liked him.

He liked me soft and vulnerable, in dresses with full skirts and small white collars. He bought school girl cardigan sweaters for me to wear. I could be that for him.

Until the night I noticed. Until I noticed he didn't like me only because I was vulnerable. He liked me to be a child!. Some dark part of me screamed, *Wait! What! Am I being the helpless little girl, all innocent and wearing those little sweaters... and what is he?!*

Is he the daddy who takes care of you?! Is he a daddy who likes touching little girls?! Is that what we're doing here?! I was angry and afraid. I didn't like this game, but I didn't walk away. I stayed. I needed the money now.

Well, so this is how it is, I told myself, in my bathroom mirror again. *Men like that innocent, little girl look. That's who you are. That's your appeal. That's what draws them to you. You can be that, just don't let them play daddy, don't carry it too far, you'll be ok. Keep it subtle-like, not obvious. A sweet vulnerable girl in a sexy black dress, that's got appeal. This is who you are.* I stared at myself for a long while in that mirror because I did not know the girl who looked back at me.

~

I do not remember why I left the VanClyde Hotel, but I did leave. I walked around the corner and down the next block to a new place, just opening. An ancient, one-hundred year old brick house on the fringes of the nightclub district. It was a new, inviting, eclectic, bar and restaurant. And I wanted new, a new start.

~

Old wooden floors and brick walls met me as I entered. To my right I noticed a large dining room, running the entire length of the house, the bar at the far end. *They must have torn walls down for that.* The man behind the bar, talking to a vendor, did not look up, so I slipped up the stairs. Wandering through two smaller rooms, I could imagine people dining, siting in the booths against the wall. It was cozy and intimate. An old gentleman sat on a chair, soft fuzzy white hair hanging over his face. He wore an old sweater, buttoned top to bottom. Bent over a strange guitar, absorbed in the music he was playing, he startled when I stepped off the stairway, as though I intruded into his world. His face was inviting, his smile genuine. I liked him instantly! I waved a bit, he nodded back, silently, then lowered his head again to his instrument, retreating from the world as he played his soft music.

I moved on, continuing my tour, walking through the large meeting room on my left, through the kitchen, tucked across the back, overlooking the large walled-in courtyard downstairs.

I took those back stairs, from kitchen to courtyard, and was surprised by a thin old man poring over sheets of music, sitting at a table, his little goat-tee shaking as he muttered to himself. He, too, was startled to see me, and stared at me long enough to make me really uncomfortable. He motioned for me to sit opposite him.

"Have a seat, young lady. What you doing here, wandering around this old place?"

"Well, I'm just checking things out, thinking I might want to work here."

"Why you want to work here, little place like this, not much action going like those big clubs up the street." He was friendly and I instantly liked him.

"Yeah, I've been working at the VanClyde and... just thinking I might want a little change." I pulled the sleeves of my sweater down over my hands, keeping the needle marks on my arms hidden.

"Sure you do, nice girl like you! What you shooting all that dope up your arms for? You gotta stop doing that stuff!"

"What makes you think I do that! I just walked in here, you don't know me. You don't know anything about me!" I was angry now, defensive. Who did he think he was! In my haste to leave, I knocked the bench over. I struggled to set it upright, he reached over to help, grabbing my wrist to slow me down.

He had the most intense eyes I'd ever seen on any person. He stared at me, held my gaze, my eyes were locked into his. His hold on my wrist was gentle, yet I couldn't break away. He was tall, pathetically thin, with sunken cheeks, yet there was a vibrant health about him that was mesmerizing. I could easily have pulled my hand away, but I didn't want to.

His hand moved from holding my wrist to restrain me, to shaking my hand, introducing himself.

"My name's Charlie," he said. "I'm the piano player here, we have a sing-along some nights, 'bout 9:30 or so. Put them little red song books on the tables after the dinner crowd leaves. I can play about any song any way people want. I been around a long time. You have a seat," he motioned to the bench across from him.

Clair

~

    For the next hour we sat, sipping cokes, our backs warmed by the sunlight, as he told me his story, tried to get me to tell mine. I wouldn't.

    He just nodded, pulled at the strands of his wispy grey beard, looked my face over. I felt his eyes move from my hair, to my chin. He studied my face carefully, then placed his boney hand on my shoulder.

    "Young lady, you stop runnin' that stuff up your veins. You clean yourself up right now! You hear! You walk away from those big clubs, come work here. You're right, you need a change. Go inside, talk to Harry. He'll hire you. You work here and everything'll be all right! Go on now, go in there and tell Harry I sent you. You remember my name? It's Charlie."

    "Yes sir, I'll do that!" I said. I believed Charlie.

    It had been a long time since I believed someone.

Chapter 12 – Fresh Start

I stared at Charlie, taking a moment to decide. It didn't take long. I could maybe make this work, a fresh start. I would be away from upstairs hotel rooms. I would be away from out-of-town businessmen. And Charlie liked me.

It was a short walk, across the patio with its red and white striped umbrellas, unmatched tables and chairs scattered about. The floor was rough stone, not smooth cement, and in my haste, I stumbled and almost fell. I caught myself, embarrassed, but Charlie was again muttering over his music sheets and didn't notice.

Inside, I faced the tall, thin, blonde fellow behind the bar. Young. He looked up, surprised. "Well, where'd you come from? That door only leads to the patio! You just drop out of the sky or something?" His words were challenging, but his smile and voice were full of mirth and joy.

"No, no, I came in through the front door, but you were busy so I went upstairs." I waved toward the front stairway, as way of explaining. "I found my way to the patio from there."

"Well, I'm Harry, and I own this place, so now that you're here, what can I do for you?"

"I… I was just talking to Charlie. We, ah, or rather he, thought maybe I could get a job here?" He wasn't quick to answer, just looked at me with his sparkly blue eyes and teasing grin.

I hurried to add, "Charlie said it was a good idea!"

"Oh, he did, did he? Well, then, I guess I have to hire you." He shrugged his shoulders and continued washing glasses, "Since Charlie said so!" I sensed this was a joke I didn't get. "You ever wait tables?"

"Yes sir," I said, in my best good girl voice. "I've been working at the VanClyde last few years, in the Dining Room, both dinner and nightclub hours. I've had lots of experience."

My voice was shaky, I was unsure, uncomfortable, cautious. I forced myself to make eye contact, pulling my eyes from the bar top to look at him, into his eyes.

Gone was the sassy me. This was the me who stood on the corner outside Marley's, wondering where to look for a job. *What had happened to me, as I passed the doorway from Charlie to Harry?*

After a quick tour, Harry asked, "I need you next week, Friday. Our grand opening. Can you be here?"

"Yes, sir, I'll be here!" My voice said I was excited, but my heart said, *I have a week to pull myself together. I can do that. One week!*

I never went back to the VanClyde. I went home to sweat it out, to wean myself off dope and drink. It was not hard because I had something to look forward to now, and I was determined to make this work. *This time I will do it right! This time!*

Gertie only asked once why I was home. She smiled and shrugged her shoulders when I said, "I have the flu!" on my way from the bathroom back to my bed. Trying to throw up when there's nothing left to throw up is gruesome and only made the children afraid of me. My headache was almost unbearable and the shivering drove me back to bed every time I tried to stay up.

Every few minutes, I recited to myself, *It doesn't matter, in a few days I'll be good as new. In a few days I'll stop throwing up, I'll feel better. In a few days I can just play Mommy.*

~

It was true! In a few days I felt better, marvelous by the end of the week. Proud of myself, hope began to creep into my heart again. *I can do this! I am a strong woman! Look at me! I did this all by myself!*

I took the children to the park and pushed them on baby swings and held them in my lap as we went down the slide. We went to the library and sat on the floor and looked at pictures in all the books. In a few days they came to cuddle with me when I sat on the couch. I didn't have to ask them, they just came. On their own. These were the best days and I was very happy and I wanted this to last, knowing that I couldn't not work for long. Work put food on the table and paid the rent. But I pushed those thoughts away, and drew my children close and read them another book.

And it was true. In a few days, we were out of milk, out of bananas and cereal and bread. In a few days the landlord came to collect, and the water bill arrived. Gertie held her hand out to be paid. These were the things that reminded me that my real job was to make money, not cuddle and read books to toddlers. These were the things that made me ready for my new job. So that night I told myself in the mirror, *This time I will be mommy and make money. I don't know how, but this time I will get it right.*

I liked My Old House, I liked the people. Harry was bartender and owner. Miguel The Cook, of course, was the boss of his tiny upstairs kitchen, and scolded everybody in Spanish. And Very Old Man carried his Spanish guitar from room to room, to bring old world charm to dinner guests. And of course, there was always Charlie, playing his own version of honky-tonk piano for the late-night sing along. No one drank on the job here. I watched them. *They are a family, the four of them.* I was jealous. *Maybe I can be part of this family.*

~

Since I had no regular customers to remember and cater to, no need for file card notes, I created other challenges for myself, so I didn't get bored. I also looked for attention.

How many orders at a table could I remember and quote to the cook without writing them down? I started with four...worked up to ten. I could stand at the table, hands in my pockets, listening. Steak, rare, salad with French dressing, baked potato, mixed vegetables. Five items each for ten people.

Always, someone at the table stopped me with, "Don't you want to write this down?" Answering, "No, sir, I don't," made me proud. I loved the looks they gave me, gave each other, when I served them correctly. As long as no one had changed their seats, I was ok!

Miguel The Cook shook his head and worried as I wrote the orders for him, but I could tell he was impressed.

I could also remember ten drink orders at a time. Harry the Bartender was proud. When I stood at a dinner table of eight or ten customers, he told people at the bar, "Watch her, now." I was the star of the room again!

Most of the customers were young couples out for dinner. They paid the babysitter well, but not the waitress. If the husband left a ten dollar bill on the table for me, his wife reached back and snatched it up as they walked away. My income had dwindled and I was not paying my bills, so I added more days and hours to my schedule to avoid "after hours customers". I wanted to be a good girl this time. Even if I was a tired good girl.

∼

By the time Charlie came in at nine, I had cleared dinner things and placed little red books on each table so people could follow the words and sing along. Boisterous College Boys filled the room on weeknights, sang, drank beer, and flirted with me, the only waitress. I had fun, knowing if I acted on their flirting, they wouldn't know what to do. They were so young! I watched them, laughing and teasing, fake punching each other when the joke was especially good. Watching them, I knew I had never been that free and innocent, and I envied them.

It took a few months for me to realize this was not a family, it was a nightclub after all. It took a few more months for Boisterous College Guys to know Charlie, to know me, and to know Harry. Once this was home to them, that fine thread of meanness that is in every person began to unravel and show itself.

They began to pat my butt too aggressively, grabbed my arm and pulled me down on their laps. For them it was only fun. It would never go further, and I knew that. The quicker I jumped off their knees, the more they laughed and ordered another pitcher of beer, grateful, I thought, that I didn't accept their boyish version of flirting. I didn't like it, but knew they were no threat, and that I could handle them. Sometimes they tipped well at the end of the evening.

Charles was not so lucky. Poor Charles! This gentle man, eighty three years old, was my first gay friend.

Every night we worked together, and every night I thought about the first day we met on the back patio, him muttering over his music, friendly, telling me about himself, while I sat, awkward, angry, and defensive.

Charles had never found a place to be safe, not anywhere. He had never, in his long life, pretended to not be gay. Nor had he been proud to be. He simply was. As a young man he had been physically chased out of town, because he was gay. He had been beaten up. His family would not speak to him, because he was gay. He had been fired from jobs he loved, because he was gay. Music and theater were the only homes he knew. The only places he could be safe, and then only sometimes. He held a soft spot in my heart.

Then came the night College Boys learned about Charlie. I never knew how, but they knew he was gay and they knew he had a colostomy bag. Their mean thread turned ugly one night. The night they drank too many pitchers of beer.

They put a triple laxative in his drink to cause the bag to fill and Charles to stop in the middle of a song and rush to the men's room. They thought making his bag burst would be funny. I didn't and forever after watched his coffee cup, placing it out of sight from Boisterous College Boys. Cutting the Boys off after four pitchers of beer. I could protect Charlie. Here was someone I could protect! Poor Charles, no longer chased out of town, but here, chased off his piano bench to lunge for the bathroom!

∼

He thanked me by inviting me to parties at his house....the house famous for random sex in side rooms...and a very large painting of a penis hung proudly over his couch.

I was shocked, even though I had thought nothing could shock me anymore. I was glad to know this did. I loved Charlie, but was uncomfortable in his house. I didn't like it there, with these people so out of control. It reminded me of myself and I didn't like that either. I was glad I didn't like it because then maybe there was still some hope for me to be a nice person after all!

∼

Weekends the Boisterous College Boys were gone, and the crowd was older, professional. People I knew from the VanClyde. They knew me. I was surprised to see them here, in my safe place. I didn't want them here and I was a little afraid. I don't know why, but I was.

When I went to the bar, placed my little round cork-topped tray down and gave Harry my drink order, he asked, "Who's that couple, sitting by the fireplace, ordering these martinis?" I told him they owned the famous French restaurant up the street. Or later, "Ok, now who's that guy sitting alone, scotch neat, always here every Saturday?" I leaned over the bar, closer, "He's on the radio." I knew all these famous people and I felt important. I was showing off and it felt good! As long as the famous people didn't remember me, I'd be ok.

Harry never asked how I knew these people, but he watched Mr. Lawyer follow me back to the bar, lean his back against it while I placed the drink orders. He watched Mr. Lawyer or Mr. Doctor whisper in my ear and fold a note into my pocket. He watched others do the same on other nights. I pretended to be shy and not notice. Only later, when he couldn't see, only then did I read the note and follow their instructions. I knew the step I was taking and I was afraid. Afraid I would fall off the cliff once again. Could I do this and still feel good about myself?

But I was more afraid of the landlord because I didn't have the rent money and I was more afraid that maybe there wasn't enough money to cover the checks I had written. My income had been cut in half, leaving the big hotel, coming to this small bar. I was more afraid of that!

~

As this became a popular place, other lawyers and doctors and businessmen came for dinner with their wives. Their wives didn't notice the glance, the recognition on their husbands face, my quick turning away. The eye contact that said we knew each other.

These men knew me and I could not hide. Maybe I didn't want to. Not paying my bills scared me more than seeing men in hotel rooms.

~

The world changed again the night Harry passed a twenty dollar bill across the bar to me.

"Hey, kid, here, take this." I looked at the money without touching it, knowing what was coming, hoping it wasn't, willing my heart to slow down. I forced my eyes to meet his. His voice soft and tender, like love. He leaned over the bar and whispered in my ear, "Go find us a room when you get off, then call me and tell me where you are. You can leave early, I'll close up." I reached for the money, quickly slid it into my pocket and wondered if this was what everybody did. If there was no "other life." I still didn't know I could say no to sex.

So, once a week, that twenty dollar bill slid across the bar, and once a week I found the room. "Next time, find something farther away, so we can be more discreet," he said, one night, at the Hotel a few blocks away. I liked that Hotel. Harry did not, "Someone might see me here!" I knew he meant someone might see him here with me, but I tried not to notice.

I did notice that I was visiting men in hotel rooms to pay my bills. I did notice that I was sleeping with my boss because I liked having a relationship.

But I wanted to work here so I could change my life! I was afraid.

Harry didn't notice when I left early on other nights, he didn't notice who I talked to or who I left with. Charles didn't notice. Or I didn't think they did because they didn't say anything. *If they really cared about me they would have said something.* That's what I thought. That's how I knew no one cared what I did. That I was an invisible person here, too.

∼

I found comfort, again, with my best friend, my only friend. But only occasionally, only once in a while. Only on some days. That needle and syringe, the warm, clear liquid that rushed through my veins, into my brain, washing away guilt and fear. Bringing the blessed sense of well-being, promising that everything would be ok.

I thought I was only running away from the turmoil in my soul. I wish I had seen that I was sliding into a pit that I would not be able to climb out of.

∼

A civic-minded, all-men's club began to rent the big meeting room upstairs, every Wednesday. I hurried to bring their food and beer before the dinner crowd began downstairs. These young, good men were looking for projects to make the city a better place.

And they liked me. I was my most sweet, innocent self for them, and they became my big brothers. Asking questions about my life. Hearing that I was a struggling single mom, working long hours to support my three children, they felt sorry for me. I helped them feel sorry for me so they would leave generous tips. They did.

And they never touched me, never patted my butt or pulled me onto their laps, never asked to meet me later. That's how I knew they cared about me. This felt really good and I liked to be with them.

But downstairs I had to be the sassy and flirty girl. I was alluring and wore a button that said, "If it feels good, I'll do it," and people liked that. A lot of men asked what it meant and I responded, "What would you like it to mean?" Not very many men walked away. I should have been wearing a button that said "Beware".

Harry The Bartender took me to afterhours parties with other nightclub owners. In back rooms, with large movie screens. The images were grotesque. Beautiful people having ugly sex. I wiped away tears as I watched. They were real tears, spilling over the rims of my eyelids because I was appalled at the films! I was disgusted. I had thought nothing could disgust me and again, I was happy to know something did. Maybe somewhere inside I was still a real person.

~

He was married, Harry was. I knew from the beginning. I knew he had two children, a little boy and a little girl. His wife never came to his bar. She avoided this place. I thought, *She should be here helping. She should be his partner. She should be helping to build his business, not me!* I believed she didn't care about him, and that helped me not to feel guilty.

And then, she called me, one afternoon. Asked me to come to her house to talk. I went.

She served tea in pretty little china cups. I looked around, at her house, at toys scattered on the floor, at unfinished homework pages still on the kitchen table. I listened as she told her children to brush their teeth, as she shooed them off to bed.

Then I listened as she became the first wife ever to ask me what she was doing wrong, what she could do to make her Harry come home to her every night. "Her Harry", she said.

I was stunned at her honesty, yet braced myself for the anger I knew was to come.

But she had asked me the question and I felt I owed it to her to, at least, give her an honest answer.

"You should hang around his bar a lot."

She countered with, "I hate bars. I don't even like the taste of alcohol. I've never liked bars, or large groups of people. I don't know what to do in those places."

I let her talk, for a long time. I listened to her anger and finally her heartache. Then I shared mine.

"If I had a husband, someone who married me, gave me a home, let me stay home and care for my children…if I could just be a homemaker…I'd give up *everything*. I'd give in on *everything*. You have it and you are throwing it all away just because you don't like bars! This is his dream, and you are running away from it. You act like you don't want him."

She glared at me with angry, hateful eyes. I waited. Her shoulders sank, she reached for the blanket on the couch, tucking her knees against her chest as she wrapped herself, cocoon-like in the blanket.

It was a long time, as we sat silently, before she could look at me and ask, "What should I do?" I watched tears run down her cheeks. I knew Harry would be very angry and wouldn't like what I was going to say, yet I went on, because right then, sitting there in her living room, I liked her a lot more than I did him.

"Be present, just be there," I told her. "Come in with a sexy dress, drink sloe gin fizz, it's a mild, girlie drink, you'll like it. Nurse it along for an hour. Bring a few girlfriends along and laugh. Sit close to the bar. Get over being disgusted. You have to love what he loves. Just be there and be proud of him."

An hour later, I left, moved by her honesty and her cleanness. But I also knew she'd never do it.

I was wrong! The next night she was there, with her friends, drinking that sloe gin fizz, for an hour. And she was there several nights every week after that, always surprising us.

And Harry never slid another twenty dollars across the bar to me.

I wished I was her.

Chapter 13 – Golden Boy

But I was not her. She had a husband and he bought her a house. He worked at a job while she took the kids to band and soccer. She cooked yummy meals and made a home that he went back to every night. Even after meeting me in a hotel room, he had gone home to her, to his wife.

I began to wonder if I had been wrong to ask Smitty to leave. Maybe just having a husband was the most important thing in the world.

If I just had a husband now, if he worked while I made a home for us, I wouldn't care if he slept with other women, or if he went off on adventures. If I just had a husband, I would be a good mom, I knew I would. Drugs and other men would mean nothing. I'd give up everything, anything, just for that, just for my husband.

My heart beat faster, every day, as I thought maybe it could happen for me! I cut pictures from magazines, pictures of what my house would look like, what color my kitchen would be. I'd put frilly curtains in Lucy's room, and a pink quilt on the bed. I'd do bright colors in the boys' room, yellow and blue and red...the colors of crayons. I began to be hopeful!

Until the morning I woke early and stumbled into the bathroom. I was dying of thirst and leaned over the sink to fill a glass with water. I lifted my head back to drink, and caught sight of myself in the mirror. I had looked in that mirror every day, getting ready for work. I used it to put on eyeliner, then mascara, a touch of color on my cheeks, leaving my hair curly-fluffy. Every day, the same things until I no longer saw me. I only saw the face needing make-up.

But that morning, that one morning, I saw me and I wondered what had happened to the girl I had been, the girl who had been excited to have a baby every year.

I was pale and thin again. My hair was limp and my eyes grey and, more than grey, they were blank, yet the girl in the mirror scolded me. *Face it, you stupid girl! Stop wasting time being dreamy about a husband and house and pretty curtains on your windows! No one will ever want to marry you! Not ever! Who wants some girl with three babies? And where do you think you gonna find some nice guy, some single guy to marry you and have money for you to stay home?* I finished the water, hoping with each swallow that magic would happen and I would know the answers.

No magic came. I set the glass on the sink and forced myself to look in the mirror again. *Ok girl, there is no knight in shining armor that is going to come swooping into a bar, look at you, fall in love, and rescue you and your children. This is not the movies. This is your real life. Stop dreaming, get on the bus, and go to work!* Always those words, *Go to work!*

As the hard fist of reality reached through the mirror and punched me in the stomach, I threw up. As I washed my face, I let husbands and nice kitchens and frilly curtains go down the drain. Then I threw up again.

This was the morning I remembered my father's words, "No one will ever love you as much as we, your family, as much as we do! It will never be better than this, so you should appreciate us."

I sat on the edge of the tub and thought about living at home, with that family. I thought about being alone with The Secret, the secret that could send my father to jail. "It will drive your mother insane and put your brother and sister in an orphanage. Is that what you want?" My Dad said that to me often. It would be my fault, if I didn't guard The Secret. It would never be better than those days! His words circled my head, over and over. I couldn't make them stop. I realized he was right, and threw up again.

Then I washed my face for the third time, went to the kitchen and made toast. I drank a glass of milk, took my pills, hid my unused needle and syringe in a sock in my drawer, fixed my hair, applied extra make-up, and walked to work. I wanted to be there early, to stop dreaming, to shut my father up, and to avoid my children. I had kept The Secret, I had protected my brother and sister, my mother, but I knew I was failing to protect these, my own children. This was my new secret to hide. *I am a failure and no one will ever want me. If this secret gets out, they will take my children away! They will be in an orphanage!*

~

I liked this job, because here I knew what to do, here everything made sense. People came to drink and have fun and sing-a-long with their friends. I was here to help make that happen. I knew how to do that. I knew how to smile and laugh, bring drinks, and serve steaks.

I knew how to make the most of my "If it feels good, I'll do it!" button and I had charmed Civic Interest Guys. And I decided if Harry ever again slid the twenty dollars across the bar to me, I'd smiled and slid it back.

Then I noticed a young woman, new to me, stopping in every night before opening. She sat at the bar, in her nurse's uniform. Harry leaned forward to hear her quiet voice, as she smiled and tossed her long hair over her shoulder. I knew those looks. They were familiar with each other.

"Can I get you something from the kitchen," I asked. Every afternoon, I asked her and every afternoon she brushed me aside with a wave of her hand. She didn't answer with words, just the wave of her hand, that said "go away".

I didn't like her and I was not nice to her. I wanted very much to pound my fist on the bar and say, "I know what you are doing! Stay away from Harry. His wife is a nice person." But I didn't say that. I pretended to ignore her while giving both of them cold, steely looks. When

Clair

I decided to stop sleeping with him, I thought it was a good thing to do. It would be good for him, for his wife, but it had made no difference. I had been replaced.

∼

Taking a taxi home every night at three in the morning was expensive and I wondered if I could manage having my own car. Maybe it wouldn't cost that much more and I knew Civic Interest Guys would help me find one.

I started with tired looks and slow service so they would ask, "Are you ok? You seem pretty tired tonight."

"Oh yes, well, I couldn't find a ride home last night when we closed, so I had to walk, It took about an hour, but yes, I'm ok. I'll catch up on my sleep tonight!"

A few weeks later I added, "But I'm thinking about buying a car so I can get home earlier." And then, "So, anybody know where I can buy a good used car?" Finally, "How can I get a loan to buy a car? With really cheap monthly payments"

They were eager to help! Mr. Dave had a used car lot, with a nice station wagon that would be "just perfect for you and your children... I can let you have it for what I paid for it...glad to help."

He talked to a Banker Man, and a loan was ready if I came and signed papers. I went on a Monday morning when the bar opened late. I sat across from Mr. Banker Man as he explained the terms to me.

"Sign here, on this line, and date it. The payments are as low as we can possibly make them." I looked at the paper and the payment was lower than my taxi bill every month!

"Just bring me proof of insurance, and the car is all yours."

"Sure, no problem...how do I do that?"

He gave me a list of agents, and was genuinely sorry none of Civic Interest Guys sold car insurance. I'd have to do this on my own. I took the list he handed to me, "Ok, I'll call someone today, and be back to pick up the car this afternoon."

It was not to be. The first agent would be happy to see me in about an hour. "Just bring your driver's license, and the paperwork the bank gave you, and we'll set you up. It should only take about ten minutes." I did not have a driver's license.

I called the next number on the list, and made an appointment because I knew I could be more persuasive in person. *I need someone who will forget to ask for my license.*

I wore a longer skirt, a white blouse and a cardigan sweater, shoes with flat heels. I prepared my speech and practiced my innocent girl smile in the mirror before going.

After handing me forms to fill out, getting my signature on the right lines, he stood and said, "Ok, just let me make some copies of these papers, and your license..." he waited, hand outstretched. Fumbling in my purse, I went through documents in a brown manila envelope.

"I know it's here!" Allowing panic to creep into my voice, I dumped everything on his desk. "I don't know what happened, maybe I dropped it somewhere!"

"Well, then, no problem, I'll just hold on to this form, and you can bring your license in when you find it." I gathered my things, stuffed everything back in my purse, and called the next person on the list, and then the one after that.

On my fourth appointment, I took my children with me. I filled out the same forms, answered the same questions, and became just as confused as I tried to find my license. I had a large purse this time. "It's here, I know it is! I tossed it in here this morning." Twice I stopped looking for the small license, set my purse on his desk, and went to bring a child back to a chair. "No, Matthew, honey, don't touch those books!" And then, "Oh, Michael, babe, no! Those drinks are not for us, here, come sit with Mommy. I have to find my license. We'll be done in a minute."

Sighing deeply, I straightened my skirt, and once again started The Search. This Mister Nice Person, feeling sorry for me, finally said,

"Here, I can see you're struggling, I'll just give you these papers. Take them back to the bank so you can pick up your car. Just don't forget to bring your license in when you find it so I can make a copy of it."

I was an overworked, frazzled young mother, spewing forth grateful expressions. As long as I was in his office. When I was on the bus going home. I sat up straight. I knew he'd forget about my license in a few days. I wore my proud "I did it!" smile.

The following day I drove my red and white station wagon to work. I had a bank loan, and my car was insured. No one knew I did not have a driver's license and I felt very powerful, definitely in control of my life. Definitely the boss of me!

One evening, when business was slow, Harry leaned across the bar, "Hey kid, they are making it legal in Indiana for women to be bartenders! You should do it. I can hire another waitress, and you can work some nights for me." He handed me the application.

Wow, you are probably the first person to ever have a car with a loan and insurance but no driver's license…now maybe you'll be the first female bartender in Indiana!

I mailed my application on the way home the same night Harry gave it to me. I mailed it at the main post office so it would get there faster. I wanted to be first.

~

My Old House was one of the string of bars and clubs along two blocks of Main Street. Several owned by "The Brothers," others were independent. Some opened early in the morning, dark, smoky, dirty, places that smelled of stale beer, old cigarettes, and urine. People drank beer or whiskey at ten am. Entertainers there were people to be made fun of, to laugh at and ridicule. A tragic, overweight, old lady dancing in a skimpy outfit. I often wondered if she knew they were only making fun of her when they tossed quarters on her little stage. She just beamed a toothless smile and thankfully picked up those quarters. No one cared.

Other places were nightclubs, not opening till three or four in the afternoon. They were dark also, but clean and shiny. Cute waitresses served pretty drinks with fruit tucked under the little paper umbrellas. Here the entertainers were talented singers and dancers who picked up ten or twenty dollar bills from their stages.

Scattered between cheap clubs and fancy clubs were the occasional places to eat, to buy cigars, or to play poker in a back room.

This was our neighborhood, up and down Main Street. We wanted the best for each other and always hoped for just one person, even just one, to find a life away from Main Street.

~

And one afternoon, as I parked my car behind My Old House, checking to lock the door before going in to work, I saw one of The Brothers walking toward me. He owned the little seedy bar next door. Leaning against my car, comfortable in his expensive clothes, he lit his cigarette with a flashy gold lighter I knew was expensive.

I wonder why he's trying to impress me, a little nobody waitress. He chatted as though we knew each other well, as though we were best friends. We were not best friends, only casual friends, so I listened carefully, cautiously, saying as little as possible. Finally I stood up straight, walked a few steps to stand in front of him, and said, "Ok, what is this about? What do you want?"

His head jerked around in surprise, but he met my eyes and gave me a straightforward answer, "I want you to come work for me. I need someone to manage the Top Top next door, days. I've watched you, and now that you have a bartender license, I think you could do it. It's a rough place, and you're little, but you're tough, so I think you could keep order and manage the business side. I'll come in and take over nights, and you can go home. I know you have kids, so this might work good for you, working days instead of late nights. What do you think?"

What did I think? I was flattered, and shocked! I barely knew him, I thought he barely knew me. The idea was intriguing, "manage the business side!?" This was a promotion! I forgot about caution and being suspicious. I quickly said "Yes!" and was excited.

Then I walked into my bar and looked at Harry, at Charlie, and I couldn't tell them. I didn't know how. Harry and I still really liked each other. I loved when he'd lean one elbow on the bar, smile and talk to me as though I was an important person. Charlie still gave me that little shake of his head that said, "I know what you doing and you should stop."

We had regular customers, people I liked, and Civic Interest Guys upstairs…these people who smiled when I walked up to their table, these people who liked me. I knew their names. It would be hard to leave.

It had not been hard to leave the VanClyde. In less than a year, I no longer remembered the name of the hostess who trained me, nor the names of any girl I worked with! I could not even remember the names of band members. We worked together every night, yet I didn't know if the other waitresses had children or how they managed. We had done our jobs well, without knowing each other. It had been easy to leave.

At My Old House, I knew everyone and it would be hard to leave, yet, I wanted this better job. I finally told Harry and Charlie.

"Working days will be better for me and for my family. I won't be exhausted. I'll sleep at night, when my children do. I'll be a better mom." Charlie only rolled his eyes as though he knew better, but Harry said, "Well, you're not really leaving, you'll just be right next door. We'll see you every day."

Civic Interest Guys were most disappointed, "Does the Top Top have a meeting room?" I shrugged my shoulders and said, "Well, no, it's a little place. But I can stop in here and say 'hi' to you on your meeting nights." They liked that.

I took three days off to prepare for my new job. *I'll be sharp, and prove I can be good at business, that I can do more than serve drinks.*

I took books from the library about managing a bar, and I didn't touch the needle and syringe still in a sock in the back of my drawer. I tried to sleep without pills, and I made myself start the morning with only coffee to wake me up. *Now I will have a fresh start. This time I will make it because I'll be working days, I'll be a business person. This will make a difference.*

I wanted a new look, to go with my new job, and dyed my hair a soft, natural blonde. I also taped a picture of a woman in a business suit on my mirror to inspire me.

~

The Top Top was a rough bar. I was glad for a good salary because I would have no "added income" from tips or "after hours dates." These men drank beer, played pool, fought over cards, and never paid for sex.

My first morning, as The Brother showed me how to take inventory and order liquor, how to hide the cash, and what to do when trouble started, I sat back in the booth, and smiled. I loved this challenge...of keeping order, being in charge. Of being a boss.

When The Brother left, as I gathered up the paperwork, I surveyed the long, rectangular room, a door at each end. I looked at the booths on this long side, vinyl seats with duct tape patches, the color worn from a thousand people sliding in and out over the years. The tables were checkered with cigarette burns, the varnish worn off. Nobody cared.

I looked at the bar, on the long wall opposite the booths. The mirrored-back was ancient, various liquor bottles jutted out from the shelves in no particular order, their black pour spouts sticking up in all directions. I marched behind the bar to turn the bottles so the labels faced out and I adjusted the black spouts to all point in the same direction.

The man working there opened six bottles of beer and passed them across the bar for men waiting there, poured shots for three. He didn't care about labels and spouts. It was his last day.

The high spot was the pool table at the back. Placed at a slight angle, dimly lit, it drew a crowd from opening to closing. The table was never empty, there was always a game, and money on each game.

Music came from a tape player behind the bar. The familiar smell of stale beer and whiskey mingled with the cigarette smoke. The floors and tables were sticky, and nobody cared.

∼

My first weeks were hectic. I opened at eight every morning, washed the tables and mopped the floors, kept the inventory, placed the liquor order, handled deliveries, opened bottles of beer, poured shots, and talked to customers. They liked talking to me. Most days I was the only girl. Women didn't come here, not young ones, only older, hardened women looking for a free drink, or to pull their man away before he lost his paycheck on the pool table.

I kept the phone behind the bar handy for when I needed to call the police, about once a week. Tommy The Beat Cop made his rounds each day along Main Street. He checked in here every hour because he worried about me, the sweet, vulnerable little thing,

"And what are you doing behind the bar at the Top Top, of all places," he asked.

"I need the daytime job," I told him, smiling sweetly, "so I can sleep when my kids do."

I wondered how the men could play pool and drink all day, until I saw how much money they made! Pool was not a game. This was their job, and they worked it seriously.

Some games, with large amounts of money on the table, became intense, tempers flared. In an instant, a beer bottle was cracked on the edge of the table to create a sharp, jagged, weapon. The instant a hand went around the neck of a bottle, I reached for the phone. I didn't try to talk anybody down. I didn't ask questions. I just called the police. Nobody cared. They were all here the next day.

I did my best to never come from behind the bar. It was difficult when the waitress was off because state law forbid customers to carry drinks, not from the bar to a table, not from one table to another. Only waitresses or bartenders could carry drinks. From behind the bar, I couldn't serve the booths or tables, so everyone sat at the bar when I was here alone.

The law also said a person must be seated to be served alcohol, or to drink it. On crowded days, with only ten bar stools, I pretended to not notice the men finding little spaces to stand at the bar. I passed their drinks to them anyway....nobody cared.

The pool players left their bottles on the far end of the bar, next to the pool table. Others devised schemes to get me from behind the bar, but it never worked. I kept the bar between me and them. I was in charge there, safe, and I liked that very much.

I decide who can have another drink, I decide when or if I call the police, I decide who stays and who cannot, I am the boss. I like being the boss. It feels better than charging for sex. I like this power.

I had no power, though with one very, very little old man who came in and sat in a booth about once a week. He had bushy grey hair, and I could see a scrawny man under the oversized coats he wore winter and summer alike. He brought his own bottle, in a paper bag and camped out for the afternoon. The same booth every time. Didn't order anything. Homeless, he sat there in the winter to be warm and in the summer to escape the heat. It was against the law for him to bring his own bottle, illegal to drink it here, but I pretended not to see. I had learned to overlook a lot, working at the Top Top.

To my dismay, I could not ignore when he messed his pants and didn't leave...just sat there, asleep or passed out, I didn't know. On that day, on those days, I did come out from behind the bar. Not one man bothered me because they knew I was about to do what they didn't want to do. I would go to him, touch his shoulder, take his hand, then his arm, physically escorting him out.

"Too bad, nameless little old man, but you have to leave, you smell too bad." The first time I had told him to leave, he only stared at me with blank eyes...yellow eyes, sunken deep into his wrinkled, yellow face, eyes that were a picture of a life deep in misery. Telling him to leave always went unheeded. I had to walk out from behind the bar to usher him out! To hold his arm until he stood on the sidewalk, looking up and down Main Street. I wiped off the seat, sprayed the room with deodorizer, and took my place behind my safe bar again. Everyone breathed a sigh of relief, and took up their game again.

~

Beneath the power, beneath the good salary, I began to see the squalidness of this bar, where I spent my days. The floor always sticky, and no amount of washing cleaned it. Too often The Brother didn't come in that night until 8, or 9, or maybe 10, sometimes not at all. I couldn't leave until he came, or sent someone in his place. I think he forgot about me. Invisible.

Nights, the crowd was bigger, meaner. I was glad the law said I couldn't serve a drink after two am. I waited for the last drinker or pool player to leave so I could clean up and lock the door and be out of there. Ready to open again in the morning. My new exciting promotion, my new job, was now exhausting, and I grew tired of pudgy drunks and men who never showered.

~

And then, one bright and sunny summer afternoon, into this picture, walked a Golden Boy...tall and thin, he was, clean white shirt, well-fitting jeans, and hair the color of golden strawberries, kissed by sunlight. He'd come to play pool, his friends were here, welcoming him, glad he'd stopped by. He nodded to them, turned to look at me, and came to the end of the bar. I handed him the beer he asked for.

He didn't play pool that afternoon. I didn't mop the floor. He leaned on the bar, this beautiful, lanky person, and talked to me about books he'd read and loved, Atlas Shrugged being his favorite. I told him about Steinbeck and we compared their philosophies, Ayn Rand and John Steinbeck. I couldn't believe this person was here, in my dirty bar, talking to me about serious literature. I couldn't believe he chose talking to me over pool with his buddies!

In the weeks that followed, he was here every day, standing at the end of my bar, waiting for me to talk to him. He was in construction, working on the new city-county building down the street. With time on his hands, unable to work because it had been raining every day.

I was thankful for that, because now it was not raining in my world anymore.

Chapter 14 – It's Only A Little Tarnish

On the day the rain stopped, the sun in all its glory shone over downtown. I could hear the buzz of construction. Workers climbed the rafters of the new building, pedestrians put hands to foreheads, shielding their eyes from the sun, looking up to watch workers walk the scaffolding, tools in hand. They were fearless, those hard-hatted men. As ground-level watchers went on their way, each to his own cubicle in his own office building, to do his own job, each walked with a spring to his step and joy in his heart. It did one good to watch the fearless.

But not for me. I unlocked the door to the Top Top with a heavy heart, knowing there would be no sunshine strolling through my door today. My Golden Boy would be walking those steel beams high above the city.

I was glad for the routine business of running the bar, an easy way to dispel my sadness.

"Hey, Joe, how are you this morning? You got my order straight today? Three cases of Old Crow, not two. You got 'em?... good."

"Oh, Tommy, finally, you here to spray my roaches? It's about time! Maybe you can take some with you, I got lots to spare!"

Mike The Brother, now Mike The Owner to me, stopped by and I was eager to sit and review the books with him, proud of my work, mostly needing the distraction. Anything to break the boredom of this day. Waiting to see if my Golden Boy would come here after work.

~

Clair

"Hey, kid, you're doing good. Nice profit, neat books you keep here, easy to understand. You handling the rowdy guys ok? Any trouble over the pool table?"

"Nope, I just reach around and call the cops. No trouble at all. Mostly I keep myself behind the bar, but I'm good at smacking any hand that reaches me. Or refusing drinks, that always gets them!"

"Yeah, I think they're learning not to mess with you. And I like having a cute little thing behind the bar that's tougher than these guys. They think you're a challenge, and that's good for business."

I watched him walk out the door, even from the back his clothes looked expensive. His haircut was perfect and he walked as though he owned the world. For a brief moment I wished I was still a one hundred dollar girl.

But only for that fleeting moment. Until an empty beer bottle pounded on the bar called me back to this day and this hour, in my squalid bar and my ruined life. I could only shrug my shoulders, because, after all, I did this to myself.

And then it happened! My Golden Boy sauntered in that back door, just as he did on those rainy days when he had nothing else to do. Fresh off the steel girders, hard hat left behind, that golden red hair glistened with sweat. He ran his hand through it, trying to smooth it before he looked at me. Two steps inside the door, still trying to tame his hair, he stood still and smiled at me. The smile that melts hearts. The grin that says, "you are the most special person I've ever met!"

I watched him walk toward me, to stand at his spot at the end of the bar, his jeans grimy along his thighs where he'd wiped his hands all day, his white t-shirt stuck to his chest from the hot, humid day. He looked marvelous to me, my Golden Boy.

I handed him a beer, his usual. "I didn't expect you here."

"What?" he grinned, teasing me, "you haven't been waiting for me all day?"

"Well, I thought since you went back to work, you know, you wouldn't have time to hang around here."

"Baby, I have a wife who kicked me out a long time ago, I have a kid who I don't even know is mine. I have a job to go to most days, and then I have you...the only thing I have to look forward to. And you thought this wouldn't be the first place I come when I get off work! Well, it is, and now you know. Standing here, watching you work, listening to you talk, this is where I belong!"

He came every day after work. Didn't play pool. Endured the teasing aimed at him from the men around the table,

"So, you gonna get in the game or just go talk, huh?"

"You gonna let a girl take you out of the game?"

"Ha-ha, money or the girl, what's it gonna be?"

Seeking to bring him back to them, to a good game. He only laughed and waved, bought them a round of drinks, and turned to watch me from the end of the bar...waiting for me to have a few spare moments again to stand and talk with him. Still lighting up my dirty, stinky bar. Still lighting up my life.

At last call, I locked up the bar and took him home with me. I made coffee and sat on my couch to listen to his stories. About growing up in the backwoods of Appalachia. About a little shack he called home, a little shack with no electricity and no running water. About an outhouse that never got cleaned and about possum and raccoons that turned soup and turnips into meals. About getting old enough to walk barefooted beyond his own hill and valley and explore other places. Each night I hung on every word of the story he would tell.

"In all my walking over them hills, I still remember the first time I came to a place that didn't look anything like where I lived," he began. "The buildings were all painted. I don't think that roof ever leaked at all! And the chickens were in a fence. I was awestruck. And a boy saw me, a boy about my age. He looked at me strange, I looked back at him, his arms and legs and face all clean and shiny, black hair short, I could see his ears. He made that wave of his hand that said come closer.

"I did. He smiled and said, 'Wanna watch TV?' Just like that, 'wanna watch TV?' I had no idea what he was talking about, but I followed him into his house. And my whole world changed in that one moment. Staring at the TV showing pictures of a world I never heard of, at the things in his house. I went back every day, and saw water come out of a pipe over a basin, and an outhouse in the house. I learned a new word…'flush' and was fascinated. I don't think I ever had to pee so much in my life!"

I listened and loved the innocence of that little boy, an innocence I had never known. I sat up, to watch his face. "Then what?"

"One day that boy took me for a walk over another hill to a town. He took me to his favorite place…a library. Those books changed me. Changed my world, and I was never the same after that day. I couldn't get enough of those books, don't know why, I just couldn't.

"Well, I don't know how it happened, or when, but eventually we left the mountains, and moved here. And all those things I'd seen on that day became usual. Everybody had them, I had them. And we laughed the day my mom came home wearing her first pair of shoes. First time she ever had something on her feet. Well, they weren't really shoes, they were boots. Gosh, how she loved those boots, wore them everywhere. It was summer, but she wore those boots! Guess that's probably why everybody's still always calls her Boots!"

He laughed, enjoying his own storytelling.

Night after night he told stories to me. He wanted me to tell stories, but I had none. None I wanted to tell. None in which I was that innocent, naïve.

He sees me this way, though, sweet, innocent, child-like. I've made him think of me like that. I've worked hard to be that way with him. No, I'm not telling my stories.

I sent him home after a few hours. Not sure why. Protecting my innocent image, maybe, now, with Gertie gone and a new babysitter here, I wanted to be careful.

A few months earlier, Gertie had been unusually quiet for two days before she came to me, finally, to say, "I love your children, they have just about become my own. I can't bear leaving them, but," She reached for the tissue that was always in one of her pockets.

"But, I'm just too old! Almost 85 now. My sister wants me to come live with her. I know the kids love me, but I think I have to go. I just can't do it anymore, I'm too tired."

Dropping her face in her hands, wrenching sobs spilled through her fingers. My heart ached, listening to her, and I knew she was right, and I didn't try to make her stay. I was proud of myself for that. At least for that.

From an ad in the newspaper, I found Jodie, with a little boy about the age of my boys. Never married, single mom, walking with a disjointed hip, partially dragging one foot. With a child. In her farming community, in her little town, she felt out-of-place.

"I'm 30 years old," the words rushing out to me when I interviewed her. "I want to be on my own, I don't want to live with my parents my whole life. I don't want to leave my boy."

I could see that her hip problem left her with a slow, awkward gait, but she managed her boy well. I liked her, and she thought coming to the big city, managing the house for me was her chance of a lifetime. I liked that too.

Her only condition was that I take her home to spend weekends with her parents. I agreed because "I have a car!"

With the additional child, we moved to a bigger house, older, close to downtown. Lots of big rooms for children to play in, a small yard even. I was proud to give them that.

I had a fresh start, again here with Jodie. She hadn't heard me throwing up in the bathroom, she hadn't heard me come home at four am, she hadn't heard me stumble up the stairs and fall into bed. She hadn't watched strange men leave in the morning. She hadn't watched my children turn to her, turn away from me.

Jodie sees a hardworking, struggling mom. A good mom. Sweet. Nice. I didn't want her to find a man here in the morning. No, I didn't want to ruin my fresh start, so I sent Golden Boy home every night. Wherever home was. I forgot to ask.

Clair

This was the month of May. Idyllic May. When trees sprouted leaves and flowers bloomed, and my future seemed full of promise and love. A real home maybe, now, with My Golden Boy! I would stay with my children, getting so big, three, four, and five years old. Not my babies now. Little people.

Three-thirty every day, Golden Boy walked through my door at the bar, every night he drank coffee and sat on my couch and told stories to me. Every night he left without being told. Every night I went to bed feeling cherished. "I will put my needle and syringe away for good, before he finds out about them. We will build a home together."

∼

I had a day off, once at the end of May. Golden Boy came to my house. "I have a surprise for you!" His eyes were lit up and his face glowed. "Here's something I want to show you, it's your day off. This will be fun! You'll like it."

Jodie stared at him, suspicious that he'd walked in without knocking. The children stood around, waiting for the surprise from this strange man who made their mom smile.

He took my hand and pulled me into the bedroom. "Come here, I have to show you alone." He closed the door. "Here, sit here, on the bed."

My heart raced, I held my breath. What good thing did he have for me? A ring? Would he ask me to marry him? From my seat on the edge of the bed, hands demurely in my lap, I looked up at him, eager, trusting, happy, waiting.

He knelt on the floor, pulled a rolled-up cloth out of his pocket and spread its contents on the bed beside me.

And there it was, a needle and syringe, a cotton ball, a bottle cap, and a two ounce bottle of paregoric. His eyes glowed as he looked up into my eyes, waiting for my response.

For a moment, just a moment, the room turned black. I almost fainted. I didn't want him to see my disappointment. I could only stare at him, at his face, my mind grasping for the right thing to say. I did not want him to know these were familiar to me. I didn't want him to know.

"Wait till you see how much fun this is," he said. "See, we cook the camphor off and we have a bit of opium! Not much...but enough! Let me show you."

Gently tied my arm off, found a good vein, and injected the golden liquid. He watched my eyes, waiting to see the pleasure he'd given me, proud of himself.

Bombarded my own thoughts, I was afraid. *I should tell him I've done this before! I should tell him heroin is better, way,* way *better! Thank goodness I haven't been shooting up in my arms anymore so there are no needle marks!* But I didn't. I didn't tell him any of these things. Afraid it would change the picture he had of me. Maybe he wouldn't cherish me, or be gentle with me, or be proud of me still. Or stand at the end of my bar every day, glowing.

So I pretended this was all new to me. I let him be proud of the gift he brought. I felt nothing from that tiny surge of paregoric. It was only paregoric, after all, but I pretended to enjoy the mild high it could give.

This ended the month of May, and ended the life I had hidden. I was no longer a person who got high alone. I had a partner. I only had to pretend this was as new to me as it was to him. I didn't know if I could pretend that much.

He was still my Golden Boy, and I knew he loved and cherished me. But this was the day a tiny bit of tarnish began to appear along the edges of that beautiful, shiny hair.

Just a tiny bit, that tarnish, easy to ignore. It's only a little tarnish, after all.

∼

He rushed in another day. "Hey, get your car! I want you to run me by my old house so I can get some stuff I left at my wife's house."

Sure enough, I can do that. Maybe getting his stuff out of her house would rub some tarnish off.

"Here, park here, in this lot next door, wait in the car while I run in. Wait here for me."

Car radio on, I leaned back, daydreaming, eyes closed, window down, sunshine and a light breeze on my face.

Bam! Bam! My face was smashed into the steering wheel, my hair grabbed with two fists and my face pounded into the steering wheel over and over and over. Blood poured down onto my skirt. I peed my pants. I couldn't stop it.

When will this end! Please stop! I was frozen and didn't think to defend myself. The pounding continued forever, until Golden Boy pulled her away and forced her into the house.

It was his wife.

Coming back to my car, he handed me a few wet towels. "Here, you can clean up."

He climbed in the passenger side, leaned close against the door, away from me. I could hear his words, that he was angry with his wife, that he had smacked her a few times to punish her. He ranted, on and on.

I wanted to scream, "Shut up! Shut up and help me!" But I didn't. He was in a different world and didn't see me. In his world, this was not a big deal. I was not the first woman to ever get beat up! He was here, in my car, talking, but I knew I was alone, because he really didn't see me. I dropped him off somewhere downtown.

And then, I had to go to work. A shot of heroin would take the edge off my pain, and I knew where to make a quick stop before work. But nothing could hide the cuts, and no amount of makeup could hide my swollen black eyes and green and yellow bruises that developed over the next few days.

Everyone at the bar joked about wishing they could see the other guy. I laughed it off because I didn't want anyone to know that I didn't deliver a single blow. I just took it, and peed my pants.

This was the first day I looked at my Golden Boy and cried. The tarnish had begun to grow, the shine was fading, and I wondered if there was any polish that would ever rub it away.

But then he became my Golden Boy again, gentle and tender, with stories to tell, with soft eyes and tender words, and he stood at the end of my bar with an armload of books we could read. There was a polish after all!

Chapter 15 – Billy Joe

A person can live with a little tarnish, I decided. Depends on the beauty and value of the object. A little tarnish here and there, mostly hidden, on a beautiful vessel, makes one want to keep it and cherish it.

So it was with my beautiful, literary Golden Boy. I saw the value in this man, so unlike any other I knew. A man who chose me over the pool table, a man who wanted a lengthy discussion after every book he read, a man who wrote poetry, and a man who sat speechless for an hour just to watch the sun rise. Yes, I could certainly overlook that tarnish growing along his edges.

My swollen, blackened eyes healed. The bruises faded, and the scars along my lips and cheekbones faded to nothing. But the needle marks up and down my arms grew. Bruises from them also. I turned up the air conditioning at work so no one would ask why I wore long sleeves on such hot days.

And my tarnished Golden Boy, he and I played a game together – he the adventurer, the initiator, proud that he'd turned me on to shooting paregoric in my veins, proud that he'd shared with me this pleasure, this high, and me a child-like disciple, ready to follow, eager to learn. The game suited me well.

Needle marks I gave myself when alone, with my own heroin, these became well disguised, lost in the ones he gave me.

I wanted to say, "Hey, let me show YOU something. Forget paregoric, try this packet of heroin! Sooo much better."

But that would change the game, I would then become the

leader. He would see the tarnish on me and walk away, no longer wanting to play. The tarnish on me was greater than the tarnish on him, so I did not tell him the truth. I knew there was no polish to take away the now black tarnish on me.

On my next day off, he bounced through my door again, eager and excited, "Hey, come on! Your kids are taking naps. Let's go! I want you to meet some people!" He took my hand to lead me off the couch, away from my book, his arm around me as we left the house. *He's including me in his world. He wants me to come be a part of it.* I was elated!

~

It was a small 2nd floor apartment in an old house off Creighton Avenue, next to the Makoleys Supermarket. Billy Joe and Susan lived there, with their children.

Toddlers padding around barefoot on sticky floors, diapers sagging almost to their knees. Shaggy, sandy haired Billy Joe sat with his wife Susan. They sat at the kitchen table, planted in the center of the room, the center of activity, the center of their lives, that table was.

He jumped up when we came in, knocking the chair over, excited to have us there, excited that Golden Boy brought me.

"Hey, you, it's about time you brought her!" He reached out to shake my hand. I accepted, taking his in mine, expecting the one-two-up-and-down gesture we all make. I felt the trembling in his fingers, his palms were sweaty, and the closeness brought his faint body odor, odd in some way, to my attention. And he didn't stop shaking my hand. On and on it went, each shake more pronounced, deeper, higher. I had to pull away, jerking my hand back, hugging it to my waist, glad it still belonged to me.

This was Billy Joe as I came to know him, I wanted to name him Dynamite Billy, because he was at super speed all the time. Super speed without the drug!

"And, hey, this is my wife, Susan," he tilted his head toward her by way of introduction. She glanced at me, then back to the table, as though I was not there, her attention elsewhere, her pale stringy hair covering her face, Susan the Mouse.

It was a table strewn with cotton balls, old needles, tissues, spoons, lighters, cold pizza, old half-eaten sandwiches, beer bottles, moldy glasses. And two new full bottles of paregoric, standing erect among a pile of empty ones. Empty bottles piled together in the middle of the table, a center piece, a picture of their lives here.

Golden Boy and I, we took our places at the table, bringing extra chairs from another room. We watched Susan pour the amber liquid in her spoon, even as Billy Joe paced. Back and forth behind her, around the table, into another room, back to us.

"Sit down, man, you making me nervous with that. Sit down," Golden Boy said, trying to sound scolding, annoyed, his half-smile defeating it.

He sat on the edge of a chair, Billy Joe did, "Oh, man, this ain't enough, two bottles. I gotta get some more. Already did the store on the corner, can't go there!" Back to pacing, back and forth.

"Sure you can," he said, my slightly tarnished Golden Boy, "take her with you, show her how to score, they don't know her!" I knew in that instant he meant me. I was the new person there. I didn't want to go. For a brief moment I didn't want to go, but then, as though someone flipped a switch, I wanted this new experience, I wanted to be part of this group, I wanted to belong here, I wanted to go!

"Sure, take me, I'll do it," I stood up to show I was eager. "Just tell me what to do!" So it was me and Billy Joe walking down the stairs, across the street, down a block, to the corner drug store. I had to skip a few steps to keep up with him, and I listened closely to his instructions. He talked as fast as he walked.

He waited for me outside, him having been there earlier it would raise suspicion if we were together. I sauntered up to the pharmacy counter, picking up baby aspirin, Johnson's baby powder, and a carton of formula on the way.

"Can I help you, mam?"

"Yes, sir." I jostled my packages a bit. "Paregoric please." He reached under the counter, shoved the notebook and pen my way, I signed my name, my made-up name, and he set the 2 oz. bottle on the counter for me. I tossed a quick, "Thank you, have a nice day," over my shoulder, as I walked away.

Dumping the baby items, I laid the few dollars on the front check-out counter, nodded to the cashier, and left the store. Easy! So easy! We walked two blocks ahead, turned a corner, another two blocks to a drug store and did it again.

Back at the apartment, I was euphoric! Billy Joe bragging on me, "Man, what a natural! You shoulda' seen her! What a genius, walking up with all those baby things in your arms, like you got a teething baby that needs paregoric! Man, I can't believe it! How come we never thought of that?"

My Golden Boy sat a little straighter, nodded at me, proud. Our eyes met, mine excited, happy, proud. His blank, eyelids drooping as he retreated to the serene world of his slight opium high. An hour later, Billy Joe was back to pacing. "Come on," he said to me. "Let's go make some money!" I did not look at Golden Boy; this time, I did not need to.

"Wait." Billy Joe stopped, rushing into the bedroom, coming back to hand me a bulky, oversized sweatshirt, tossing another over his shoulder.

Walking across the parking lot, we entered the supermarket, he grabbed two boxes of Cheerios before we got to the meat department. We took our time, found two of the most expensive steaks for each of us, tucked them under our shirts, paid for the cereal at checkout, and left the store.

Walking to another neighborhood, a better one, he taught me what to say. Here the houses were nice, but not rich. I rang a doorbell. "Yes, mam, I'm Carol. My dad owns the grocery over on Broadway, do you know it? No, well, stop by sometime. Anyway, our meat cooler is being repaired and we don't want everything to go to waste, so could I

But I Can Learn

interest you in buying a few steaks, half price?"

I met Billy Joe around the corner, ten dollars in my pocket. "Oh, man," I thought. "This was so much fun! And so easy." I could barely suppress a giggle. He gave me the fifteen dollars he'd scored.

"I don't do it for money," he needed to say, it was important. "I just like the thrill of getting away with it, of putting it over on them." I understood that. He was the first person I had ever met who was proud to do a wrong thing.

Later that evening, at home with my own children tucked into bed, I walked across the street and scored my own tiny foil packets of heroin with the most fun money I'd ever earned.

~

A few weeks later, I closed the bar, locked up, walked to my car and started for home. East on Wayne Street, right on Samson. I drove this every night. At Lincoln, I saw the light, red. It was red, but would turn green by the time I got there.

There was a man, in his own car, on Lincoln, counting on making it through his yellow light. He sped through and we collided. His car careened across the corner parking lot and stopped, crashing into the building. My car stopped dead in the intersection! I was unhurt. That was my first thought. My second thought was, "Wait, drugs! What do I have in my car, what's in my purse! Oh, wait, nothing, I'm ok, I'm not in trouble." And seconds later, I lifted my head to see the other car. Too many seconds later I thought of the other driver. "Is he hurt?" He was not my first concern, he was my last. And I was ashamed.

Stepping out of the passenger side of his car, unable to open the driver door, he crossed the lot to talk to me, glad I was not hurt. We were not sure whose fault this was, both of us trying to cheat a light, but when the police arrived, when the tow trucks took away our totaled cars, that was of no consequence. It was my fault because I was driving without a driver's license. I'd forgotten about that! I was arrested and released on my own merit, and I fell into my own bed at five am, wondering how I would survive this.

How will I keep my sweet girl image? I don't know. But I did know how to reach for my own needle and syringe, taped along the back of my dresser now, and soothe myself to sleep.

I could hide a needle and syringe, "my works", but I could not hide the accident, because my car was gone.

I could not hide my arrest. Agents from the insurance company came to my home, came to my bar, looking for ways to charge me with insurance fraud. They left defeated, paid all the damages, wrote the bank a check for the car loan and cancelled my insurance.

This was the last day I stood before myself in the mirror, talking to the girl I saw, challenging her to do better, to be better. I looked at that girl, at myself, and I knew on that day that it was hopeless.

I would never meet a nice guy who would marry me and make me an all day mommy. I would never have a home, a kitchen where I would bake cookies and can tomatoes. I would never be a good wife. I would never be a good mommy. I knew I was in trouble and needed help.

I went to my "only slightly tarnished" Golden Boy. In a frantic moment of honesty, I pulled up my sleeves, "Look," I said. "See my arms? I'm not just using the paregoric we score together. I'm using heroin, every day! I have to quit! I have to stop! I'm in trouble!" I did not confess to having done it before I met him, only that I'd gone over the edge since meeting him.

"Wow! Heroin, really!?" I could see his eyes light up, interested and excited, before he quickly turned them to me, to what I was saying. That I was falling apart moment by moment.

He pulled me close to him, sitting on my bed that morning, one arm around my shoulders. The other hand rubbed my arms, soothingly, as though he could wash away those black-and-blue track marks. I couldn't tell.

"Babe," he began. "This isn't a problem. If you like doing drugs, then you should do them. It's no big deal. And if you really don't want to, then you won't. Don't fight yourself. Stop saying you don't want to when you do. I don't care if you use heroin or what, I just want you to be happy and enjoy whatever you're doing. Be free to do whatever you want! Drugs or not, it's your real free choice. Only you decide what you really want. Just be free!"

I sat up straight, away from him a little, so that I could see his face. The face I so loved. The face that seemed free, unchained. "Be like me," he said. "Play with drugs for the adventure, experience everything the world has to offer. It's like the rush I get walking a construction beam high above the street! It's exciting!"

He could not understand that I did not play with drugs. They were my lifeline. I did not feel the rush of adventure, never adventure. Never excitement. Only escape. Escape from guilt and failure. I tried explaining these things to him. And he held me closer. "If that's what you need, if this helps you, then its ok. But be careful so you don't get arrested. And what can I do?"

My answer could only be, "Well, nothing, really, I guess." He did not understand the power, the hold anything could hold over a person. Except adventure. He knew about that. He wanted to experience everything! I gave up trying to make him understand. And the tarnish grew a bit more.

~

I didn't have to be in court for sixty days. Some of those days I plunged into fun with Billy Joe to distract myself. Each time I climbed the steps to his apartment, I knew I would do something new that day. His wife, Susan The Mouse, did not talk to me, nor did she ever leave that kitchen chair. Not that I ever saw.

But Billy and me, we sold more steaks door-to-door, and other days he took me to newer, fancier neighborhoods. "Look here," he'd show me. "See that big house there? Those people are on vacation. Let's go check it out." He knew how to pick the lock. Inside, I watched him find a few items worth takings, setting them by the door. I added a few things and checked to be sure no one was watching before I stepped out to the back porch, anxious to leave.

"No, wait," he held my arm, pulling me back in. "The fun's just starting! Don't you see, look at this big fancy house. We gotta enjoy it! Let's go fix us something to eat. Here, how about these steaks in the freezer? Let's cook 'em." And so we did. They were delicious. We left our dirty plates on the counter for the owners to find.

We took long, hot showers and left the wet towels on the floor. We took a nap in their big puffy bed and left it mussed up so they'd be sure to see. He had so much fun in that house that day! And for a few hours I forgot I had to be in court in forty-seven days.

Golden Boy loved the stories we came back to tell, sitting around that kitchen table. But as we left, walked down the stairs together, he always, always put his arm around my shoulder and said, "Remember, Babe, please remember. Be careful, be very careful."

I was careful. The night I got off work early, and went to their place, Billy Joe was putting a gun in his pocket. "Hey, wait! What's going on?" I was quick to ask, shaken, alert, cautious, afraid. He was more nervous than usual, pacing faster than usual. "It's the drug store in Kendall. Little town like that over there, not much police. I'm gonna hit it tonight, just before they close." He adjusted his belt, rubbed his hands together, then combed his fingers through his hair, trying to keep it off his eyes.

He stopped pacing, turned to stare at me. "You wanna come? Yeah, come, you'll like it." He sat in the chair beside me, took my hand. "Come with me. You've never seen anything like it! Oh, man! When I walk in a store, point my gun in a man's face, in that moment, to that man, when I point that gun at him…I am God!" I stared at him. His face contorted, angry. Not my Billy Joe, not the fun, fun person I knew. I was afraid.

I looked away, looked at Susan The Mouse, and said, as lightly,

But I Can Learn

as casually as I knew how, "No, well, no, I think I'll just stay here with Susan. You can tell me about it when you get back."

"Yeah? Well, ok, then." He hitched up his pants, adjusted his belt, again. And was out the door.

We sat there for a long time, not used to being alone together, The Mouse and me. She'd never spoken to me, barely looked at me in all the months I'd been hanging around. Her babies bounced around, in between chairs and under the table. Still she didn't move, didn't get up. The smell of messy diapers permeated the room. I picked up a little boy, looking around for clean diapers, finding none, I settled for a dish towel. I changed him, and walked over to place him on his mom's lap...the silent, never moving Susan The Mouse.

It was then, only then that she put her arms around her babe, held him to her chest, and spoke to me. Without looking up, she simply said, "Someday he's not coming back, my Billy. You know that, don'tcha? Someday they gonna catch him. Put him in jail. Or someday he's not coming back cause they gonna shoot and kill him!"

I was glad I could sit with her and wait, me, with my thirty-seven days left before court.

Chapter 16 – I Need Help!

We waited, sitting there, waiting for Billy Joe to come home. Susan didn't talk, just sat there with the baby in her lap. I couldn't just sit, looking at her blank face, eyes that looked at nothing, just the table.

"So, Karen," I began. "It's like, after ten, and do you want to put the kids to bed?" I pointed to the boy asleep on the floor. "Or maybe we should feed them something?"

She didn't answer, didn't hear me, maybe. Just stared at the table. As I opened a cupboard door, the roaches scattered, but I found peanut butter and jelly. With lids on, so I deemed it safe. The bread next to it was moldy.

I pulled a knife out of the pile of dirty dishes, and washed it, found a few hot dog buns, a bit stale, but not moldy, and fed the children, washed them up, put them to bed. It was only when they didn't argue with me about bedtime, that I realized I had never heard them speak, not ever, in all the days I'd been there! I wondered if they could.

I went to each one, sat on the edge of their bed and asked what their names were, but to no avail. They only stared at me. *Maybe they can't hear!*

Thoughtlessly I blurted out, "Do you want a cookie?" All their little heads bobbed up and down while they smiled. "So you can hear. Oh, no, I shouldn't have asked you that because I don't have any cookies!" To assuage my guilt, I promised to bring some next time.

Susan didn't move or look at me when I took the baby from her and put him in the crib. He'd fallen asleep in her lap, his head lopped over to one side.

Clair

This irony was not lost on me. *Why am I here, caring for these children instead of at home, caring for my own?* My heart beat faster and faster as guilt descended on me again, hammering into my head, pounding my heart. Before I exploded, before it killed me, I straightened my shoulders and said, out loud to make it real, "I AM caring for my own children. They are home, in a house with a yard, with a babysitter who doesn't come and go. She lives with us, she cooks them good meals, reads them stories, takes them to the park, and she loves them almost as much as I do. And there are no roaches in their home." I told myself these important things to make the hammering stop pounding at me.

The guilt that I wore like a steel cloak, the pounding in my heart, these things I always chased away every few hours with little silver packets of heroin. It was the only thing I knew.

But they did not go away on this night. The pounding was lighter and slower, I could breathe normally, but I didn't feel good. I wanted to feel good, to feel proud of myself. *I should feel proud of myself! After all, my children don't live like this, with sticky floors and dirty clothes and roaches and rats and no food! Feel good about that!*

I turned to look at Susan. She reached across the table, took two little foil packets from the pile in the center, fished the needle and syringe from her sweater pocket. Still didn't look at me, still didn't talk.

Will I end up like that? I didn't think so. I was more controlled. Still the boss of own self. I walked over to the table, took two packets for myself and left.

I didn't see that I was fast becoming just like her.

~

Walking down the stairs, I felt sad, alone. Guilt I was used to. Guilt was true. Guilt made my heart beat fast, but sad and alone! I feared my heart would stop beating. I couldn't catch my breath. I sat on the bottom step and pounded my fist on my head, and my stomach, and my hips. But hitting myself didn't make the sad-aloneness go away, so I pounded on the railing and on the steps. It still didn't go away. I covered my face with my hands and tried to cry. Maybe if I could cry, cry really hard, that would help, but I didn't know how to cry. No one ever taught me to cry.

∼

I walked up my own porch steps, too tired now, too depressed to move quickly, yet anxious to get inside, anxious to push relief into my veins again. Anxious to feel it descend over my head, down through my arms into my fingertips, down my legs into my toes. "Just a few more steps, and I'll be there. Just a few more steps!"

Inside, I closed the front door carefully, not to wake anyone. Turning to walk up the stairs to my room, I saw him, Matthew. Sitting on the top step, in his flannel jammies and little bare feet.

"Matt, honey, why are you up? It's 2:30 in the morning! Why aren't you asleep?"

"I was waiting for you to come home!"

"Why, is something wrong? Why are you waiting for me?"

"So I could see you. I want to see you."

I sat on the step with him, pulled him onto my lap, wrapped my arms around him, rested my cheek on the top of his head, absorbed his little boy smell, and cried.

Now I could cry. This four-year old boy, my son, so full of innocence, an innocence I'd never known, this boy, had a sadness, an aloneness about him that tore at my heart. It made my sadness fade. It made me cry. I cried for him. I cried for myself. Now I cried...hard.

∼

In the morning, I crept out of bed carefully so I wouldn't wake him. It was early, we'd only slept three hours, I should still be asleep, but I needed a shot badly. My skin was creepy, I was chilled to the bone,

Clair

I needed a fix before I started throwing up. I needed to take care of myself before I could talk.

~

I felt the sickness fade, as I sat on the edge of the bathtub, trying to steady my breathing. And then I knew. *I think maybe I need help.* I stood and stared at myself in the mirror and said it out loud, to make it real. *I think I need help.* I said it again. I left the house and went for a walk because I didn't know what else to do. Just walk anywhere.

This is crazy! I know how to score drugs, where to steal the best things. I know where to go to turn a trick for a hundred dollars, or for ten. I know how to con people to do anything I want them to do, but I have no idea how to stop being a stupid junkie. How do I stop forever? I've stopped before, I've gotten clean, but I just do it again! Does anybody stop for good? Has anybody ever? These are the things I said to myself, that I said out loud as I walked toward town.

And then I saw it! I turned a corner and saw the church on the next street. The tall steeple, the gleaming cross on top, the sprawling buildings that filled the whole square block. Big, and fancy. I was drawn there. *They'll know what to do! They'll help me! I'll go there!*

~

The minister was gentle, offered me a comfy chair, a cup of coffee. The familiar smell of it calmed me.

"And what can I do for you today?" he asked. He was full of confidence, I could tell by the way held his coffee, leaned back in his chair, crossed his leg. He had the answers to everything, I could tell that too, there were a lot of books on his shelves and I trusted him enough to tell my story. I told him all of it, unable to stop once I'd started.

For the first five minutes, he didn't move, just stared at me. The smile faded first, then his posture changed from relaxed to stiff and rigid. When he leaned forward, elbows on the desk, looking at the bookcase behind me, at the picture on the wall, at his hands, looking anywhere so he didn't have to look at me, I knew for one fleeting second that I should stop. He didn't want to hear this. But I couldn't stop talking. This was my help. He had to be my helper, where else could I go but to a church!

When I got to the end, finally stopped talking, only then did he look at me. "And why are you here? What can I do for you today?" he asked, his face rigid, lips a straight line, eyes like steel.

"I need to stop, I need to know what to do! How do I do it?"

"Well, young..." he began, paused, and quickly looked away before he continued. I knew he had started to say young 'lady' but couldn't get the word out. I wasn't a lady and I was embarrassed.

"Miss," he began again, more composed. Now he leaned forward slightly and looked at me. "This is Fort Wayne, not New York City or Chicago or Detroit. We don't have drug problems here, we don't have treatment places, I don't know what to tell you. You'd have to go to a bigger city, I guess."

"But I can't go to some treatment place, even if it was here. What would I do with my children, how would I pay my bills if I wasn't working? I can't do that. Isn't there some doctor or something? Can't you help me? You must know something..." I was beginning to panic. I was afraid, and angry and could no longer sit in my chair.

When I stood, he stood, one foot back defensively, hands clenched. He was afraid of me!

I sat back down because I needed him to understand and think of an answer for me.

"Please," I began again. "You are a minister, you've been to college, you must read lots of books and go to seminars and stuff. Look at all the books you have! You have to help me!"

Lowering himself into his chair, he crossed his legs again. I could see by the quick sharp moves when he leaned forward that he was irritated.

"Look, miss whoever you are. I don't even know if this is your real name. But I do know this, it may be 1968, and we may be a modern city, but I do not believe, not for one second, that there is heroin here. I think you are making this up. It's a good story, I'll give you that, but if you came looking for a handout, you came to the wrong place. I'm too smart for this. I think you need to leave now."

I did. I walked away. I did not look at him, I did not say a word. I just walked away.

I was embarrassed, and desperate, and afraid. So I walked again. Just walked, not knowing where to go, I just walked around town.

And then I saw that familiar limestone building, old, preserved, cared for. With its arched windows, gabled roof, and turret corners. I knew the people in this building would help me. *I'll go in here, here they'll believe me, here they'll know what to do.* For one second, as I opened the door, I wondered if this, too, was a stupid thing to do, but I had no other choices. I was desperate and needed help. It was here or nowhere.

Here, the police station.

I walked up the marble steps into the enormous lobby, each footstep echoing loudly. I looked around, awkward. *Maybe this is a wrong idea after all!*

Three large, uniformed officers breezed past me, then stepped back to ask, "Can we help you? You need something?"

"Oh, yes! I need help. I want to know... can you tell me how someone gets help to stop using drugs?" I blurted it out. I said it fast, before they could walk away.

"You know someone needs help? Your boyfriend using drugs?" Bombarding me with questions.

"Stop!" I shouted. "Stop." I pushed my sleeve up, thrust my bare arm toward them, forced them to look at one arm, then the other. At the track marks, the green and yellow and purple bruises.

"It's me. I need help! I have to stop. I can't do this anymore!" I was surprised that tears ran down my cheeks. I was also surprised at my anger.

But I Can Learn

The first officer took my arm, "Come with us, over here." Up the grand staircase on my left, they ushered me into a small room on the second floor. "Wait here, someone will be with you in a minute."

I sat in the metal chair. It took a while before my breathing settled. Settled as much as I was able to make it. Before I could look around, to see where I was, to notice the room. The table in front of me, metal, bolted to the floor. The chairs, bolted to the floor. I realized this was not an office. No desky items on the table, no bookcases, no lamps. *Where am I?!* I began to panic. *This was a mistake! I shouldn't have come here. Why did I come here?! I need to get out of here!*

But I couldn't leave. I tried. I went to the door and it was locked. I pounded and yelled and yanked on the doorknob but nothing happened.

"I think I'm going to throw up!" I yelled over and over, hoping someone would hear me. "I'm sick and I'm going to throw up!" Hoping that would get their attention. It took only a few moments, but felt like hours before someone answered me. Two men, in regular suits, not police uniforms, came in, walked to the table, tossed their notepads down, ordered me to "take a seat". I did. I crossed my arms over my chest to stop shivering. My nose was running and I needed a kleenex.

They introduced themselves, Detective Mean and Detective Nice. I looked at each of them, searching their faces for sympathy. I needed them to feel sorry for me. *Please feel sorry for me.*

"Ok, so tell me, where do you buy your stuff? What's your dealer's name?" On and on with questions. Questions I couldn't answer. Couldn't answer because I didn't know what was happening and the room was spinning.

"What does it matter who I buy from or where? I just want you to help me stop."

A uniformed officer opened the door and set a wastebasket and box of kleenex on the floor, glancing at me before he left. Detective Mr. Nice brought the kleenex to the table. He set the trash basket next to me, "in case you throw up." I was grateful.

He took the chair across the table, assured me "We'll take you to the hospital in a few minutes, to doctors who will help you." I was more grateful. "But first, sign this. We need to go look over some things at your house before we take you to the hospital. Just sign here." He held a pen out to me. I leaned over the desk, threw up in the wastebasket, wiped my face, my nose and eyes with the kleenex, and signed his paper. I didn't read it.

They looked angry, these men did. I laid the pen on the table, pushed the paper toward them, and said, "I don't even know why you're so mad. I'm just here for help. It's not like I'm selling drugs or anything."

"We'll see about that!" Detective Mr. Mean said, jamming the paper I'd signed into his folder. "Let's go. Stand up!"

Willing my legs to hold me, to steady me, I did. He stepped forward and handcuffed my hands behind my back, taking away my ability to brace myself against the table. He took my arm, Detective Nice took the other arm as they ushered me out of the room, down the long flight of stairs, into a squad car. *Soon this will be over,* I told myself. *Just do what they ask, they're here to help. It will be ok, just do what they say.*

~

They drove their car onto my back lawn. Three or four police cars already there. Two more parked on the street in front. In my house, people in every room, I didn't know why.

"Why are you turning all the chairs over? Why are you pulling my books off the shelves? Stop that! What are you doing!"

I realized Jodie and the children weren't there, she probably took them to the park. I was glad they were not there, to see this, to see our house torn up, to see me in handcuffs.

"Please, can I sit down somewhere," I begged. "I need to sit down!"

A lady officer removed my handcuffs and let me sit on the couch, handed me a blanket to wrap myself in. I was shivering badly.

The officers talked, conferred, looked in drawers and thumbed through books. No one paid attention when I left for the kitchen, for the little red pills still in the cupboard, hidden in a corner of the top shelf. My fingers found the envelope.

Suddenly Miss Lady Officer rushed through the room, out the back door into the yard. Another followed her. The screen door slammed shut. Startled, I dropped the envelope.

"What's going on?" I asked. Their attention was riveted to the yard and they didn't answer me.

And then I knew. I saw Jodie coming up the sidewalk, children in the wagon, two walking, tired after the park. They are here, my children.

"They can't be here," I yelled to everyone. "They can't see this."

Detective Mr. Nice put his radio to his mouth, and called for Child Protective Services to send someone out. The lady officers kept the children in the yard, kept them out of the house, away from me. I could see them through the screen door. Huddled around Jodie. Eyes wide, confused, crying. Lucy, only five, listening to the officer. My boys, the little guys only three and four, crying, hugging Jodie.

They don't know what's happening. I don't either.

I ignored the officer watching, standing next to me, making sure I didn't go into the yard to interrupt as the children were placed in a squad car, as they cried, "Where's my mommy, I want my mommy!" *They are afraid. So am I.*

I bolted to the door, to rescue them, to bring them back, but the officer grabbed me. I tried to wrestle away from him, but a wave of nausea sent me to the kitchen sink.

Finally, I turned back to him, to all of them, the four tall, unyielding officers watching me, the detectives coming toward me.

"Let me go. I change my mind. Let me go to my children. Let me bring them back."

"No, mam, we can't let you do that."

"Why not! They are my children!"

"Because you are under arrest."

"No, I'm not! I am not!"

At that moment, the detectives stepped forward, replaced my handcuffs, gruffly led me to the car in front.

"You are under arrest for possession of narcotics, possession of paraphernalia, intent to…"

I stopped listening. I didn't hear the rest of the list. It didn't matter. Whatever he was saying didn't matter.

My world had come to an end.

Chapter 17 – Psych Ward #1

I waited in the back of the police car, handcuffed. *No, wait, someone has removed them. A bucket there, on the floor, they don't want me throwing up all over their car.*

"I need a bathroom, please get me to a bathroom quickly! Someone!"

My body was in pain, screaming and desperate. My mind, worse. Rocking back and forth, I groaned, loud, hoping to drown out the words of my children, "I want my mommy, where's my mommy?" The pain in my heart was greater than the pain in my body.

The car came to a stop. I expected to see the jail, was ushered instead through the emergency room doors at the hospital. *Oh my gosh! The police, they really do care about me! They are not taking me to jail! We are here, at the hospital. Just like they said. This will be ok. I'm not really arrested. They are just helping me.*

As one officer went to the desk, the other took my arm, sat me in a chair, to wait. I cried, quiet tears, not sobs, glad I was here, in the hospital, not jail, not facing the horrors I'd heard of kicking heroin in a jail cell. I was relieved.

The officer handed me a kleenex. "You ok, miss?"

"No, Mr. Officer, I am not ok!" The release of tears preceded my ability to control any of my own body fluids. I made a mess.

Everyone sprang into action then, wrapped me in a blanket, placed me in a wheelchair, rushed to the elevators. One nurse, two police officers. I was ashamed and did not look at them, only at the hand of the nurse, frantically pushing the button for the top floor. Psychiatric Unit the sign said. I didn't care.

~

For three days I could not leave my room. The first meal brought to me on a tray smelled of grease and onions and caused instant, violent vomiting, on the floor, on my bed. The next days, only jello, juice, and crackers sat on my tray. Didn't matter. I couldn't eat them either. At least they were odorless. I worked to swallow the pill the silent nurse brought. Most of the time I didn't throw it up. If I did, she brought another. They wanted me sedated. So did I.

On the fourth day I ate part of a cracker, took a few sips of the juice, waited. No rush to the bathroom. No throwing up, no diarrhea. *Maybe I can eat the jello.* My arms and legs ached, my stomach hurt, I could only walk hunched over. But I could walk. I could walk around my room. That was when I noticed it was bare, only a bed. That was when I found my locked door.

On the fifth day, the food tray gave me toast and oatmeal. I didn't throw it up. On this day Mr. Doctor came to my room. He brought a chair with him. Sitting there, he motioned for me to take a seat on the bed. I waited as he checked my chart. He looked stiff and professional in his grey suit, and white shirt. He began to read out loud.

"OK, I see you are twenty four, have three children, hmm… single." His voice was soft as he thumbed through pages, pondered each fact. I thought that was good.

Pulling his eyes from the chart, he looked at me and then stopped talking. A flickering moment of recognition. I saw the jerk of his shoulders, the frown that crept over his forehead, the eyes puzzled, then cold, staring at me. No longer talking. He stood, clutched my chart to his chest, turned his back to me, walked to the door, to leave.

I found my voice. "Wait, don't you want to ask me any questions? Talk to me? How can you help me if you don't talk to me?"

"That's not necessary. You are much better now. There's no need to keep your door locked. I'll adjust your medications…and…see about getting the rest of your furniture in here."

"So can I leave? Can I go get my children now?"

He stopped at the doorway, turned to look at me. "No, you've been arrested and cannot leave this floor. This is a locked ward, mostly for psychiatric patients, but it will keep you here too."

"But my kids, I need to bring them home."

"No, you don't, and I would advise you to stop being hysterical. Your children are in foster care, wards of the state now, you might say. They are no longer your responsibility."

"But I'm their mommy!"

"No you're not. Not anymore." He left the room. Left the door open. I heard the click of his shoes as he walked down the hall, away from me. I was afraid he would not come back. I sat on my bed, thinking of the moment he seemed to know me. I tried to remember him. "Was he ever my customer, at the hotel?" Maybe. I struggled to find a comfortable position on the bed so I could think. My body, no longer in violent rebellion, still rumbled in protest. I was sick, not as sick as I was, but still sick.

My thoughts bounced off the walls. I couldn't make sentences stick together, my mind reeled more violently than my body.

I needed to remember Mr. Doctor So Nervous. What sort of things he liked. If he knew I remembered him, he would be embarrassed and afraid and it might maybe make him be on my side, help me get out of here. These were the things I thought.

It was exhausting. I fell asleep thinking, *I have to remember him.*

~

I woke to a dark room. I was cold, shivering. I reached for the blankets. They didn't help. I was too cold to go back to sleep, shaking too hard to keep the covers on. Nausea threatened to overcome me again.

Clair

A nurse brought the little white pill and a glass of water.

"Here, it's past time for your pill. We didn't want to wake you. This will help."

I was grateful and quietly submitted to opening my mouth, moving my tongue around to prove that I did indeed swallow it. *Why wouldn't I swallow it? Would anybody choose to be that sick?*

Now I felt mean and angry. *Stupid people! Why were they late with my pill? That's why I'm shaking! Of course I'll swallow it. Do they think I want to be sick? And if I didn't swallow it, what would I do with it? Sell it? Ha! Like I can just walk up to someone here and say, 'Hey, wanna buy this pill?' I'm here with a bunch of crazies. They probably don't have any money. Of course I'll take the pill! Stupid nurses!*

I did not say these things. I smiled, sat quietly on my bed as she left the room, left the door open. I waited, watched the door, waiting for her to come back and lock it. She didn't.

I ventured into the hallway. Holding my hospital gown tightly around myself, bare feet. My room was at the end of the hall. I glanced in rooms I passed, looking for other patients. I found them at the end, in the dayroom. A nice room, tables and chairs, a few couches. Some patients were in hospital gowns, like me, and some had regular street clothes.

Turning to the orderly, I demanded, "Hey, I want my own clothes." He pointed to the nurses' station, just across the hall, directly opposite the dayroom. With a clear view of the crazy people.

The nurses were staring at me. One came from behind the desk, leaned against the wall, alert. I smiled sweetly and kept walking.

She stepped into the middle of the hall, watching me as I reached the elevator. It did not have a down button. The round mirror on the wall made bizarre images of the nurses, of me.

I pointed at the mirror, announced to her, to everyone, "I see you don't want the crazy people getting out of here. You don't want me getting out, either. But I'm not crazy, only arrested, you know!" I wanted to make sure everyone knew this. It was important. Wandering back to my room, I found a nightstand, lamp, chair, the tray on wheels, and extra blankets. I crawled on the bed, exhausted again, and noticed three magazines on the nightstand. Old, tattered, covers torn. Used. *Like me.* Covering myself with all the blankets, I held the magazines tightly and smiled. *Someone cares about me.*

~

I swallowed the little white pill each time the nurse brought it to me and wandered around the dayroom with the crazies and made crafty things with the lady who taught us how to glue beads on a board to make a picture of a tree and a bird. I think it was a bird.

I was compliant and a model patient because I wanted out and I wanted my children. They must be scared to death! I resolved to not be afraid and to become alert and plan what to do.

~

For weeks, I waited for Mr. Doctor to come back to my room. I knew I could make him be my friend and help me get out of here and get my children back. I saw him at the nurse's station and I saw him talking to patients. *I suppose he gives them good advice about how to stop being a crazy. He should come talk to me and give me good advice about how to stop being a junkie.*

He didn't. He didn't come to my room, he didn't look at me. I knew he checked my chart and changed my medications because each day I got one less little white pill. Last night I did not get a sleeping pill. Today I will get only one white pill. I must be getting better!

I went to the dayroom every day. I made a basket, painted a picture on canvas, and strung beads to make necklaces for the nurses. I did all of this exactly as I was told. *Don't be creative, just follow instructions like a good girl.* But I was bored. Very bored.

When two more days passed and I did not get a little white pill, and I did not throw up, Mr. Nice Detective came, sat in the chair, and explained, "You are still arrested, but you don't have to go to jail right now, there is no bail. You are out on your own recognizance."

"What does that mean?"

"It means they trust you to show up for your hearing on July 17th. Here's the paperwork, see which courtroom you have to be in, and what time? Don't fail to show up! If you do, you will be arrested again and they won't trust you to be out without bail then. This is very important! You can probably get a suspended sentence for this, since it's a first. If you keep out of trouble, keep your nose clean, get a job, and show up for this hearing, that is."

Ok, ok, I get it, I'm not stupid! I didn't say that. Instead, I said, "Oh, thank you! I'll stay clean and I'll be there for that hearing, I promise." Then, "Wait, what about my children? Do I get them back now?"

"I don't know, that's not my area. I'm sure a caseworker will get in touch with you soon. I know you won't get them back before you go to court, though."

"Can I see them?"

"Probably not, I don't know. Wait for the caseworker to call you, ask her. Good luck, miss."

Alone in my room, I was confused. *Why can't I see my children? I got help, I've been here for weeks. I do all the crafts. I'm off drugs. I've done all the right things.*

I was afraid and began to shiver again. I gathered every blanket in my room, wrapped myself in a cocoon and tried to sleep. The shivering didn't stop and the fear didn't go away. I took blankets from rooms next to mine, brought them back to my pile, to quiet my pounding heart, my shaking arms and legs, to chase away the nausea that overpowered me again. It took a long time until I slept.

∼

I was startled awake as the overhead light assaulted the room and I shielded my eyes. The orderly pulled the extra blankets off me.

"Who do you think you are?" he bellowed. "You can't go stealing other people's blankets! You're not even supposed to go into other people's rooms, you know that! Now these have to be laundered! Get up, dinner is in the dayroom. You need to start eating with everyone else. Come on...up, up, up!"

"Ok, ok, sorry," was the answer I gave, as the good girl. It was not the answer I felt.

So I had my supper in the dayroom with the crazy people. The depressed people. The suicide people. I reminded myself, with every bite, *I am not one of them! And besides, this food tastes pretty good, and tomorrow I get out of here!* Nothing else mattered.

∼

The morning sun was bright as I walked out the door, onto the street, in my own clothes, free, confident. The heat felt good on my skin and warmed my heart and I smiled at the new start I had been given. I walked to my house, up onto the porch, my own porch.

As I opened the door I was flooded with a memory of the time I walked through this door, Matthew waiting for me. At two am! My heart pounded with guilt, but I braced myself, shoulders straight. *You beat heroin. You are strong now. You can do this!*

I walked through the house. Passing overturned chairs, setting them upright. Putting books back on shelves, toys back in their boxes, straightening the cushions on the couch. I walked through the dining room into the kitchen. Here I remembered my children screaming as they were put into police cars. "I want my mommy, I want my mommy!"

I pounded my fists on the counter, my forehead into the cupboard door and screamed back, "And I want my children! Bring my children back!" My voice echoed in the empty house. My empty house.

I couldn't just stand there, in the kitchen, place of pain and fear.

Back through the dining room I wandered, into the living room, the room I'd put back together. Putting myself back together.

And there he stood, my Golden Boy, with his fair hair and shy smile. I stopped, not sure of him now. He walked toward me slowly, eyes locked into mine, wrapped his arms around me, pulled me close to his chest. One hand on my head, holding me close. I sobbed.

"It's ok, babe, it's ok now," comforting, leading me to the couch. He was sorry they wouldn't let him see me at the hospital.

"I tried, babe. I tried every day. Sometimes I came two, three, four times in one day, looking for a different person that would let me see you. No one would tell me anything, they made me leave. I was so afraid and worried for you and I didn't know what to do!" Tears formed in the corners of his eyes, spilling over, down his cheeks. He wiped them away quickly and I pretended not to notice.

"It's ok, I understand." I was glad he was here, now. That I wouldn't be alone in this house. We sat, on the couch, for a long while, quiet. I was hopeful.

Until he slowly sat up, facing me, to explain, "Here's the thing, babe. I know you say you want to do this 'no drug thing', and I get that, I really do. That's cool, if you that's what you really want.

"But here's the thing, you know, if you change your mind, that's cool too. Whatever you want, I'm with you all the way, doesn't matter to me as long as you're happy. So, I want you to know, I saw this doctor today and scored thirty morphine tabs. They are here in my pocket. Better than heroin cause it's pure and clean. You know, just in case you change your mind. I am always here to give you what you want."

The room began to spin and I barely heard the rest of his rambling speech, "we only do what we really want to do, living free isn't about denying ourselves, life is about following our impulses, taking the moments, experiencing everything."

I stood up, moving away from him, "Why are you telling me this? You know I want to stay clean, I want my children back! I don't want what you have in your pocket!"

"Yeah, I know, I know. I get that, no problem. But here's the thing. People are always telling you, me, what is good for us. What we should want. If you really don't want this, then don't. It's only hard if it's just what other people are telling you. I'm here to give you what you want, not to just give you what others think you should want. That's all I'm trying to say!"

I did not know how to answer him. Confused, I returned to the couch, my head in his lap. He stroked my hair, my back. I fell asleep.

~

Hours later, the middle of the night, I was suddenly awake! Wide awake, startled! Alarmed! I stood up, walked around, still afraid. Terrified! *Why am I afraid?* I checked the doors, they were still locked. I went to the windows, looking to see someone there. No one was. *What woke me?* Caught in a tornado of panic, I knew danger was lurking but could not find it.

Then I knew. *The caseworker came, here, in the middle of the night, looked in my windows and saw him here, Golden Boy. Saw that I have a man in the house, a man I am not married to. If I have a man here she will never let me have my kids back! I should make him leave! No, it's too late! It's too late because she already saw him.*

I ran upstairs, into my children's rooms, touched their pillows, hugged their stuffed animals, smelled their jammies. *Now I have lost them and will never see them again because the caseworker was here, looking in the windows.*

I was alone with the awfulness of myself.

I left their rooms, walked down the stairs, down one step, then another, until I came to the spot that only a few weeks ago I sat with Matthew. My sadness was unbearable. *I have lost my children forever. There is no hope of ever getting them back.*

I continued down the steps, to the couch where my Golden Boy slept. He stirred briefly as I reached into his pocket, as my fingers found the prescription bottle. I knew his needle and syringe, his "works," were in the other pocket. I took them too, made my way to the kitchen, placed one tiny morphine tablet in the syringe, put the needle in place, inserted it into the glass of water, pulled back on the plunger to watch what little water it took to dissolve the morphine.

It only took a few seconds. The pounding of my heart stilled, the condemning voice in my head quieted, my muscles relaxed, and I was at peace once again.

Finally, for the first time in my life someone is here to give me what I want, not what they think I should want. There was a strange comfort in that. I wondered why it seemed so wrong.

I grabbed a blanket, cuddled next to him on the couch, my head in his lap again.

Chapter 18 – Fired!

The first moment I woke, I felt the sun streaming through the window, warming my face. I looked around, remembering I'd fallen asleep there on the couch with GoldenBoy, the night before. My head in his lap, his hand on my shoulder, they comforted me then. Now only pillows were under my head and blankets were tucked around me. I was alone. The second moment I was awake, I remembered. My children are gone! I didn't want to remember, so I plodded out to the kitchen, made coffee, hoping to chase away the panic rising from my stomach, catching in my heart. It was hard to breathe and I did not want to be here, alone.

Coffee in hand, I turned from the counter and saw my empty kitchen. No children at the table eating cereal. I went to sit on the back porch, and remembered police cars and crying, pleading children. My heart raced. *I can't do this!*

Running back through the house, to the couch, I wrapped the blankets around my legs. *Stop! Stop thinking about that. Think what to do. How can I get my kids back? I have to get my kids back!*

I made myself think about the night before. *The caseworker was here. She watched in the windows and saw GoldenBoy. She saw me here, with a man overnight and she'll never let me have my children!* My hands began to shake. Coffee spilled on the blanket and I couldn't sit there. I paced the living room, then the dining room, reciting, *Calm down. Don't panic. Find a way out of this.*

Slowly, somewhere on the edges of my fear, a tiny thought began to rise. *Or was she? Was she really here or did I imagine it? I didn't actually see her! Maybe she wasn't here and I have a chance!* I didn't know, but I could hope. As hope chased away panic, my heart calmed, and I knew the first step was to go back to work.

After brushing my teeth at the bathroom sink, I splashed cold water on my face, ran a brush through my hair, and saw the needle and syringe on the back of the toilet. Two tiny morphine tabs beside them. Left there, for me, by my Golden Boy.

I hadn't put the prescription bottle back in his pocket after using that one tiny tab. The bottle with those thirty morphine tabs. Twenty-nine after last night. Now twenty-seven.

Staring at the two tiny lovely tablets, I hoped he didn't give many more away today. Then, *I hope he does. I hope he doesn't come back with any left. I hope he gives them all away! I did one, but no more. Just that one. I'm not doing it again!* I knew I should flush them, but I couldn't. But I did stop looking at them.

Taking extra care with my makeup, winding my hair in rollers to tame fly-away curls, I told myself in the mirror, *Be sure to look your best. The Brothers will be proud of you, that you turned yourself in to get help, and they'll be glad to finally have you back at work.*

I leaned into the mirror closely and examined my eyes. Clear, not pin pointy. That's good. I chose my best skirt and blouse, ironed my apron, walked to work. The morning air was refreshing and I felt good.

∼

Arriving early, I used my key to open the bar. I was checking inventory when he strolled in, the Brother who owned this bar, here on Main Street. He was not alone, I noticed. Jerry was with him. I knew Jerry, he filled in wherever they needed him. He was a nice guy and I liked him. With a quick nod of his head and a wave of his hand, the Brother motioned Jerry behind the bar and me to sit across from him in a booth.

"So, tell me what happened." I did, editing the story as I went along. Not lying, only giving him the most important parts. "I just wanted help, I knew I needed it and I didn't know where else to go." I didn't tell him about the night before.

He listened patiently, not interrupting. Watched my eyes, never looked away. I felt awkward.

As I finished talking, he reached for my hand. "I wish you had come to us first. We could have taken care of you without the police. We would have handled this. But here's the thing. Now you've been arrested and the police are involved. You'll have a record. I don't know if they'll make it a felony or a misdemeanor, but you can't work here anymore."

"Don't fire me! I didn't do anything wrong. I'm a good worker! This won't happen again." I couldn't stop the tears rolling down my face, onto the grimy table as I pled for my job. I didn't care how I looked or how embarrassing I was as I grabbed his hand, wouldn't let go, and begged to keep my job. I'd never get my children back without a job. That much I knew.

Pulling his hand away, he leaned back, away from me.

"I'm sorry, really I am. But I can't help you now. Unless you want a drink, you might as well leave. No, wait, sit here for a while, I'll get you a drink."

He slid out of the booth and walked away, then turned back to look at me and said, "I'm sorry, really I am." I believed him.

~

Outside the bar, I shielded my eyes from the sun, looked up and down the street, my street lined with bars and clubs, a few stores. I knew everyone. These were my people and I had belonged here.

It didn't feel like my street now. I'd been kicked out and was unsure what to do or where to go. *Wait! Whitey, he runs the PlayBar and knows everybody. He likes me and he'll tell me what to do. How to find a new job.* I crossed the street and walked up the block to the PlayBar.

~

Sitting at the small round table near the door, the table that sometimes served as his desk, Whitey, his glass of whiskey in hand, listened to me, nodded occasionally, watched my face.

"Look, you're a nice girl, and you know I like you a lot, always have, but I don't know what to tell you. I can't give you a job here, you know that. You've been arrested and will lose your license. But you gotta stop shootin' dope! Stop now before you're in any deeper. Look at me, only forty-five, and I got yellow eyes and a shot liver from drinkin'. I won't live much longer, they tell me. I know that. But you, you're still young. You can pull yourself together."

I looked into his eyes, saw the dark yellow for the first time. When had this happened, and why hadn't I noticed? I was overcome with sadness for this most handsome, gentle man, and realized he was as hopeless as I was. I forced my attention back to what he was saying. "You're a young, pretty girl, and you got kids. You have a lot going for you. Get yourself together before it's too late."

"But I don't have my kids, and if I don't have a job I'll never get them!"

His stared at me, "Yeah, it's a sad. But look out the window. You know by now that everybody all up and down this street, in every joint, everybody's got a sad story. There's a hundred out there. I didn't know how to make it different for me, and I'm sorry I don't know how to make it different for you. I wish I could, sweetheart, but I don't know how."

His voice was quiet, I could barely hear him. He stood, came around to the back of my chair, leaned his chin on the top of my head and folded his arms around me. "I don't know what to tell you, kid, I wish I did."

The bartender came for him to sign something, a small fight broke out over in the right corner, and I knew he was busy and I was in the way. I left.

I stepped out to a different world. No sunshine. Now dark clouds covered the sky, and cold rain settled over us. Here, rain didn't wash everything clean. Here, rain brought life to rotted garbage laying in the alleys and against buildings. I leaned over the curb and threw up because I was afraid. The rain brought a stench that matched my mood.

I walked home. In the rain, cold rain.

~

In my house, my own home, I turned the heat on. *How can it be cold in July?* I took a hot shower, laid my wet clothes out to dry, draping them over chairs. I made hot tea, took my mug to the couch, still wondering what to do. *I don't understand what's happening. I did the right thing, and now this is a bigger mess.* I sat paralyzed, numb, unmoving for hours. Maybe it was only minutes.

~

Footsteps on the porch startled me. I was alert, afraid, then remembered, "It's my Golden Boy, home early. He can't work in the rain. He's here!"

Running to greet him, I threw open the door, and there he was, not Golden Boy, but Mr. Morgan, the landlord. He stepped inside, brushing past me.

"Mr. Morgan, umm, I...it's not rent day, is it?"

I followed him to the living room, watched him look around quickly, scanning my home, and was glad I had put everything back in order last night. There was no sign of the police search.

I asked again, "It's not rent day. I'm all paid up till the end of the month."

"Well, no, actually, you're not, your last two checks bounced. I should have come and talked to you after the first one, but you with all these little kids, and working, I figured I'd just wait and you'd make it good. But now, with the second one! I've got my own business to run and I don't do charity!"

His voice firmer with every sentence. "You need to find another place. I gotta rent this house pretty quick. I'm already out two month's rent from you." He continued to survey the room, as though assessing how much time it would take me to move.

"How soon can you clear all this stuff out?"

"I don't know!" I stumbled over my words, looking for something to say, grasping for time. "I'll make it right, really I will. You can't just throw me out!" I was begging and embarrassing myself again and I didn't care.

"Well, maybe I can't throw you out today, but I can call the cops about these bad checks. If you don't move quickly, I can just call them and they'll handle it!"

He walked into the dining room, looking at my stuff again. "Can you be out tomorrow?"

"Sure, I guess." I stared at the floor, defeated. On his way out, he paused at the door, glanced back, and said, "Just leave the key in the mailbox."

Long after he left, I sat on the porch steps and thought about how I could have changed the day, one defeat and rejection after another and then I was angry. *What a vulture he is! Walking around here like a big shot! Why was I so pathetic! I could have smiled at him.*

I paused and pictured myself standing close to him, tilting my right hip to one side, touching his shoulder. Smiling just so. I knew I could have made him forget the rent. *I should have. Why didn't I think of it while he was here! I was so stupid and now it's too late.*

And the Brother, how could he fire me! I worked double shifts, and I overlooked stuff they did! I kept that place running, they couldn't have done it without me. He didn't have to fire me!

I sat, letting anger rush through my veins, giving me energy. And then I remembered. I rushed inside, up the steps, to the box I kept hidden in the medicine cabinet in the bathroom, behind the hair gel, under the razor blades. My emergency stash, always with a couple of hundred dollars there.

But it was empty! *How can it be empty!* Despair took over, anger gone. Defeat was no longer only a feeling. I could touch it. I saw it on my face as I noticed myself in the mirror. I could smell it in the room.

And then, I saw them again, the two little white tablets, there, still beside the needle and syringe. I reached for them, held them in my fist, ready to flush them down the toilet in disgust, but paused, hesitating, and I couldn't do it. *I should do it. I should. But what if I can't stand it, later, and I need them? They're like money in the bank, saved for a bad day. I should save them. I won't use them, but it will be good to know I have them. I'll feel stronger, knowing I have them. Yeah, I'd better save them. Don't waste them, flushing them down the toilet. That's stupid. I'll save them.*

And I did. I hid them. I searched through the medicine cabinet. Found a bottle of Rolaids. That would work. I dumped them on the counter, wrapped my two little morphine tablets in a tiny square of toilet paper, tucked them in the bottom of the bottle, added the Rolaids on top. Bottle back on its shelf. Ordinary looking. Safe. I felt better.

I started down the steps, stopped and sat, my face in my hands. I wished I could cry now. *What will I do? What can I do?* I was tired, too tired to move. Slowly I looked around, slowly I realized I was on the same step I had sat with Matthew at two am, so many weeks ago. *Was it really weeks ago? I don't know.* I missed him.

I felt the same sadness and could only sit, doing nothing, numb.

~

I looked up to see my Golden Boy at the bottom of the steps.

"What's wrong? Why are you sitting here in the dark? How long have you been just sitting there?"

"I don't know." That was the truth.

He sat on the step beside me, took my hand. "Well, we can't have that! You can't just sit here in the dark, looking all sad! Let's go downtown." I looked at his cheerful face, I listened to his soothing words, pulling me into his world!

But not tonight! "I can't! I can't! I have to move out tomorrow." I fought to, for once, for just tonight, to pull him into my torn-up world.

"Look at all my stuff, what am I going to do. I don't even know where to go. And they won't let me come back to work. I got fired and everything's gone! My job, my kids, and now my house! Why is this happening to me! I didn't do anything wrong, I only wanted help!"

But my Golden Boy, he wouldn't join my despair. Taking my hand, he walked me back up the stairs.

"Hey, come on! None of this moping around. Did you use the stuff I left for you?"

"No, I don't want it, I threw it away, flushed it down the toilet! I don't want it, I just want my kids back." I lied. I don't know why.

"Ok, ok. But you didn't have to flush it. Next time just give it back to me." He breezed past my lie and I was relieved.

"Come on, wash your face, put some make-up on. Hey, wear that red skirt I like. We'll go downtown, that old fat lady is dancing tonight. And you can watch me play pool. I'll win us lots of money!"

With his hand on my cheek, seeing his smile, I couldn't help but think everything would work out. I'd be ok. I'd worry about moving later.

∼

The PlayBar was dark and crowded, full of life. I glanced at the table by the window, Whitey still there, still with a glass of whiskey. He didn't see me. We walked through the room. Through the loud music and the smells of beer and fried food. To our friends, waving from the booth, there in back, between the stage and the pool tables. They scrunched over to make room for us. Billy laughing and smiling, talking to someone I didn't know. Nodding to me, this new person introduced himself. "Detroit Mike here. And so, glad to finally meet you!"

He looked happy to see me. Even Susan the Mouse seemed happy to see me. Their happiness was contagious, everybody smiling and laughing. I looked around the table and smiled. *These are my friends. I'm glad I'm here.*

Motioning for the waitress to bring me a Coke, I ignored the open bottle of Jim Beam on the table, it's lid lost somewhere. Sticky shot glasses were scattered around, leaving little wet circles on the already scarred table.

"No, I'm fine. This Coke is good." I waved the bottle away, smiled and laughed a little louder. The music blared, but we talked over it. Until the dancer stepped up on the small stage in the center of the room. In her barely there bikini. GoldenBoy was right. This was the old lady's night. She danced and twisted and moved her hips and tried to shake her limp breasts and everybody cheered. She enjoyed the attention and smiled big enough to show her three teeth. Her limp grey hair hung in greasy strands and rolls of fat hung over her outfit and shook like jelly. She didn't seem to know that she was not beautiful, she was not sexy.

Urged on by the laughing, cheering crowd she became braver and more outrageous. She left the stage and made her rounds to the tables and men put dollar bills down her bikini top. Oblivious to their ridicule, she reached over to kiss them, but they only laughed and pushed her away. She stumbled, caught herself, and laughed with them. They pounded each other on the back. Congratulating their success, proud of her humiliation. For the first time, I wondered why Whitey had her here. *Six nights a week he has pretty young girls, so why does he do this?* I couldn't watch anymore.

I reached my hand across the table to get Jack's attention, to distract myself, needing to talk. About anything. He was Susan The Mouse's father, after all, so we should have something to talk about. Pulling his eyes from the dancer, he looked at me and poured Jim Bean in my coke, spilling a little on the table. Through misty eyes, tears threatening, he smiled at me, tilted his head to one side and said, "I know, Babe, you got a bad deal. We all did. But you're here now, with us, and it's ok."

He held his glass to me, I reached for mine, clinking it to his in a toast to the future, and drank it down. Jack poured more whiskey in, "There ya go! Who needs the coke, huh?" I drank that in one gulp and wondered, would I be like Jack, still sitting here when I was fifty, still shooting up, with watery eyes and shaking hands, unable to find my own veins anymore, still looking for the next high? I hoped not.

Hours later, Jerry stood at our table. He handed a small paper sack over to me.

"Here, I found some of your things behind the bar, thought I should bring them to you."

I dumped the contents on the table. Everyone was interested. A comb, a list of phone numbers, just stuff. They went back to their drinks, to watching the dancer.

I sorted through the rest. *Just stupid stuff, I should throw it all away.* But my fingers found the button, the badge I'd worn every day, pinned to my blouse. My slogan.

Turning it over, I read the words to myself, this white button with red letters. "If It Feels Good, I'll Do It." I remembered being so proud to wear it, laughing when customers asked me what it meant. I had really liked that button. But not on this night. *It isn't funny anymore.*

Chapter 19 – Arrested Again?

I hated this new job, watching people try frame after frame for their new perfect glasses. "Just stand there and watch, don't talk, smile. Don't give advice. Let the customer choose." *Be a robot!*. My supervisor didn't say that last part, but I knew that's what he meant. Him, with that huge smile pasted on his face, his white shirt, brown tie, and perfectly combed hair. I forced myself to listen to his instructions.

"Guide clients to the proper display, men, women, or children's frames. Do not suggest which frames you think look best, as they may come back later and blame us if they don't like them. Here we have a box for each customer with their prescription, when they choose a frame, place it in the box and walk them over there to a technician. Done. Greet the next customer as though you are their best friend." *I don't have any best friends*. I didn't say that.

Every day I felt angry and pretended I wasn't. I didn't know what to do with anger. It didn't fit on my palette of emotions, the ones I had perfected, choosing ones that would draw people to do what I needed them to do. But anger? What could I do with anger? Anger would never make people feel sorry for me, would never make them do what I wanted. Anger pushed people away, so I hid it. Always.

Every day I watched the clock, anxious for the shift to end at nine PM. I didn't mind walking, even in the dark, to Golden Boy's apartment where I lived now. This was my neighborhood, and the walk was always uneventful, peaceful. Gave me time to settle my thoughts, forget the eye-glass place. The walk in the dark was good.

Until the night the police car was there, parked by the front door as I left work. *Relax, it's not for me. I haven't done anything.* I told myself to keep walking and ignore them. I took only two steps, and they were there beside me, pulling my hands behind my back, handcuffs again.

"Wait, what'd I do? What's wrong?" I tried to get away, but their grip was tight as they tossed me into the back seat.

"We have a bench warrant for your arrest." I didn't know what a bench warrant was and was afraid to ask. Another silent ride in a squad car.

At the police station, I was handed off to another officer. Holding my elbow, he led me down the stairs into the belly of the ancient building.

Still protesting, still shouting, "This is a mistake, I haven't done anything! You can't do this to me!" I wrestled my arm away from him, and stumbled down a few steps before he caught me. My knee hurt, but was only scraped.

Strange odors accosted me as we reached the bottom level. Cement floor, cement walls, cement ceiling, peeling red and blue and purple paint. As he led me to the left, I looked at the large cells to my right, some with four or five men in each one.

I had a small cell of my own, here on the left hallway, away from the men. My cell had the same wood bench, the same drain in the floor. No window, same peeling paint. Mine was red.

The officer removed my handcuffs, stepped away, closed the barred door, locked me in. I knew now that I needed to choose a different emotion, a different color from my palette.

"Wait, sir, please, answer me. Why am I here? What's a bench warrant? What'd I do." Because I had made my voice soft, pleading, submissive, he answered me.

"A bench warrant means you failed to appear at a hearing."

"A hearing! A hearing for what! I don't remember a hearing, when was I supposed to be there, and for what?" Turning away, he merely said he didn't have that information.

I listened as his footsteps took him up the stairs to the safe place that looked nice and didn't smell. I sat on my wooden bench and yelled, "I bet they send you to a special class to teach you to not talk and to never, ever look at our faces."

Then it was quiet there. I could hear the men prisoners on the other side. I could hear them talking, mumbling. I heard someone pee in the drain. I heard someone throw up.

I was alone and afraid I might be sick.

No, I won't be sick, I haven't been using that much, I'll be ok. I won't be sick. I'm only shaking because I'm nervous and my skin is creepy because it's cold in here. That's all, I'm not sick.

Still sitting on my wood bench, I stared at the drain. For minutes or hours. I heard men brought down and put in a cell. Some slept and snored, others yelled, most were silent As I was silent. There was nothing to do but wait. I threw up in the drain.

Each time an officer brought someone down I asked about the time. It was midnight, then two am. I threw up again, almost missing the drain.

I jerked up as an officer turned the key in the lock to my cell, opening the door, ushering me out.

"What's happening?"

"Someone posted your bail."

"Who? Who did that?"

"I don't know, ma'am, just come this way."

~

Out on the sidewalk, I looked up and down the street, and there he was, my GoldenBoy, in his car, waiting for me. I wanted to run to him, but made myself walk casually. I don't know why. Maybe I didn't want to look desperate. Inside the car I threw my arms around his neck and cried. "Thank you, I should have known you'd come. I'm such a mess, I was so scared."

"Yeah, I had to find out how bail you out and that took a while, sorry." He smoothed my hair with his hand, touched my cheek. "You're shaking!" Reaching out to me with his other hand, he opened the glove compartment, and there it was. My syringe, loaded and ready to go.

He helped me shoot up, waited until I was calm, till he could hold my hands without them shaking. It was then, only then, he locked eyes with me. "You know we have to talk about this. But not tonight, tonight you need to rest, but we'll talk tomorrow." I was afraid of "the talk." But knew that I did have a rescuer, my precious GoldenBoy would always be here for me.

At the apartment, while he made coffee, his back to me, I checked the box, there on the top of the dresser, the box where he kept the morphine tabs.

Only two left! Did I use all of them? Or was he using, too? No, I know he isn't. It was probably me. Maybe that's what he wants to talk about, tomorrow, not tonight.

Rummaging around in my one black plastic bag, there in the corner where I left it, I found my bottle of Doriden, took one, and crawled into bed. Waited for the powerful sleeping pill to work because I didn't want to think.

∼

As we sipped our coffee in the morning, sitting together on the edge of the bed, he was ready for "the talk." I wasn't.

"Babe, you have to get control of this. Sometimes you go crazy. Look at me, I hit up once in a while, maybe once a week, just for a good time. But you do it all the time and it's not good for you, you have to cut back. Or they'll keep arresting you. Will you do that?"

"Yeah, sure, I get it, and I'll do that. I just got carried away, you know, my kids and all. But I can do it, not a problem." And there it was, that grin of his, the sparkle in his eyes as he looked at me, his hand on my shoulder. The ways I knew he loved me. I hoped this was the last time I would lie to him.

~

When he left for work, I rushed to the bottle, two morphine tabs, still there, he didn't take them with him. I was glad. I used one, pocketed the other.

And then, as I placed the now empty bottle back in his box, an idea exploded and filled the room! *I need get my own prescription I could do that! No one would know how much I was using if I had my own. I would be in control.* The boss of me again. I went back to the bottle in the box and made a note of the doctor's name.

I made an emergency appointment, Dr. Conner, eleven o'clock. I planned what to say, rehearsed it over and over. Practiced in the mirror in the bathroom down the hall, learning to put pain on my face.

He watched me slowly walk into the exam room, this young doctor. Hunched over, I was, one hand on my back, teeth clenched, limping. I was the perfect picture of a woman in great pain. He offered me a chair, as though he knew I could never get up onto the exam table. He leaned forward, and listened to my story.

"Sorry to bother you, but, well, I'm from Virginia, and I was in an car accident and need surgery on my back. I'm on my way to my parents in Seattle so they can take care of my children and help me out." He interrupted with, "How old are your children?"

"Oh, my babies are small, three, four, and five, and I'm not married, so I really need to get to my parents. When I'm in so much pain I can't drive, and my doctor gave me a prescription for those little morphine tablets, you know the ones that dissolve under my tongue?"

He nodded his understanding, and looked sympathetic. I continued. "Well, last night, when I was checking into that motel, getting our suitcase and the children all out of the car, I left my purse on the seat, and then later I noticed it was gone!" I stopped talking, struggled to find a more comfortable position, held my breath, frowned, then continued.

"Someone stole my purse, and my prescription, my medicine!

My folks are wiring me some more money, but I really wonder if you could write me another prescription so I can drive the rest of the way there. I have a little money here, that was in my pocket and didn't get stolen."

He nodded sympathetically, reached for the prescription pad. "And let's take your blood pressure, just to make this legal." It was strange that he didn't tell me to roll up my sleeve. That's how I knew he didn't believe my story and that he didn't care.

I hobbled out of the office with a prescription for thirty ten mg tablets of morphine in my hand. My very own prescription. No one would know I had it. I did it again the following week, a different doctor. It was easy. I felt powerful.

And then I stumbled on Dr. O. When I started telling my sad story, he put his hand up to stop me. "Come on now, your back isn't really injured, is it? You don't have to make up a story for me. I'm here to help you." He asked questions about how I was doing, how I felt. He wouldn't write a script for morphine, but if I said I was depressed, he found a bottle of pills in his drawer for me, and told me to come back in a week. That week I said I was tired because I worked long hours at the glasses place. Another little bottle from the drawer. And always plenty of Doriden to help me sleep. Most of what he gave me I didn't want. I gave it to others who came to the apartment because they wanted it. And because I knew if I gave stuff away they would not think I was using much myself. I don't know why he did it and didn't care. Paid twenty dollars for the office visit and left.

The next time I went to work, the owner fired me. And scolded me. On and on he scolded me until I walked away. I left the building. He was right to fire me. I forgot to go to work too often. I showed up high too often. Walking back to the apartment, I worried about getting another job.

∼

"I just got fired again!" I announced to GoldenBoy. Looking up from his book, he stared at me, and I knew he didn't care about the job. He looked stern. I made myself look pitiful. He didn't notice, not this time.

Motioning for me to sit with him on the bed, he began, "We have a big problem here. Your first court date is next week, I guess we forgot, but I just found this card on the floor, under the bed. Looks like somebody official gave it to you."

"I have to get another job right away then."

"No, you have to get clean first. You can't go to court with track marks and pinpointy eyes." He took my hand, pushed up my sleeve. "Look, look at this! Look how bruised you are. I can't understand, I keep trying, but I don't get it. People come home from work and have a drink to relax and they don't keep drinking. I don't understand why you can't enjoy a hit now and then like I do and not keep going until you're strung out." He lifted my chin to make me look at him and I saw tears welling up in his eyes. "I want to help you, and I just don't know how. But right now all I can do is help you get clean before you go to court, cause I want you to come back and be here. I want you here, with me. I don't want to lose you. I can't lose you!"

"I can't go back to the hospital, they'll know if I do! I've kicked this by myself before, I can do this on my own."

"I don't believe you can. So I talked to Billy and Susan, and Mike too. We think you should take that Doriden for the next few days, take enough that you sleep through it. That way there'll be no withdrawal. We'll give you pills every few hours. We have to go to work, but we'll come back and give you the pills when it's time. You'll sleep right through it and then be ready for court. I think this court date is for your drug charge, or maybe that car accident. But not your kids, so it shouldn't matter that you don't have a job."

It sounded good, his plan, and I felt how much he loved me, to have a plan. No withdrawal, no pain, just sleep it off. I could do this and my kids' casework would never know. I agreed.

Clair

No one considered they would be leaving me locked in this room alone and the only bathroom was down the hall, out of the apartment. A bathroom shared with other people. He gave me three Doriden, I swallowed them and went to bed.

The next day I threw up in the sink, stumbled to the door. My head was spinning, everything look fuzzy, and I could not stand on my own. I crawled to the door but it was locked. I needed to use the bathroom. I tried to pound on the door, to get someone to come, but it was a feeble attempt. My pounding was soundless as my arms slid to the floor. I could not stay awake.

~

I woke up in great pain in a strange place. Each breath drove a knife deeper into my chest. I was on a couch. Soft pillow, warm blankets. Trying to sit up, I could only groan. The pain was excruciating!

And then I noticed the people in the room, all of them, standing, looking at me. Waiting.

There was Harry, my boss from My Old House. And there, standing next to him, his Nurse Lady friend, the one he chose after me, instead of his wife. Other Civic Interest Guys were there, watching me, waiting. All of them, looking at me. I didn't like it and I was afraid.

"Where am I, and, and... what happened?" I struggled to sit up but couldn't. I asked again, "What happened. Where am I?"

Dragging a footstool over, Harry sat beside me. "A few of us were talking, wondering what happened to you. We hadn't seen you around anywhere for a while. We figured your court date was about to come up and wanted to see if we could help, like if you needed character references or something."

"How'd you find me?"

"We asked around Main Street and somebody said maybe you were staying at Eugene's apartment, up on Ballard Street. Dave and I went to see if you were there, but when we walked in the front hall, you were there at the bottom of the stairs, unconscious. We didn't think we should call an ambulance, so we brought you here, to Carol's, since she's a nurse. She's been taking care of you. Do you remember any of this? Do you know how you ended up at the bottom of those stairs?"

    I didn't. I didn't know anything. Only that my head hurt and it was painful to breathe. I could barely keep my eyes open. I wanted to sleep again.

    Nurse Lady brought me a glass with a straw, encouraging me to drink water. "I think you were taking very large amounts of some sleep medicine, but your vitals are good now. Slow but good. If you rest, and drink lots of water, you'll recover ok. Just sleep now."

    I did. I slept a lot. I learned that I had several cracked ribs. Looking in a mirror after a shower I saw my arms and legs, my chest, bruised. One side of my face, bruised. Huge green and yellow splotches, black centers. It was ugly.

    "What happened to me?" I asked Nurse Lady every day.

    "I don't know. They just brought you here like this" was the answer she gave me, the same answer every day. The answer that was no answer.

    I needed to know what happened. Where was GoldenBoy? The others? How many pills did they give me? Why was I at the bottom of those stairs? But the people who came to see me here, in Nurse Lady's apartment, did not want to talk about what had happened. They wanted to talk about what was to come. They were excited.

    "I got your court date postponed one week."

    "You have a job, file clerk, in Sam's office, you can start next week."

    "There's a small apartment a few blocks from there, we put a deposit on it for you."

    "I picked up your clothes and stuff from that old place. It's here for you. We can move you to your new place when you're ready."

    They had a plan but I did not think I would ever be ready. I wanted to be ready, I wanted to be the person they thought I could be, but I did not think I would ever be.

Injured, laying on that couch, I had lots of time to think. To think about how many times I'd tried to be a good and better person. How many times I'd failed. How many times I'd turned a "fresh start" into something rotten.

Why were Civic Interest Guys trying to help me? Why do they do this...the job, an apartment? I wanted to feel grateful, but I wasn't. I was terrified. Of failure, again. Of letting people down. Again.

I sat on NurseLady's couch, a cup of warm cocoa in my hand, alone, staring at the wall.

Well, maybe not this time. Maybe this time I can hold it together. I'll go live in their apartment and I'll go file their papers, and I'll go be Miss Prim in court. I'll go be whatever they want me to be and maybe, just maybe I can be happy. Maybe this time pretending will turn into real.

I thought about this for a few minutes, picturing myself in a modest dress, filing at a desk, in a nice office. I pictured myself in an apartment they picked out. And I hoped they would be happy with me. I hoped I would be happy letting them be the boss of me.

Chapter 20 – Civic Interest Guys

And they were happy! Civic Interest Guys found a project! Every month, each month, they met, I had been their waitress. Served their meals, carted pitchers of beer up the stairs to their meeting room. About fifty of them, young men, married, starting new families and new careers and looking for a cause, a public cause to devote themselves to. I knew because I listened while pouring mugs of beer for them.

I knew they liked me because they joked with me, and someone at every meeting commented, "Hey, what's that button you're wearing? 'If it feels good I'll do it!' What's that mean?" It was always asked with a smile and sparkling eyes, and I always smiled back and answered, "What would you like it to mean?" I knew they liked me because they laughed a nice laugh, not a malicious, selfish laugh like the men downstairs. I liked them back.

They must have been shocked when the news trickled down Main Street, to their meetings. I wondered which customer sat there, ordered a Schlitz and announced, "That cute girl used to work here, the one that's was the bartender next door? She's went and got arrested!"

"Arrested! You're kidding! What for?"

"Heroin! Can you believe that! Who would have thought!"

They must have been shocked the day they left their offices and came looking for me. The day they stepped into my world, peering through dirty windows, stepping through doors that led only to the underbelly of our town. Did they think this world existed only in Chicago, New York, or Los Angeles?

They must have tried to deny what they saw! "How can this be here?" Or maybe, "Heroin! Here? We're a city with churches and parks and parades and little league! How could we have not known about this?"

I thought about all of this the day they moved me into the new apartment they had picked out for me. A nice apartment on a tree-lined street, a park across the street. A park with a pond and rose gardens and tennis courts.

A nice upstairs apartment, furnished. Small living room, kitchen, and a bedroom, all separate rooms! All immaculately clean, there would be no roaches here, I could tell. The bathroom was next to the bedroom, same apartment, not down the hall to be shared with others. A nice apartment. I liked it.

Three of them moved me in, I carried my one plastic bag of belongings, they carried a few boxes filled with other things they decided I needed, groceries, a few dishes, towels, things like that.

"Well, that's it. I think we got everything. Anything else you need?"

Standing in the hall, they seemed hesitant to leave. It would be the first time I was alone since they picked me up from the bottom of the stairs. *If I was them, I would be afraid to leave me alone, too!*

I listened to their footsteps as they left, down the stairs, out the door. Watching from the front window, parting the curtain just a little, I saw them standing together, talking, leaning against their cars. I crept down the stairs, opened the door a few inches, and sat on the bottom step to listen.

"I still can't get over how much drugs there are here, in our own city! And heroin! I'm having a hard time getting used to this."

"I know, Joe, but this is 1968, and we're a bigger city now, maybe we should have seen this."

"Well, this has really shaken me up! I mean, it makes we wonder, if we didn't see the trouble she was in, I mean, it makes me wonder who else looks good to me and smiles and does their job well, but carries a needle in their pocket! Who else do I know that's drowning in a secret life! It scares me! Scares me for our kids!"

They were afraid! I could hear fear in their voices. I understood they would no longer be as carefree as they once were. Now they would walk with careful steps and measured words and wary eyes. I knew I had done this to them, stole their innocence, and I did not want to hear any more. I climbed the steps back to my new apartment.

I put away my new dishes, lined up the cans of soup in a perfectly straight line. Folded the towels in the bathroom, folded them again. *I want them to look perfect!* I folded them again. And again, until each one was the same exact size and no edges showed. *There! That looks great!* I felt better.

I dumped the contents of my black plastic bag, the bag of my own things, I dumped them on the bed. One by one I folded my shirts and placed them in a drawer. Hung my jeans and skirts on hangers. Sorted my underwear. And there it was, my own works, my needle and syringe. I didn't want to look at them. I tossed them in the trash. And there, the bottle of Doriden. "Maybe I should save that. After all, it's a legal prescription. From a doctor. It must be ok. I can keep this."

Sitting on the edge of my bed, I wondered why Civic Interest Guys hadn't gone through my things before turning them over to me. Maybe I hadn't taken away all of their innocence after all! I felt better.

∼

The next day I went to the new job they had picked out for me. I could walk there. That was nice. I found the office I was told to report to, Mrs. Hager, with her hair in a bun, her white blouse buttoned to her chin, and the hem of her skirt just below her knees, and "sensible shoes" I think they are called. My curly hair was a bit windblown and sun streaked. I'd taken care to iron my best skirt and blouse, but it didn't button all the way up and my skirt was above my knees and I was embarrassed.

"Well, there's been a change of plans here, dearie," Mrs. Hager informed me in her clipped, all business voice.

"We were going to put you at the reception desk, that's the easy job, just answer the phone and file incoming mail. But Mr. Chambers, up on the third floor, well his secretary was in an accident and will be out for several months. They told me you can type? Think you can handle that job till she gets back?"

"Oh yes, mam. I'm sure I can, I'd be glad to fill in upstairs if you need me to." I used my soft voice, the one that belonged in here, in this marble building. Here with the very proper Mrs. Hager.

Mr. Chambers must not have been very important because he had the smallest office, up there on the third floor. I had a little office beside his, facing the hall, clear view of the elevator. After scrubbing off my red lipstick in the ladies' room, I felt hopeful.

~

Knowing that staying clean would not be easy, knowing that Dr. O didn't talk to me enough to help, knowing that Mrs. A was only the children's caseworker, not really mine, I pondered, in the evenings alone in my nice apartment, I pondered who could talk to me about how to make a new life and be happy. I could not think of anyone, but "someone must know, surely somebody knows how I can be happy here."

So, I went to AA. *Maybe if I just say "drugs" every time they say "alcohol", maybe that will help.* I went to three meetings every week, sometimes four, maybe five if I was really lonely. They were nice people, most of them. The men were friendly, eager to explain the twelve steps, which one they were on, how long they'd been sober. The women smiled tight little smiles and only said "be sure to read the Big Blue Book every day." I decided not wearing lipstick was not enough and that I would buy a longer skirt with my first paycheck.

In my third week, Mr. OlderFellow did talk to me. Small and thin he was, ravaged by years of addiction. But his eyes sparkled and his silver hair crowned him a winner. He didn't tell me to read the Big Book, he gave me one of my own. Every meeting he sat next to me.

Every meeting he drove me home. I was cautious, on guard. Too lonely to not accept the ride home, too lonely to not invite him up for coffee, I braced for the advance I knew he would make, the advance I hoped he would not make. The credibility of AA hung in the balance. Here I would decide if people really did get clean, stay clean, be good and be happy.

A month later, Mr. OlderFellow offered to pick me up and take me to his home in a nearby city to have Sunday dinner with his wife and family. I was delighted. Maybe this sober AA thing was for real.

~

We drove up the long driveway to his home, out there in the country. A large house, classic wrap-around porch, shutters at every window, flowers in the gardens.

"Wow, you have quite a place here! What's that huge building over there, the green one?"

"That's where I work, my business. I'll take you out and show you after dinner." I was impressed.

The dinner was lovely. Yellow flowered tablecloth, real napkins. A blue plate piled high with fried chicken, bowls loaded with mashed potatoes, and three vegetables! The children chattered between mouthfuls, his wife was polite but quiet. She did not look at me. I wished she would, I was wearing my new longer skirt and hadn't put on any makeup. After dinner I offered to help clean up.

"Oh, no, I can do this, he's anxious to show you his shop, you go on, I'll take care of this."

And so we did, walked out to his shop, the large building with no name, and I entered a world I had never seen...rows of huge vats, two, three stories high. A tall glass window at each one revealed lovely green or yellow or red pills. Each vat filled with pills! We walked through valleys between mountains of pills.

"What is this?" I asked, unable to hide the excitement in my voice. His face lit up with pride. "I manufacture prescription medications!

Clair

It's a legitimate business. I have all the permits and inspections." I was in awe.

By the third aisle I began to wonder why he invited me there.

Impulsively, on the last aisle, I shouted, "Oh, I know this one! My doctor gives me Doriden to help me sleep good every night."

He turned to face me, shouting, "How long have you been taking it?"

"I don't know, a pretty long time, I guess." I could see by his wide eyes, stiff shoulders, and shaky hands he was upset and I wished I had said nothing. He spewed forth a sermon on its dangers and side effects. "Seizures!" "Heart attacks!" He fired words at me, words like bullets meant to pierce my defense. I stepped outside. I did not want to hear the sermon. I was anxious to go home, to be away from there.

I sat on my bed that night, after swallowing two Doriden. *Why had he said all those things, why did he want to take away the one tiny comfort I still had?* I didn't understand. Then I was angry. True, he had never made a sexual advance, but showing me all those pills! Does he take pills instead of drinking? I was confused and realized I would never go to another AA meeting, I pulled the blankets over my shoulders, and retreated into oblivion.

∼

Each morning I walked to work slower, slower every day, dreading getting there. This was supposed to be "my good life", but going to a boring job every day, making just enough money to pay my expenses, not a penny left over, no movies, no eating out, not even an occasional treat at the grocery store. Sitting alone every night, every weekend alone. Week after week after week! I wanted to shout at each person passing by, "Where's the 'good life'? Huh? I'm being good, so where is it!?" I did not say those things. I walked on to the job someone had decided would make me happy.

But I Can Learn

~

My boss was a really nice man. He gave me a book, "The Cross And The Switchblade." Each day he stood in the doorframe of his office, crossed his arms, smiled with anticipation.

"So, are you reading the book? What do you think of it? Do you like it?"

"Well, it's a nice story about a bunch of drug addicts in New York City and how they... 'found God', ...or something like that. Nice for them." I didn't see what it had to do with me, why he gave me the book, what he wanted me to say. He looked disappointed, standing there, waiting for a better response.

Swiveling my chair to face him, I asked, "So, are you trying to say I should move to New York where those people are?" Recoiling as though I slapped him, he stepped back into his office, went to his desk, came back to shut the door, but not before I saw the forlorn, disappointed look on his face. I guess I wasn't getting the point of the book he wanted me to get and I felt guilty, and sorry that I was disappointing yet another person.

~

And then it finally happened, the day the caseworker arranged a visit with my children. A real visit this time. Not a visit in her office, and not at McDonalds with her sitting at another table. "I'll bring the children to your apartment Sunday afternoon, about two o'clock, and I'll come back at four to pick them up." I was ecstatic!

For two hours we would be a family again! My children were coming here, to my home. I knew they would be as excited as I was, and I planned the visit carefully.

I see us snuggled on the couch, reading books and talking. I can almost hear their laughter as we play games. I can feel their touch, how they will want to stay close to me, unable to let go, needing a knee or foot or hand to always be touching me, to stay in contact. Cereal, I have to buy cereal, kids always like cereal. Oh, and ice cream, I have to be sure to pick some up! I could think of nothing else, as I waited for our special day.

Mrs. A came, on Sunday, just as she said she would. I was waiting at the front of my building, watching each car. She found a parking place there in front, got out, came around to my side, opening the back door. My heart leapt as my three babes stepped out, stood next to her, next to the car, shyly looking at me. I was quick to wave goodbye to her, quick to usher my children up to our apartment. Not my apartment, our apartment!

I brought out the books first. "Here, lets read some books. Come sit with me, here on the couch."

Three little faces stared at me, three little children still standing at the top of the stairs, here in our apartment. They didn't come rushing up to sit here with me, as I had pictured. They seemed afraid to really come into the room.

"Ice cream!" I shouted. "How about some ice cream?" I ushered them one by one to the table, they sat as little wooden dolls, unspeaking. "What flavor would you like, strawberry, chocolate, or vanilla?" Still no answer, just eyes staring at me. Changing tactics, I asked, "Would you like chocolate?" That only required a head shake "yes" or "no". Success! We were communicating!

We did read books, we did play games, these children of mine, willing to please. And I, desperate to please.

We walked to the park, I pushed them on the swings, cheered as they slid down the slide. We spread out a blanket and had cookies and Kool-Aid. Silent children who didn't look at me.

And then it was four o'clock. Mrs. A came, right on time, of course. She parked in the same spot, opened her back car door, and my three little stoic children came alive. Jumping into the car, they told her "we played games and had ice cream." And then, "How long till we get home? Do you think they had supper yet? Will Uncle Ted still be there?" The long awaited visit was over.

    I climbed the stairs back to my apartment and cried. I could not walk to the couch. I could not walk to the bed. I collapsed in the hall as sobs broke from somewhere deep inside me. I did crawl to the bathroom and throw up.

    Leaning against the sink for strength, I stood and viewed my little bathroom, the towels folded perfectly, not an item out of place, not a speck of dust on the floor. I grabbed a towel from the rack and threw it on the floor.

    I walked through my bedroom, there, so neat and tidy. So perfect. Not like me. I messed up the bedspread as I walked by.

    Through the living room I walked, slowly, feeling out of place. *Have I really been living here, in this place, this nice place? This magazine place?* Sitting on the pale blue sofa, I wanted to feel at home, tried to feel I belonged here and knew I didn't. As I tucked my feet under me and wrapped a fluffy, white afghan over my lap, I hoped to be comfortable. It didn't help.

    Dumping the afghan on the floor, I walked to the kitchen, opened every cupboard door, moved the cans of soup around, moved everything around. Standing back, I surveyed my messy cupboards. *Almost, but still too tidy, not like me.*

    I put three cans of vegetables down on the shelf with pans, moved the glasses over, and put the bread on the shelf with them. Everything out of order. That was better.

    Taking the mayonnaise out of the fridge, I left it on the counter, to spoil. To become unusable.

    Surveying my apartment, my disorganized apartment, my messy apartment, I felt better. It felt right.

Chapter 21 – Mr. Broadcaster

In the morning I dressed for work and started down the stairs, on my way to my "supposed-to-be-happy" job before I realized I was wearing my short skirt and low cut sweater. Rushing back to my bedroom I donned my longer skirt and modest pink blouse. I quickly threw the mayo in the trash and moved all the canned soups and vegetables back to their original tidy places, trying to remember this was the new me, not the old one.

Walking to work, I tried to think about this out-of-place feeling. *Well, I was never really a child because I was the mistress of my father even before Kindergarten. I wasn't a good mother because I couldn't stay home with my children. And now maybe I can't be a good secretary to Mr. Chamber of Commerce because I hate my job and am bored to death. I am restless and depressed. I don't like it here.*

∼

Tom, Mr. Blue-Tie Civic Interest Guy called me at work that day. "We have a project we'd like to talk to you about, one you can be a part of. Can we meet you after work? We'll take you out to dinner."

"A project! What sort of project?" I was excited, something to break boredom.

"Too complicated over the phone. How about five-thirty at the Grill House, just a few blocks from you?" I said yes.

Walking into the Grill House, seeing those five men, Civic

Interest Guys, in their suits, white shirts, ties, I was glad I was not wearing my short skirt and low-cut blouse. I was glad I had changed to my longer skirt. In this place, for them.

Over dinner, interrupting each other with enthusiasm, they explained their plan, the plan that would "change the youth of our city forever".

"Here's what we're thinking. You already know we never thought there was a drug problem here, but obviously there is."

Mr. Steve, Black-Tie-Glasses was eager to explain, "We can't stop what's already here, let's face it, we wouldn't know where to begin. But young people, the teenagers who aren't using drugs, we think we can reach them. Maybe we can stop it before it even starts."

"And how in the world do you think you can do that?" I couldn't help but ask because I had no idea what they were talking about.

"By educating them," he continued, excited. "Warren needs Powerful Drug Education. If young people see the danger, the harm in using drugs, then maybe a lot of them won't even try it."

I shook my head in disbelief, "And just how are you going to do that? You just said you don't know anything about it! You guys going to read a lot of books, or what? Make a movie?"

We'd finished our dinners. They leaned back in their chairs, and smiled. All five of them. It was Sam, Mr. No-Tie, who leaned forward and said, "No, we think young people will only listen to a personal story, like your story. If they hear it from you, what's happened to you, what you've lost, then they most certainly will not be eager to try drugs. Every time they're exposed they'll think of you, they'll remember what you said. They'll listen to you."

And it was Robert, Always-Green-Tie, who pushed a typed page over to me.

"Here's a list of the youth groups we've contacted. The highlighted ones have already scheduled a talk. We're calling school principals, too. All we need is you, for you to agree. One of us will take you to each meeting, you won't be alone. Together we can really do some good, save some kid's life! What do you say? Want to do this with us?"

Five men, five eager faces, looking at me, and I didn't want to do it! I didn't want to be talking about the worst parts of me, the parts I hated, about my failure as a good person. I started to say no. *But look at them, they're full of hope and dreams, eager to do good, to have purpose. I remember listening to them, when serving their dinners and beer, hearing them talk about their need to have a project, a purpose. Can I say "no" to these kind, hopeful faces, waiting for me. Maybe I should say yes. Maybe I should do something unselfish.* I asked if I had to use my own name, and they said that I could use something like, "Sandy." I liked that and said, "yes".

It was Mr. Black-Tie-Glasses who drew the picture of each meeting for me. "First, one of us will talk about why we're there, that will only take a minute or so. Then another minute to introduce you. Then it's your turn. You can write out what you want to say, or just ad lib it. Just tell how you first got started using drugs, maybe like who first gave them to you, or why you even did it, you know, what led you to start. Be sure to talk about the bad stuff, you know, like getting arrested and being in jail. You'll know what to say."

"And then one of us, whoever brought you, will take over and let the kids ask questions. They'll have a lot. Most of them you can answer, but if it's something like the harmful effects to our health, well, we've all been reading all the literature, everything we can find. We can answer those."

Twisting in his seat, Mr. No-Tie interrupted with, "By the way, how did you ever get started? I don't think we've ever heard."

It took only a second to realize I didn't know. I really didn't know. They stared at me, waiting. The silence became awkward. Shrugging my shoulders, I used my casual voice. "Well, my parents were alcoholics, drinking every night, so that kinda screwed things up at home." I lied because I was afraid to say I didn't know. A lie is better than being stupid.

Clair

~

Sitting on my couch later that night, I wrapped myself in the afghan again, and waited for the two Doriden to make me sleepy. I pondered the evening. *Something feels really wrong, something about doing this, telling "my story." I don't like it and I don't want to do it.* Carrying my fluffy afghan to bed with me, I knew I would do it anyway because I didn't want to be a selfish girl who didn't care about kids who might start using drugs if she didn't.

In one month I wondered if we were helping anyone. Kids loved to hear about police cars driving into my yard.

"How many were there?"

"How much mess did they make when they searched your house? Did they find anything?" and "Did they handcuff you in the front or the back?" were common questions.

They didn't think my story was sordid. They thought it was exciting.

But in two months, I came to love the meetings. My boss gave me time off work with pay when we did assemblies at schools. One day a County Narcotics Detective attended a talk.

"I think you're doing a really good thing, he said. "I give a few Drug Ed talks, and it would sure be effective if we could team up and work together." I shook his hand and smiled politely, so he wouldn't know I was afraid of him.

I stood in front of teenagers in the afternoon, and parents, teachers or pastors in the evening and told them to never, ever, even try a drug. "What if you like it? What if you like it as much as I did?" I was proud of that statement because I thought it made people think. I felt important.

Most of all, the part I loved best, was the drive back to my apartment. I never wanted to get out of the car when the Civic Interest Guy of the night parked at my building. I never wanted to climb the steps to my apartment and be alone. I wanted to stay in his car and talk. If I could be sad and depressed, I knew he would have to stay, to help me feel better. Me, the poor girl who was willing to be so vulnerable in front people. Just to be helpful.

"It's lonely, without my friends, and with my children gone."

Or, "I've made my life so hopeless, it will never get any better."

And Mr. Civic Interest Guy, whoever he was on that particular night, always responded with, "I know you're lonely, but you'll make new friends."

Or. "You're pretty and smart, with so much potential." I didn't believe them.

I became a master manipulator with slumped shoulders, sad eyes, and tears. They became helpless men, wanting to help, yet unable to escape the guilt I gave them every time they let me go upstairs to my apartment alone. They did not want to let me down and be the reason I started using drugs again. I knew how to bring that threat into the car, that unspoken threat.

They had families at home, wives waiting up, worried. I didn't care. I held their attention as long as I could, before walking up the stairs, leaving them to feel sad and guilty, trapped between abandoning me and going home to their wives. I didn't care. I had escaped lonely for one hour.

~

Businessmen often came to the marble-floored fancy building where I worked every day, at my desk. I began to smile and greet each one with a lingering handshake and a slightly tilted head, only cause I was bored. My eyes said, "You are the most special person to walk through my office this week!" My posture said, "I think you are a very attractive man!" I did this because I was bored and lonely. In my heart, I was still the druggie girl, pretending to be a good girl. Again, I couldn't live in both worlds. It was easy for the bad girl to take over the trying-to-be-good girl. It was too bad.

I began to have a dinner date once a week, then three times a week, often with coffee in my apartment later. Each night, as I lay in bed, waiting for my three Doriden to lull me to sleep, I wondered. *Why, when I am so poor, why am I having sex with businessmen for free?*

And then I met Mr. Radio Broadcaster, most handsome single man with time and money. He introduced himself after a particularly long Drug Education Talk. His smile was beautiful, unguarded, his handshake warm and lingering, his voice calm, soothing. I liked him immediately. Holding his business card and pen out to me, he didn't even have to ask for my phone number. I took the card and quickly wrote my phone and address.

In seconds, Mr. Civic Interest Guy was at my side. Smiling politely, he shook Mr. Broadcaster's hand before whisking me away.

"So, what was that all about? Who is that guy? Do you know him?"

"No, I'd never met him before. He was only saying how much he appreciated what you are doing with this program. You should be really proud."

Flattery never failed to distract someone from asking more questions. I did not mind being dropped off at my apartment alone on this night.

I put the coffee on and waited for the Broadcaster to knock on my door. He did.

At midnight, I crawled out of bed, swallowed my three Doriden, and stood watching him sleep.

"Boy, I wish my dad could see me now! He'd hate it that I just had sex with a black man." I knew he'd be really mad. Not that he'd ever find out! Still, I felt good thinking about it.

We became friends, the Broadcaster and I. Each night I had to give a talk somewhere, he'd be at the top of my stairs at home, waiting.

"I thought you could use some company after your talk. I didn't want you to be alone and I brought a bottle of wine. How'd it go tonight?" We talked for hours, sitting on my couch with the fluffy afghan. Because he listened with the same intensity of Golden Boy, I liked him. He took me to his favorite places. Introduced me to his friends. Respectable radio people. And then he introduced me to Gypsy, who sold dope in a house on a dark street. *I wonder why he took me there.*

In four months, "Don't Use Drugs" talks dwindled to three each week. In six months, they were few. I dreaded answering my phone. Civic Interest Guy called every Friday. "Well, we don't have any talks scheduled next week. I think we've just about covered every school, church, and civic group. I'll let you know if anything comes up." He sounded relieved.

I know, they're just tired of carting me around and having to sit in the car and talk to me for an hour afterwards. I didn't say it out loud, to them, but I knew it was the truth.

Mr. Broadcaster was not at the top of my stairs every night.

"Hey, I got promoted and I'm working nighttime radio! But maybe we can have lunch some time?" I could only answer, "Yeah, maybe. That'd be nice."

There'd be no more long talks over glasses of wine, I knew that. After three weeks he stopped calling. *It's just cause he's sleeping days and working nights.* I told myself that because I didn't want two rejections in the same month.

On Monday I wore my short skirt to work and waited. Mr. Black Suit Blue Tie, not a Civic Interest Guy, was the first appointment on my boss's calendar. I did not say, "Go right in," as usual. I came from behind my desk and ushered him in so that he could see how I wore my short skirt.

He took me to dinner that night after work, and left a nice "tip" on my bedroom dresser before he left. Alone and bored, I accepted other "dinner dates" again. With handsome men who came from my office to my bedroom. Men who didn't ask "how much" but knew and discreetly left cash on the dresser before walking out the door. I thought it would make me feel better. It didn't. I still had an ache in my heart that was bigger than loneliness. Bigger than anything. So big I had to run away from it.

Finally my Mr. Broadcaster called, "Wow, I just have to share my good news with you! I've been recruited by a major New York City station! I can't believe it! I'm moving to New York City! This is huge for me! I'm so excited!" I would have gone with him but he didn't ask me and I was disappointed.

Civic Interest Guys went to meetings and discussed a new strategy to stop drugs. They didn't ask me. I was angry.

On Thursday I went to that house on the dark street to look for Gypsy. He had a fresh needle and syringe and little foil packets of heroin.

On Friday I went to Main Street to look for Golden Boy. He had those tiny tabs of prescription morphine.

Two days, two days with my people erased six months of aloneness. I didn't go back to my boring job on the third floor, marble building. I didn't go back to my empty apartment on the second floor, overlooking the park. And I didn't care.

Chapter 22 – Psych Ward #2

It took one week. Spiraling down to ruin. One week to walk the streets, again. Everything I owned was in a brown paper bag, again. A toothbrush, extra t-shirt, underwear from the nice lady at Salvation Army with a five dollar voucher for girls like me. These things, not from my nice-girl apartment. These things I hid on top of the air conditioner in the overheated bathroom, in the gas station on Anthony Boulevard. The one with the attendant who pretended not to see me.

Other things, in my brown paper bag, two outfits. Jeans and t-shirt when I needed to be innocent and helpless. Short skirt and blouse when I walked the street. For money or heroin, both. I slept inside if I found a friend, someone who had an apartment. Two nights, never more.

"Hey," Gypsy would say. "Stay another night. Or just move in here. There's lots of room in this house."

"No, no…I'm all right. I'm just in-and-out here. I got things to do. I'll just be back later." He knew, his eyes locking onto mine for only a breath, shifting down to his feet, then around the room. He knew. He knew the rules. Never be dependent on one person, never get attached. Be in control. No one can know how much you use. Never buy from just one person. Those were the rules.

"Yeah, sure, I get it. Just don't get too cold out there. You come back anytime, always got room for you, little girl!" I liked Gypsy. It always felt good to be with him.

Some nights I slept in a hidden place under the bushes in the park down the street. Or the gas station restroom when it was too cold.

Where the attendant didn't care that the door was locked and unusable to everyone else. I was safe there. One more step down.

I cut my hair and bleached it blonde again, there in that bath room. Found the box of outdated Miss Clairol on a junk shelf at Salvation Army. I don't know why I did it.

Every time I caught a glimpse of myself in a mirror or a storefront window, I smiled. "Now I am not the failure mom! I am not the "show-and-tell" girl on parade for everyone to look at! I am the bad girl!" I felt honest, proud that I could be that honest, not a lie, that I could just be me and not pretend. Pretending had got me nothing. Maybe honesty would feel better.

I didn't see how skinny I had become, how no amount of makeup covered the dark circles, how nothing hid my sunken cheeks and hollow eyes. I stole a sweater to cover my arms, arms lined with little black dots from needle pricks, arms bruised again in rebellion at the times I missed a vein and had to start over. Somehow there was a peace in all of this not-pretending. Another step down.

I made two lives. One on Main Street with my dear Golden Boy, with Detroit Mike, Billy Joe and Susan, with Jack, sometimes sitting at that table by the window, talking to Whitey. These were my people. Here I belonged.

My other real life was Wayne Street, there with Gypsy, and Luke, and Cindy who shot up in the large vein in her neck, heroin straight to her brain. I couldn't watch.

"Why you cringe like that when you see her do that?" Gypsy would ask, laughing. I could not be like them, really one of them, because I cringed when she did that. And because I hated guns. And because I was the white girl. But I did have a life here, with them. They liked me.

I tagged along with whatever they were doing. Unless I saw a gun slipped into a back pocket. I opted out of guns, remembering Billy Joe's words, "When I point that gun at someone, in that moment, I am God!"

Every day I sat with Golden Boy for an hour or more, a table at his favorite bar. Urging me to eat, he bought food, greasy hamburgers and French Fries, apple pie with ice cream.

"You're so thin, Babe, I need you to eat, gain some weight. I'm scared for you! I'm really scared of losing you. I can't think of living without you." Never hungry, I tried, for him. His sad eyes staring at me could not make a hamburger with lettuce and tomato look good.

And every day he was sad, sorry, apologizing. "How can I stop this ride you are on? I don't know how to help you? I'm sorry I ever brought that first bottle of paregoric to your house." On some days he only cried, looking at me, wiping away tears, able only to say, "This is all my fault." I could have told him it wasn't. I should have said, "No, it's not you. I'd been running heroin up my veins long before I met you." I could have said that but I didn't. I knew it was mean and I don't know why I didn't say it. I just didn't. Two steps down .

∼

Walking the streets every day, in my short skirt, my legs cold, I looked at every person who drove by. Smiling at men, turning away from women. Especially women with children. I didn't look at them, because I couldn't be them. They didn't look at me because they were disgusted.

"That's ok," I said out loud, to no one. "That's ok, you just drive on cause you sure ain't gonna give me any money and you sure don't have any drugs, so you just drive on!"

I watched for men who slowed their car, rolled down their window, smiled.

"Hey honey, you need a ride someplace?"

"Sure."

"Well, get in, I got some time to spare."

Smiling my biggest smile, tilting my head just so, we both knew this was not about a ride.

Some days I walked downtown at five o'clock. Businessmen leaving their offices, time to spare, looking for fun.

"Hey, you whore," screamed a lady one day, standing in front of her store. "You get outa' here. You got no business here! You cheap whore!"

"I am not a whore, and I'm not cheap!" I yelled back at her. "I got a business, and I entertain and give pleasure, and I get paid. I bet I make more money than you do! And I make people happy. And I don't yell at people!" More steps down.

∼

Detectives came to know me and pulled their car up. "Hey, where ya going?"

"Well, no place. Just walking." Didn't matter if I wore my short skirt or my jeans. They'd look at me and say, "Well, get in."

Sitting in the back of their car, it didn't matter if it was unmarked or had swirly red and blue lights on top, I didn't like it and I didn't know I didn't have to get in just because they said to. I still just did what I was told. Didn't know I had a choice.

"So, you using again, I guess?"

"Oh, ok, maybe just a little, now and then."

"How much you buying? Who you getting it from now? How much you pay?"

As fast as they asked questions, I was faster answering, making up stuff as I went along. I knew not to be a snitch. Another rule of the street.

"Yeah well, there's a guy, Michael."

"Michael? We've never heard of Michael!" Embarrassed they were, narcotics detectives are supposed to have their finger on the pulse of everything, and now I told them they didn't. Didn't matter that Michael was a made up person. It was still fun.

"Where's he live?"

"I don't know for sure, I knock on the garage door, down the alley, back on Berry Street…" On and on, I wove a good story, making it up as I went along. When they dropped me off a few blocks later, I walked away, smiling, knowing I was a winner because I had distracted them from arresting me again, and I had woven a captivating story. I was proud.

Until my gas station restroom was locked. Until the streets were empty and I couldn't find an inside place to sleep. Until I found an old sweatshirt on the park bench and curled up under the bushes in the park, wrapping it around my legs to keep warm, hoping to sleep. Then I wasn't proud. Being proud didn't keep me warm. Tumbling down now, I was.

~

Four doctors in our town wrote prescriptions for those tiny tablets of morphine. Three needed a story, the reason a person needed the powerful, addictive pain killer. One did not.

There he was, kind and sympathetic Dr. T. with his tightly curled black and grey hair. His bow tie and shiny black shoes, he was old enough to have seen and heard countless stories unfold as he sat in his little brick office on Lewis Street. He knew thirty morphine tabs could keep an addict off the street. Pushing his little round stool with one foot, he sat in front of me. "Look at me," he said, his eyes sad, his voice soft, sorrowful. "These thirty pills can help you, you know. Use them to wean yourself down. Get yourself off the street. Cut yourself down more each day enough so you don't get sick. If you be careful, you be free by the time this prescription is gone. I'm trying to help you. Now, let's take your blood pressure, just to make this legal."

He was good for two, maybe three visits. If we hadn't kicked our habit by then, he wouldn't write another script. Others thought he was just an easy mark. I didn't. I thought it was sad, him thinking he could help us and us just taking advantage of him.

When I had used my three visits, I went to the booths in the back of the bars on Main Street, the booths that always held a disheveled wino with bleary eyes and dirty clothes. If he looked like a junkie, I sat with him and told him what to tell Dr. T. I traded a bottle of wine for a prescription.

Less scruffy girls, girls still sitting on the front stools, girls only on the brink of their own descent, these could also learn stories for the three doctors who needed to believe the stories they were told. I was a good teacher.

This was my life, for weeks or months, I didn't keep track. Days blending into nights. Walking in my short skirt to make money. Finding good drugs, keeping secrets, keeping safe. *Don't let heroin Gypsy know about morphine Main Street. Or Main Street know about Gypsy. No one can know how much I use every day. Don't tell detectives the truth, make them believe the story.* I was in control and now I was, for sure, the boss of me.

∼

Until the day Billy Joe slid next to me in the booth at the bar. Him, with a perfect wave that swept his hair across his forehead, his grin and eyes always excited.

"Hey," his voice low, almost whispering. He leaned close to me.

"I got this doctor in Ohio, just over the line. Here's the deal. He'll write a script for morphine, but needs a reasonable story. You do that good. And he keeps the prescription pad in the drawer right there in the examining room. So he hands ya' the prescription, puts the pad back, sometimes just lays it on the counter, and leaves to tell the nurse to give you a b-vitamin shot. You tear off three, four, however many sheets you can without being too obvious. Bring 'em back and you copy his signature, cause you're good at that too. Then we can write our own prescriptions."

"So why you telling me this? You going?"

"Nope, I've been already. I want you to go."

"And how do you think I'm going to do that?" I asked, giving him my most puzzled look. "You going to drive me?"

But I Can Learn

"No, I got something here I got to work on today. You take my car and go, just give me half of the script sheets and half the pills when you get back."

Sipping my beer, I peeled the label from the bottle, pulling it off in little strips that curled. I was stalling, wondering what the catch could be. With Billy there was usually a catch. I could get hurt. Or land in jail. But this sounded easy. He spoke so casually. Quietly, he set his keys in front of me, scooped up the pile of beer-label curls and the now empty bottle, and left. Pocketing the keys, I walked down the street to the construction Golden Boy was working on.

Watching him three stories up, walking the narrow path, I held my breath. It was still amazing to see him there, the sun highlighting the copper strands of his hair, bare arms shiny with sweat. As the courthouse clock ticked close to noon, I sat on the curb and waited for him.

I wanted him to ride with me to Ohio. He wouldn't. I don't know why, but he wouldn't.

An hour later, I sat in that doctor's office. Everything was just as Billy Joe said. My story was believable, the reciting of it easy because I knew it so well. The prescription written, the pad placed in the drawer.

"I'll send the nurse in with a b-vitamin shot, you seem pretty run down." He exited.

It was a new pad, full. I took ten sheets and walked back out through reception.

"Wait! Miss, you can't leave!" My heart stopped beating and I held my breath. "You can't leave. You didn't get your b-vitamin shot yet."

"I don't need any b-vitamins, and I'm fine!" I kept walking, out the door, to Billy's car, parked on the street. Out in bright sunshine, in this unfamiliar town, I looked straight ahead, walked to the car. *Do not look back. Do not walk too fast. Drive. Anywhere.*

Only at the edge of town did I allow my legs to relax, To catch my breath. Pulling into a parking lot, waiting for my heartbeat to slow, I saw the drug store across the street. *I'll get my prescription filled here,*

Clair

where they know this doctor. My prescription in my pretend name. Carefully copying it onto a new sheet, my forgery was perfect.

~

Driving U.S. 24, back to Indiana, I was uneasy. I don't know why I was jumpy. Jumpy at every white car behind me. Wishing I had a map, wishing I knew a different route to take home, I pulled to the side of the road. *Maybe there's a map in the glove compartment. I'll look.*

And there they were, falling out onto the floor. Pills in prescription bottles. For people I didn't know. Bottles of pills, empty foil packets, a few syringes. A gun. Didn't matter that it was small…it was a still a gun. Laying quietly, on the floor, the gun! I was scared, very scared.

Holding my breath, I was afraid to breathe. I didn't want to touch it, touch anything. I left them there, everything on the floor, passenger side of Billy Joe's car.

Drive! Just get out of here, back home. Drive! I didn't want to call attention to myself, parked there at the side of the road.

A let out a sigh of relief when seeing the "Welcome To Indiana" sign. Later, my town, finally. Driving directly to the Bar, the place I was to meet Billy, I knew I was on time. I parked his car in the back, just like he said. Glad to be inside, I waited for him. Fifteen minutes, thirty minutes. Waiting. I asked the bartender to call another bar, a few blocks away. He passed the phone to me.

"Hey, is Billy Joe there?" "Who's this?" "It's me. I have to find him right now! Is he there?" "I haven't seen him, but hold on, let me look around" Minutes passed. I waited. Heart beating hard, I could feel it in my head and neck, pounding.

"Nope, don't see 'em here. You ok?"

"No, I'm not ok. Never mind, I just have to find him!"

"Wait, Eugene is though, he just walked in. You wanna talk to him?" My Golden Boy! "Yeah, sure that'd be great" I waited as the bartender called him to the phone. I tried to sound confident, not afraid.

"Hey, I can't find Billy Joe and I think maybe I'm in trouble, can you come and get me?"

Silence. I waited. And waited. Finally he answered, stern. "Nope, Babe, I can't do that right now." More silence. I did not want to cry and I didn't want him to know how afraid I was. Terrified. I could not bear the silence, nor did I wait to hear why. I just hung up.

Needing to give the keys back, wanting to be far away from that car, with the gun on the floor, I could only wait at my table. And so there I sat, keys on the table, my head lowered to my hands, my legs, my shoulders, shaking, waiting for Billy Joe. He didn't come. Officer Daniels did.

"Ok, you need to come with me. Don't make a fuss. Just come outside quietly."

I stood to follow him out the back door, and he grabbed the keys. Fear racing through my whole body now, I feared I would throw up. In the small parking lot in the back, two uniformed officers stood by Billy Joe's car. He tossed the keys to them. Placed me in the back of his unmarked car.

It took thirty minutes for the silent ride to the hospital, the walk through the lobby, the elevator to the ninth floor again. I sat on the bed, in my room, on the psych floor, again. Arrested, again. Not one word spoken. Soundless, no words. No one looked at me.

I am not a person. I am a thing to be moved around and isolated. And then I threw up.

~

This time, Psyche Floor visit number two, was easier. I knew the routine. Five days of little white pills, five days of pain and throwing up alone, no visitors, no comfort. Be sick, be patient, submit. "I've done this before. I know the drill".

On day six, I could wander into the hall, out of my room. Into the dayroom. "Oh, here you are, come, sit right here and join us." Cheerful

Clair

Craft Lady annoyed me. Her permed hair and pink flowered apron annoyed me more. Like her cheeriness and pot-holder-making could make us all better!

"No! I will not make a basket!" I glowered at her. "Stop bothering me!"

This time, on Psyche Floor visit number two, "No" was my favorite word.

In the afternoon, Art Lady came, with her perky pony tail and rubber apron. I figured she wore that in case a crazy person threw paint at her, or maybe glue.

"No, I will not do finger painting with you! Stop bothering me!"

In the evening, the nurse brought my little white pill in a little white paper cup, juice in another. Down to only two a day, one in the morning, one in the evening, she still made me stick out my tongue to prove I swallowed it.

Handing the two cups back, I stared at her. I knew what she was thinking, about to say, so I talked first.

"No, I will not stop lingering by the elevator, threatening to escape! It's too much fun, and I am bored. I know, all your other patients watch to see if I make it. But I like entertaining them, you see, and I'm good at it so I'll do it whenever I want."

"Well, but you are a patient here, and you need to cooperate." She straightened her posture stretching out to look taller, above me, hand on her hip for emphasis.

"I am not a patient, I am not crazy, I am only arrested, and I don't have to be submissive to you. You are just a nurse, and not the police" I was angry. Angry all the time now.

~

I sat in the dayroom, watching. Sat at a table alone. I did not want to mingle. I needed time to think. Thinking was hard. I tried to find what was happening, how I got here, what would happen next, but my thoughts were like dust. Little pieces flying around the room, never holding still, never coming together to make anything. All my words flying around the room like that dust, I couldn't make a clear sentence. My mind was foggy. I felt stupid.

Every morning I watched Sharon bring her coffee-in-a-plastic-cup and sit at my table. A few minutes later Trish arrived and sat beside her. For two days I did not talk to them. I only listened to their cheery chatter and glared.

"Can't you see this is my table and I don't want you here? Go someplace else and be all happy." They ignored me. Until I said, "Don't you guys get it! You are here, with me, in a psyche ward. This is a psyche ward, for heaven's sake! For crazy people. You act like this is some high school lunchroom, or something. What's wrong with you?"

Sharon held her mug tightly, staring into it, grim-faced. "I really wanted a baby, we did, my husband and me. It took a long time for me to get pregnant. And I had a little boy, a sweet little boy, except he had no skull bones. His brain was covered only with his skin and downy little hair and he died."

Trish was bolder, she looked straight at me. "I'm here cause I'm depressed. Can't figure out why. I have a nice husband and two great little kids, but I just can't stop being sad and wanting to die. Or sleep. No reason. Nothing bad happened to me, I'm just sad."

And so we were silent, we three ladies in our robes and slippers, not allowed real clothes. Holding our plastic coffee mugs. The silence was awkward, unbearable, and I was ashamed.

Suddenly, they looked at each other, at me, and laughed their schoolgirl giggle, leaning back in their chairs, they just laughed. The sad spell was broken. We were friends.

In the evening, we sat at our table, holding plastic cups of hot chocolate.

"So," Trish asked. "Why are you here?"

I used my casual voice and shrugged one shoulder, hoping to appear as lighthearted as they were. "Oh, I got arrested for drugs, again.

Clair

They don't like me throwing up in their jail, so they bring me here."

That's how it happened that we became a gang of three, waiting for someone to make us better, to make us happy, to make sense of our lives. Trish and Sharon, moms with husbands and normal lives. And me with nothing. I liked them. Here they were my friends. Together we could be a little happy. They were cooperative and liked that I was not.

Trish had this funny way of lightly slapping the table and announcing, "Well, here we are!" She'd smile, then look at me, delighted and eager. "What are you going to do today?" I knew, even then, I was their diversion. Distracting them from their own misery. I was their TV show. They watched me annoy the nurses at the elevator, they watched me stick out my tongue boldly after taking my pill. They watched when I refused crafts…or did them the opposite of how we were told. It was fun.

Except on Thursday mornings when the orderly walked Trish down the hall for shock therapy. On those days she didn't know who we were, after her treatment. We tried to talk, Sharon and I, alone at our table, but we couldn't. I felt more awful thinking about what was happening to Trish than about my own life. Sometimes Trish didn't know us the next morning even. I was scared. Scared they might try that on me!

∼

Three weeks, I sat, waiting, afraid of shock treatments, afraid of jail, just afraid. Monday Mr. Grey-Suit Civic Interest President came to visit me.

"Hey, there's a room back here, a conference room where we can talk. Let's go there."

It sounded ominous and I didn't want to go. I stood still and stared at him, being all official and in charge, and I knew, *ok, here's where I better stop being tough. Time to be pitiful and helpless.* I didn't want to be trouble, not now, not with this man, so I followed him. Back to doing what I was told.

"Here's the deal," he began, opening a folder on his lap. "We've done some checking around, and can get you into the treatment program at Lexington. That's in Kentucky. It's a federal program and they only take narcotics addicts with a ten year addiction, but we pretty much have that documented. This can be good for you because they're experts and know what you need. They have training programs so you will leave with a skill and a good job. It's better than jail. And this will only be for six months, not years, like you could be facing. But you have sign this paper, agreeing."

I could barely breathe. *Federal Program*! The words echoed in my heart. *Federal. Was it because I brought drugs and a gun over the state line? Am I arrested for that? Federal Program!* I couldn't get over that word and was confused. Or are they are sending me away because they are tired of helping me, the hopeless person?

I was numb. And confused, wanting to ask questions, but afraid to do so. I signed the paper without reading it, choosing to trust this one time. Choosing to not be angry. I just did what I was told. I just signed the paper.

Chapter 23 – Lexington!

I walked back to my friends, the two sitting at our table, waiting to hear. Was it "Good news, I'm getting out today!" Or "It's bad, I have to go to jail!" Trying to explain to them what I didn't understand myself.

"I don't know for sure what's happening. He talked about sending me to some federal place, Lexington. It's a rehab center and could be a good thing, I won't be in a real prison, and I'll come back with some job training. I'll get a respectable job and then they will let me have my children back. That's what it sounds like. I don't know! It doesn't feel right, but I'm too scared to ask. At least I won't go to jail. This Lexington thing is only six months."

It was Sharon who spoke up first.

"That could be a good deal, but how much would you get otherwise? What would you be charged with? I mean, if you don't agree, then what happens?"

Searching for an answer, I was embarrassed and could only say, "I don't know! I don't know anything! Maybe bringing drugs across a state line, maybe forging prescriptions, maybe having a gun, maybe something else! I never think to ask. It doesn't matter anyway, cause I signed the paper."

There was nothing left to say. We sat in silence, I think for hours. Until supper trays came to distract us. It didn't work. We could not be distracted. We were depressed.

Sliding unfinished trays back in the rack, Sharon and Trish walked down the hall to their own rooms. I sat at our table, watching other patients, the teenage girl, always sitting in that corner chair. She scratches and digs at her arms, her forearms. Picking at her skin until it is a bloody, scabby mess. Something crazy happened to her one day, watching "The Wizard of Oz". By the time the movie ended, she was frantically scratching, screaming that there were bugs crawling under her skin. She had to get them out. Even now, sitting there, scratching, she whispered, "Get them out! Come out! Come out!"

I couldn't help thinking maybe she's not so crazy after all. I wish all I had to worry about was little bugs under the skin on my arms. *I wish I was her.*

∼

It was eight AM when Mr. Grey Suit Civic Interest President stood in the door of my room, all shiny clean in his sharp haircut and soft blue tie. Here to take me to court. Here to plan the rest of my life.

"A good life," he said. " I have another paper for you to sign. This will give you a chance at something better. Sign here, right here." His perfectly clipped fingernail pointed to the spot, there on page four, middle of the page. His left hand held the pen midair, in front of me. The pen waiting, waiting for me to take it and put my name there on that line.

I did it. I did it without reading the paper, without asking any questions.

Is that who I am? A girl who always does what the Guy In A Suit tells her to do?"

∼

Standing in the courtroom, I looked at the massive ceilings, at the walls heavy with dark wood. My feet plunged into thick green carpet. It was a scary place and I felt small, insignificant. Me, skinny me with bleached blonde hair. It took only a moment for me to drop my cocky "tough girl" attitude. It took only a moment for me to know, "I better look and act really small and pitiful and innocent here." I knew how to do that.

We sat at the table on the left, Mr. Civic Interest President handed papers to the Blue Suit person at the table on the right. *These men all look like attorneys. Is one of them mine? Do I need an attorney?* No one answered me. I guess I hadn't said it out loud.

Civic Interest Guy leaned over to whisper, "Remember, just say 'yes' whenever the judge asks you a question. This is your big chance, so don't mess it up."

"Mess it up! How could I mess it up? I thought I was just going to rehab." Without looking at me, he said, "Shh, we're ready to start."

The somber judge, in his long black robe, sat above everyone, being in charge, looking down at us. "I hope he's nice," I said in my most quiet voice. In this room I thought only quiet voices were allowed. The Suit Person at the other table stood and read from his papers. "A narcotic addict in need of rehabilitation." I did not understand the rest. He talked too fast, used big words and I didn't like him. I didn't like being here either. I didn't like anything.

The judge looked at me. Mr. Civic Interest President touched my elbow, "Stand up, answer "yes" to each question." So I did, stood and answered "yes", even to the ones I did not hear, even the ones I didn't understand. I just said, "Yes, Sir!" Clenching my fists, I dug my fingernails into my palms to cause pain. Real physical pain told me I was alive, that I was a real person. It also helped me not to faint, or cry.

The judged talked for a long time, so I stopped listening. I tried to remember actually being arrested and exactly what the charges were.

I remember being taken to the Psych Floor again by those detectives in their black suits, but did they actually arrest me? In a moment of clarity, I almost shouted, "Wait! What exactly is happening here!" but I didn't. I was, after all, only a speck of dust in this magnificent room full of important smart people. Little specks of dust do not talk. Little specks of dust do not resist the winds that toss them from one place to another.

∼

We didn't talk, Mr. Civic Interest President and I, until we reached my room, my home with the crazy people. Leaning against the doorframe, looking at me, he seemed weighed down, heavy.

"Well, ok, so I guess that's settled. I'll pick you up at ten tomorrow morning, and fly you down in my plane." I could not speak. I could only stare at him until he shrugged his shoulders and turned to leave.

"I hope you did the right thing here!" I said in a soft voice that he could not hear.

∼

Handing me two hospital gowns, an orderly announced, "I'll be back in a minute for those clothes you're wearing." He wanted my "going to court clothes" because here I was only allowed hospital clothes. I knew I was home. This world I understood.

After "dressing", I went to the dayroom, sat again with Trish and Sharon at our table. "So, how was it in court today? What happened?" I put on my tough girl-ness and told a story to make them laugh so they would not know how afraid I really was. Sharon wrote her address on a piece of paper and gave it to me, "Just in case they let you write letters."

"Just in case!? Of course they'll let me write letters, it's not like I'm going to prison, I'm going to a hospital, to take classes and get good job training. Of course, I can write letters!"

∼

The plane ride was silent, uneventful. Driving the car he rented at the airport, Mr. Civic Interest President didn't look so powerful.

"I never saw you in a sweater before. You look different." I smiled as I said it, to be nice. He did not smile, only recited his speech, sounding like he'd practiced it in front of the mirror like I used to do. "This is really a good thing for you, you know. A great opportunity! You'll like it here, and you'll make friends. Look at it as sort of a college, like you're off to boarding school. I know it's scary, but you'll learn lots of new things. It's good." I wondered why he kept telling me that over and over, and that afraid feeling began descending over me again. A dark cloud. I looked straight ahead and smiled again. I could smile just to be nice. I could smile to make fear go away. Until we saw the signs, "Federal Rehabilitation Center, Lexington, Kentucky."

"Proceed To Guard House." Until we saw ten foot tall barbed wire fences. Until we saw monster buildings of cold bricks. Until we saw lookout towers.

Pulling up to the gate, the guard person directed us to a small building on the left. "You can park your car there."

As we stepped into the dark, grey brick building, another guard took the suitcases Mr. Civic Interest Guy held, suitcases with things for me. Dumping the contents onto an old wood table, he examined everything, fingered the hem and seam of each garment. Some things he tossed back to the suitcase, others into a paper bag.

"These you can have," he stated, handing me the bag. "What about those other things, my books, and shampoo and stuff. What about those?"

"Those are contraband, prisoners are not allowed to have those from the outside."

"Contraband! Wait, I'm not a prisoner! I chose door number one where I get rehabilitated! Drug Education and Rehab and Community College! I'm not a prisoner! I am not a prisoner!" I shouted, stomping my right foot for emphasis. He ignored me.

I did not watch Civic Interest Person walk back to his car and drive away, leave me there. I was silent, and turned to look at the guard. He just shrugged his shoulders.

~

A Female Guard came to escort me to the main building, where hard steel doors clanged behind us at every turn. She wore her uniform tight and crisp, her badge polished. Soft brown curly hair seemed very out of place with her hard face, her clipped walk and cold eyes. Eyes straight ahead. She never blinked, never looked at me.

Entering the Intake Unit, clutching my brown paper sack, I looked at her carefully and knew that no matter how good I had been at making people feel sorry for me, she never would.

In my world, on the street, showing fear could have meant the death of me. In here, with this guard, I think she must make me afraid of her. *If I am not afraid, it could mean the death of her. If I don't show fear now, she will have to make me afraid.* I decided to let her see that I am in shock and fearful. It wasn't hard, because I was truly afraid...really afraid.

Next, down this hall, in this room. Strip. Shower. With this soap. She watched, making sure all my body creases got soaped. She hosed me down, the water gushing out hard and stinging, almost knocking me over. It smelled funny and I felt degraded and was embarrassed.

Now, still naked, to the exam room. Male doctor there, no uniform, his face blank, his words few. He checked all of my body openings to ensure I was not smuggling drugs. I was unprepared for the invasion and recoiled in shock. His large hand held me in place. I was used to invasions, but on my terms, in my street clothes, when I said "yes". But not now, not here, where I came for help. I was not prepared. I was naked and vulnerable and could not fight back. I knew I could not fight back. I could not be tough and these were not my terms. *I think I am in deep trouble here! This was a mistake!*

Handing me a drab grey-brown shirt, pants with a drawstring waist, floppy paper slippers, Stern Guard Lady walked me to orientation. Through clanging metal doors again, aisle after aisle, that harsh metal sound when each one locked behind us, the sound jarring every nerve in my body.

Orientation Nurse Lady, wore a crisp, white uniform. "Well, finally," I thought. "A real human person to care about me." I was relieved. Until I saw the badge on her left collar.

She motioned to a chair, "Have a seat there."

"So this is orientation, where we detox you before sending you to population."

"Population! What's population?" I blurted out without thinking, in my angry voice.

Carefully setting her pen aside, closing the folder with papers about me, she stared straight at me. We took the measure of each other.

"Here's what you need to know," she began. "You can pretend to be a nice girl, but we both know you're not. Nice girls don't end up here. You are not nice. You might think you can manipulate us to get your way. You might start with the first tiny thing. I'm telling you now it won't work. You are not in charge, we are. You are not the boss. We are. If you make anything a contest, you will lose. We win. We always win.

"This is still a prison. See the bars on the window. Hear those gates locking behind you. Those things are not here for decoration. They are here to keep you in. So drop the sweet, innocent act right now."

Picking up her pen, opening the folder with my name and number, she continued, "So I see that you've already been detoxed, but we still have to keep you here for three days to be sure. I'll check you frequently and if you show any withdrawal symptoms, we'll treat those. Other than that, you can rest and mingle with the other women on this unit."

"Can I make a phone call?" I asked. She looked at me, and did not answer.

Only handed a card to me. I studied the number written there: 79539-F. Looking back to her, I waited, confused.

"That's your number. Memorize it. From now on we don't use

Clair

your name. We call you by your number. You are 79539-F."

    I sat on a bed in a cubicle of a room, a spotless room, smelling slightly of disinfectant, with a metal door, a tiny window, a metal doorframe, a plain room, no window to the outside, a bare room. One thin blanket, one pillow.

    "I want to go home," I screamed. But there was no one to hear.

Chapter 24 – Prisoner?

The night was long, never ending. I startled awake at every noise, every groan coming from a room somewhere in this place. Every clang of metal slamming onto metal as doors closed somewhere in that cavernous place.

I did sleep, I knew because that time, when I startled awake, I didn't know where I was, and my door was open. Then I remembered. I am in a rehab place that looks like a prison. I am 79539-F. Maybe it is a prison! Maybe I didn't pay attention in that courtroom!

Cautiously I walked down the hall, into a small room with a few tables and chairs. Hard tables and chairs. Metal and plastic. Hard.

Seven girls sat at the largest table. Wearing hospital gowns, like me, and scruffy throw-away slippers. Eating breakfast. Someone motioned for me to take a tray from the rack, the last one. My breakfast. There was an empty seat at their table, so I took a chance. "Is it ok, can I sit here?" "Sure, where you from?" Introducing themselves by name and city, they were friendly girls, eager to talk. *Maybe this will be ok.* I relaxed. A little. And ate my breakfast. Scrambled eggs, toast, and applesauce laying on a metal tray. A square indent separating eggs from applesauce. Just a tray. No bowl, no plate. A plastic spoon. Plastic cup for coffee.

We sat, hour after hour, day after day. Eight hard-core junkies with nothing to do. Waiting to get out of Orientation, we passed the time telling stories. The only stories we had. Getting drugs, getting high, getting money, getting arrested, stealing.

"Oh, let me tell you, this one time I had the best dope! Stole it off this guy. Guess it hadn't been cut yet, cause oowee, that was sure some good stuff!" Laughing, a few girls came back with, "Oh, yeah, but I bet he beat the crap outa' you then. Stealing his good stuff." "Oh, no! I so good he never knew it was me. Uh huh, I made sure he didn't know it was me."

Proud of their stories, each one out did the other. It took only a few hours for me to grab the attention with my own stories. I wanted the attention, to be in the center again, so now I was proud of my talent for talking doctors into writing a prescription for morphine. Now I was proud that I could forge prescriptions. I had many stories to be proud of and they were impressed.

"Yeah, look at you, so tiny, and looking all sweet and innocent. I can see you really pulling that off." Here I felt important, and for a few days I was not afraid.

Maybe I belong here after all!

Day three a female guard escorted me to population, to alley 3A, third floor room. This cell of cement block walls held a bed and a locker. A large window overlooked the front lawn. Trees added shade. A perfect picture. Marred by a metal grate and thick bars. Double security.

"Here are your clothes, you can wear your own things now. The bathroom and showers are across the hall. We won't lock the doors unless there's trouble. You have an appointment in one hour, someone will run you through the drill, go to Room 112 on the first floor, and don't be late." She handed two paper sacks to me, my own things. She smiled, then.

"I'll be ok, huh?" I asked. She didn't answer, only shrugged and walked away.

Feeling hopeful now, in my own clothes, I sat across the desk from another stern-looking guard, hair in a tight bun, posture more rigid than her starched uniform. She did not look at me as she lay the sheet of rules on the desk. Keeping her eyes on the paper, she read them, one by one. Like maybe I couldn't read for myself.

"Everyone has a job here, you are on floor detail. Every morning you wash and wax the halls on the first floor, here with the offices. Afternoons you will be in group therapy. The rest of the time you are on your own. There is a small dayroom at the entrance to each alley, snacks and a TV are there. You cannot go onto another alley or floor, but you can visit other prisoners in the hall that connects each alley. You'll do fine here if you keep your head down, follow the rules, and don't cause any trouble."

"Wait, did you say 'visit other prisoners'? I agreed to come here, to get help, its Rehab! It's Rehab, isn't it? I'm not a prisoner!"

Only now, did she look up from her paper, her eyes drilling into mine. Tossing her pen down onto the cluttered desk, she leaned back in her chair, crossed her arms. I was afraid, again.

"Look, sweetie, let's get this straight! Some hot shot, probably someone in Washington, sitting in their fancy office, decided you all can be 'rehabilitated.' If we just build your 'self-esteem.' Have you wear your own clothes, call it 'Rehab' and 'Therapy.' Some of the new people working here think this will work. But us old-timers, we know it won't. You and I both know it won't. You're a junkie, will always be a junkie. You can't be rehabilitated. So just shut up, do your time and try not to ever come back here."

Pushing another paper over to me, she continued her instructions, "Now, you need to list here three people who can visit you and three people you can get letters from, they will be the people then that you can also write to."

On the way back to my room, or was it my cell, I saw three women wearing my clothes. Shocked, I started to say, "Hey, wait! Those are my clothes!" But I didn't. *They are holding hands, those three girls wearing my clothes. I am standing here alone. I'd better not say anything. I'd better be quiet, silent, unnoticed.*

~

I couldn't do my job, waxing the floor because I was too small or too weak to control the heavy industrial polisher. It banged into walls, here in the important offices, out of control.

I couldn't talk in group therapy because the other girls did and I didn't want to interrupt. The doctor took notes and did not look at us and did not talk. *Hey, doc! You one of the old-timers who thinks this won't work. That why you don't talk to us!* I wanted to say it, but didn't.

I waited for the shower room to be empty. To take a shower when I was alone, when no one could reach out to touch me or grab me.

I waited in line for meals, three times a day, trying to decide where in that line, front or back, the sound of metal doors banging open and shut would be less jarring. Eating my food again from the tray with no bowl or plate.

I sat in a little cubicle and took tests. A million questions, some serious, some silly. I didn't care. I answered them all. Truthfully. *Probably won't make any difference anyway.* I was depressed. And afraid, always afraid.

On the fourteenth day, I went to the administrator's office, Miss Tight-Bun, Stiff-Shirt Lady, on the first floor. Marched into the office, sat in the chair opposite her desk, locked my eyes onto hers.

"I changed my mind. I don't want to be here. You can send me back home. This isn't what I was told."

"And what were you told?"

"That this was rehab, and I would get good therapy, and that mostly I would get some good job training, have some skills so I could take care of my children. All you have here is typing and GED. I can type, and I'm already graduated. So, well, there's nothing here for me. You have to just send me home, cause I changed my mind. I don't want to be here."

"Ok, I can send you back, but I don't think you want to do that."

"And why not?"

"See, you are here to avoid criminal charges. It's be here, or go back to your home town and wait in jail for a month or more for your case to come up. Get a trial date. Wait another month or two to go to court. Take your chance at what sentence you will get. It could be ten years or more. On the other hand, your commitment here is for six months and you're out.

You've already got some of that time over already. So you can stay here, a sure thing, or you can go back to your home town and wait in jail. Take a chance with that!"

She explained all of this in the calm voice one uses when talking to children, disobedient children. Speechless and confused, I could only walk out of her office, back to my cell-room, back to my bed. Laying there, I counted the dots in the ceiling tile. It was better than thinking. Better than feeling. *Ok, I'll stay here. I'll just count the days till this is over. Then I'll go home.*

∼

On day seventeen, a male guard took me out of my building, across a yard, to another building. The sign on that building said, "Research".

"Ok, seeing as how you couldn't handle your other job, now they've given you this one, in this office. Here's the requests people send in, school kids, parents, teachers. They want drug information, so you pull the pamphlets from the wall, the pamphlets that apply to their questions, and send it out to them."

Letting his hand slide down my back, he smiled as he said, "And I'll walk you over here every day."

Sitting at my table, then, I mailed out little booklets to tell people about drugs. Medical information, cleaned up information. *It's too bad I can't write them a letter and tell them the real truth!* I was bored and read all the pamphlets. Then I sent some to my friends on the outside, just in case we needed more information. I liked it there, alone, in that quiet room. Alone.

~

"Hello, I'm Dr. Hall," he said, this tall, thin man who came into my quiet room. He sat without being invited. "I've been studying your tests, the ones you took when you first came. I asked for you to be assigned here because I think I can help you with some issues."

"Issues? I don't have issues! What do you mean, issues? What issues?" I didn't like him just coming in here to my alone space.

"I want to help you understand what happened with your dad. We can talk about it, there, in my office, where it's safe for you."

"I don't want to talk about that, so no thanks! And anyway, he wasn't abusing me."

"Well, you still need to come to my office every afternoon when you finish here. We can talk then."

"What if I don't want to?"

"Are you forgetting where you are? You don't get to choose."

"Well, I won't talk! You can make me sit in your office but you can't make me talk."

"Then you can listen to me talk." He turned to walk away, then stopped. "Oh, and you might want to consider that your commitment here is for six months, or longer. Up to forty-eight months. You leave only when we see that you are rehabilitated."

I didn't like it. I didn't like not being the boss of me.

~

And so I went, every day, after lunch. First I listened and argued. Then I began to talk. And he talked. I remembered things I didn't want to. I panicked. I tried to be insane, wanted to be insane, to live in another world, to be oblivious to the things he said.

"You don't really want to be insane," he explained. "Insane people live their lives in constant fear. Every moment feels to them as though they could step off a cliff. They can't tell whether a crack in the sidewalk is just that, a crack. Or maybe it's a cliff. Their balance is a little off so they concentrate on each step, not wanting to fall. Every step holds the fear of death. No, you don't want to be insane."

"Oh, yes I do," I answered. "It still sounds better to me, better than this, here. It's like I'm locked up in here with my dad! Sure, insane would be a whole lot better!"

He gave me thorazine. I felt better and decided I now liked this doctor.

~

I made friends, Cindy and Trina, and we sat on the floor in the tiny library and read Dostoyevsky and Steinbeck and Tolstoy in the evenings, after supper. Reading these again, these books I had loved as a teen girl, they now seemed to be more alive, more real. And I missed my Golden Boy, his insights, shared as he leaned over my bar on Main Street.

I went to every religious service, just to get off my alley, to fill a few hours. In the Catholic Mass I felt like a little girl again. I didn't like that and didn't go back. The Baptist person talked about committing to Jesus. I thought Jesus should have been committed to me. But He wasn't. In the Muslim service men wore funny hats and stood at each door, legs slightly apart, arms folded, "guarding against evil forces". We listened to talks about living 'in peace as Allah intended.' I wanted to raise my hand to ask, "Why are you here, in this place then, if that's how you lived your life?" But women were not allowed to speak, so I didn't get to ask my question. I was ignored and didn't like it. Ignored is worse than anything. Getting yelled at or hit or anything would be better 'cause at least then I exist. Ignored means I am nothing. I don't want to be nothing. I'd rather be bad than be nothing.

Day after day, week after week, I counted the days until I could go home. Most days I was calm. I learned a lot in therapy, even liked Dr. Hall and trusted him. Every time he made me remember stuff I didn't want to, I panicked and wanted to be dead. He put me in the infirmary, where it was safe and I couldn't hurt myself.

He cares about me, he really cares. And then, one day I knew I was better and would go home and not use drugs and I would be a new person. Most days I knew that.

Except on the day I received a letter from my caseworker. With a picture of my children. I looked at it, that picture, and yelled at the woman taking care of them, their foster mother. *My children, they are my children and now, you made them not look like my children. They are limp, just leaning against that tree, there with that dog. And look at their drab clothes! Oh, no, their soft, silky curls are gone! Their hair is cut! Short, really short! How could you cut their hair! They are my children. I am the mom! I should decide if they get haircuts, not you! You have no right to do this!*

Collapsing on the floor, I began to cry. Sobbing, uncontrolled sobbing. With a pain in my chest, unbearable pain. *I can't breathe! I really can't breathe!*

A guard came and took me to the infirmary. A nurse handed me a little cup of pills, "Here this will help you feel better." A stronger dose of thorazine let me sleep and then I was calm. Again. As long as I didn't think about that picture of my children. As long as I didn't think about my children at all. Only then could I have hope that I could go home and be a good person.

∼

Until the day we sat in the tiny dayroom on our alley, eating saltine crackers with apple jelly. The TV on, we weren't really listening. Until the news broke that Judy Garland had just died of an overdose! We knew she was one of us, struggling, year after year, fighting the same demons we were. We thought she would win, this girl who sang of dreams coming true, where trouble melts like lemon drops, and roses bloom, just for us. Where all of this is reachable, just over the rainbow, just over the rainbow our dreams will come true.

I could feel the cloud of defeat in the room. If Judy Garland, with her beauty, her talent, her money, her fans who loved her so much, couldn't make it...well, how could we?

On this day there was no color in our world, now, on that day. On this day our world here in the Federal Rehab at Lexington, Kentucky was only in black and white.

~

Going to Movie Night each week was a break in the monotony, the endless boredom.

Until the night the feature was 'Cool Hand Luke' and we watched Paul Neumann, the hero, defy guards and escape, over and over. Answering 'yes boss' or 'it's just me, boss'. Smiling while planning his next revenge. The smile captivating, we all wanted to be like him. Until the movie ended, the lights went on and we were led through those clanging metal doors again, back to our own alley. We sat in our little TV room, eating the forever snack of saltine crackers and apple jelly, looking at each other and wondering why they showed us that movie, and who were really the crazy ones in here!

Days passed into weeks, weeks into months until, finally, I was on 'short time'. Able to count days until I was released. "I will eat food that is not covered with green peppers and I will never again see red jello," I told Trina. "I will not be forced to hear Aretha Franklin eighteen hours a day, over and over, the same songs. I will have my name, not a number, but my own name, who I am".

"This isolation was good for me," I told my therapist. "I think I started only playing the part of a sweet girl, a girl who could change, who could be rehabilitated and now it's become real. Pretending merged with hoping, and somehow I really am changed! I am free for the first time in my life and I know, when I get home, I will be a new person and not use drugs."

Sleeping now without Thorazine, I was at peace each day. I knew now, I was not a bad person and I liked me. I knew I was valuable, and I had a name and I was not just a number. Dr. Hall had taught me those things.

He was very proud of me, I could tell, and that felt really good. *I don't remember anyone being proud of me ever before.* He sat at his desk, smiling, sharing the details of the aftercare program.

"You have to finish the rest of your forty-eight months on the outside, keeping clean, turning in good urine samples, holding a job. Report to your aftercare worker, she'll be like a parole officer, but we don't call them that anymore. And, we couldn't release you to the street, but I see here the Gambles, friends of yours, have offered their home to you. That's good, you'll be with a family instead of a halfway house."

We stood, on this our last time together. Me, soft, vulnerable girl, him the hero-therapist who rescued me. We shook hands, as we each wiped away a few tears. I felt good, really good.

And finally, there it was, the morning a guard drove three of us to the airport, handed each of us a ticket. Each of us going home, far from each other. We would never meet again, but on this morning we were together, a team. Rooting for each other. Excited. Happy.

We sat alone, then, when the guard left. Us in the coffee shop, waiting for our flights, drinking coffee.

And then I saw it. The window. Next to our table. I could see the planes landing and taking off. I looked down at my hand, holding a real coffee cup, a real metal spoon. I looked at the glass for my water.

And so I stood up. Announced to the room in a loud voice, "Look, everybody! No bars on that window! Whadda ya' think of that! And, oh look here, a real coffee cup…" I held it up for all to see before letting it crash to the floor in a hundred pieces. With one hand I scooped all the dishes from the table, sent them crashing to the floor. People stared at me, in shock.

Suddenly, I was angry and mean. Every wicked pleasure I had

been denied for six months, I now wanted to plunge myself into and embrace.

Angry I had been locked up, how dare they do that to me! I was resentful and vowed to my ownself that I would show them it didn't work. *All those Civic Interest Guys in their nice suits and ties, they sent me here. It's their fault! They'll be sorry, I'll make them sorry. I'll show them it didn't work! I'll show them!*

I was the boss of me again, finally the boss of my ownself.

Chapter 25 – Psych Ward # 3

I sat at the table with Golden Boy. Here in our favorite bar. This smoke-filled room with sticky tables. I was in trouble again and he had no words.

I had words, lots of them. "How did this happen? I felt so good when I was getting out of Lexington. Confident and hopeful. I knew I'd never shoot up again. I knew I'd get my kids back. Then the minute I got out I was so angry! I was mean to Civic Interest Guys."

"Wow, grass! Can you imagine! Just look at it! Grass!" I said that every time they came to visit. I don't know why! I just wanted them to feel bad, to be sorry they ever sent me there.

But my dear Golden Boy. He could only shrug his shoulders and let tears spill over onto his cheeks, not even caring to wipe them away. As he sat, just listening to me.

"And church," I went on, needing him to see that I had tried, really tried. "I lived with the Gambels like I had to, and I liked them, went to church with them even. They were odd, those people at their church, but they really believed all that stuff and I wanted to be like them. I did. And I was for a while. I made a commitment to Jesus, you know, and it felt very real. I had a bible and loved reading it. Churches had me come to tell about 'the miracle, how God had changed my life' and I liked that. I felt like I was finally doing something good."

"Is that why I couldn't find you? For months?" he asked. "I heard you were back and I looked for you, every place I knew. Everywhere. I was desperate. I knew it was my fault you got locked up. I should have gone with you when you asked. Maybe I coulda' done something. I'm sorry, babe, I'm so sorry. I have no purpose without you. I want to protect you, always, and I keep failing." He looked away, lost it seemed, in some mire of his own, remembering his pain.

"I don't know how to help you, I wish I understood where you are. Why this thing grabs you and doesn't me. I look at everything as an adventure, to take hold of, to enjoy, and then walk away whenever I want. I tried to share it all with you, all those new things out there to explore. But you, this takes hold of you in a way I don't get. I'm sorry I ever tried to take you with me, that I started this. I'm so so sorry."

Not liking this conversation anymore, not able to endure his tears, his pain, his guilt, I struggled to change the subject. I didn't like hearing him talk about me being out of control. I still wanted to be the boss of me. I didn't like hearing that I no longer was.

I went back to his question about why for a few months he couldn't find me.

"Well, during my church days, I had a Christian friend."

Waiting, I thought he might walk away now. Leaving me to sit here alone. But he just stared at me, ready to hear the story. I continued.

"Well, this guy, see, he had been the head of a Christian Rehab place in New York. I figured he surely knew how to live right. He was a bad junkie in the streets of New York, and I looked at him now, all fancy in a suit and tie, his hair combed all neat. It was good for a while. I was clean, wore nice clothes, longer skirts. Someone at church gave me a good job, my daughter got to come live with me. My boys came every weekend."

"Yet, here you are today, with me. Why?"

"Yeah, cause then I'd get excited about something I read in my bible, and tell him about it. I thought he'd be proud of me. He only said 'You don't understand anything! That's not what it means at all!' So I just quit reading it."

Now he looked into my eyes, my Golden boy, smiled and ventured, "Maybe that was for the best."

"There's more! He showed me how the bible said it was ok for us to sleep together. But every time I just felt guilty! How could I go to church, hold my daughter's little hand. How could I stand up in front of people and say, "God changed my life," when I was feeling stupid and guilty all the time! He hadn't! All that church stuff worked for some people, but it hadn't worked for me. I don't know why, but it didn't work."

"I know," he said as he pushed my sleeve up. "Look at you, all strung out again. All bruised. How can you even find a vein anymore?"

"I use my legs." He shook his head slowly. The bartender looked over, to see if we were ok, GoldenBoy sobbing now.

Needing to end this, I stood up to leave. "I can't stay here. Aftercare/Parole Lady is coming to my place at three. She's going to send me back, I know she will. I gave too many dirty urines. Three's the limit and I think I've had more than ten. She'll bring the police, and I'll be back to Lexington." There it was. The Word. Lexington. "She's sending me back." I heard myself say it and now it was real. I couldn't stop crying. So, I walked away. From my Golden Boy, the only person who ever truly loved me, I knew.

~

Glancing at the clock above my stove, I saw it was three-ten. She was late. Quickly making the bed, stacking dirty dishes in a cupboard, I combed my hair. Again She rang the bell, I opened the door. She was alone! No police escort. No one.

Sitting on the couch I tried not to look at her. I remembered the first time we met. She'd bounced into the Gambel's living room, sat on the nearest couch, tucked her feet up under herself, and announced, "I'm so happy to be here! You are my first client, and I know we'll be best friends!" Didn't even make me pee in the cup. I knew then I'd be able to get away with anything. What were they thinking, giving a rookie to an hardened street addict!

Now she was smarter. I was glad my daughter was with friends for the weekend. I broke the awkward silence with the phrases now so familiar to me.

"I'm sorry, I really am. I know I've messed up this time. But, just listen for a minute, before you send me back..." She placed her hand on my knee, interrupting me.

"Wait, what? You think I'm turning you in?" She stood, then, pacing the floor. "How can you think that! I will always stand up for you. And I'll always be here to help you. I'm your friend." She said all of this in her offended voice. My fear dissolved, I then cried. It was the appropriate response.

We sat at my kitchen table and drank coffee before she left.

∼

Alone again, my apartment became a cage and I paced like an animal, trapped. I was frantic. A familiar storm began to rage in my head, my heart, my fingers and toes. My nose was running and my eyes watered. My skin was clammy, creepy. I would soon be very sick.

I sat in the bathroom, warm syringe in my hand. I thought Parole Officer Lady would take me away from it, but she didn't. I thought she would rescue me, but she didn't. I took the shot, quickly finding a vein. Relief flowed through my body. Only my body.

Placing the bible on the kitchen table, finding the verse "we are new creatures in Christ", I underlined the condemning words again. With a shaking hand I scrawled my own two words over the page. "Not me."

I called the friends who had asked my precious daughter to spend the weekend. "I'm kinda' in trouble here again. Can she stay with you awhile so I can get straight here?" They loved her, I knew, and had the energy to give to her everything she needed. Everything I hadn't. I hadn't been able to sit by her bedside for the hour it took her to fall asleep. I hadn't been able to bring her brothers home to her, I hadn't been able to entertain her all the hours we were awake. I had failed as a mother. *Perhaps I should stop calling myself 'mother,'* I stuffed a few of my things in a paper bag.

And then, I closed the door to my house, and walked away. Tired of trying to be a good girl. I did not want the good people who believed their bibles to see that it didn't work.

~

I had to tell my dear Golden Boy! "I'm still here! I didn't get sent back!" There he was, same bar, same table, same chair, face still wet with tears. My precious Golden Boy, throwing his arms around me, face alive with joy and hope, as he shouted, " You're here! You're here! I have to tell you… I found it! I found the answer for you." He held my hands again, across the same table.

Looking at his face, looking into his eyes, he suddenly seemed different, and I did not like what I saw, what I felt sitting here hold his hand. What was it? What was different?

"What is it? What is this thing you've found that makes your face look different, that makes you different? What is it?"

"Ok, here's the thing," he began. "I figured it out. You should sue your dad!"

The words tumbling out almost faster than he could say them. "For a lot of money. We could. We could sue your dad. I heard about it on television. This girl, her dad molested her, and later, when she grew up, she got a lawyer and sued him for a lot of money. Say you need it for therapy or something. We could have enough to last a lifetime. Yeah, you should sue your dad!"

I could hear the excitement in his voice, I could see it in his eyes, his smile. I did not like it! In that moment, that moment of bringing my greatest shame out of the shadows, bringing it into a courtroom, in that one moment he was no longer my Golden Boy. He was only a man, another selfish man. That little bit of tarnish had now infected the whole. I was devastated! The one bright and shining thing in my life had now turned dark and selfish and not on my side.

Pulling my hands away from his, I steadied myself, and walked away, leaving him there, at our favorite booth, in our favorite bar, and I thought, "I will never come back here again."

∼

I walked to my favorite park, curled up under the bushes in the far corner, that dark place I knew so well. I could not sleep that night. Good heroin from Gypsy didn't help, a real, clean blanket I'd pulled from the trash didn't help. Nothing helped. I couldn't cry. Dead people don't cry... *Now I am forever alone. There is no Golden Boy. There is no me.*

∼

Morning came. I crawled from my hiding place, smoothed down my short skirt, fluffed up my still blonde hair, looked across the park and knew. "Today I am indeed a new person. My GoldenBoy is gone, and I will never love or hope or dream or be nice again." I took a moment to see if this was true. It was. I was not sad.

Walking the street the next days, the next weeks, my focus was clear. I needed to make money every day, a lot of money. Hundreds every day. Then find drugs, good drugs. *Don't buy from only one person. Don't let anybody know how strung out I am. Be in charge of my own self. Be the boss of me again.*"

One particular day, on my street, I sat on the curb, tired of five or ten dollar tricks.

I should go downtown. Businessmen will be out walking to lunch and they like me. Yeah, that's what I'll do. I need to make some good money. I'll work downtown today.

Passing a store window, I caught a glimpse of myself, here, downtown. *Oh my, look at me! I'm a mess, my hair all scragly, even my knees are dirty. I need to clean up, look fresher.* I stepped into a department store restroom. A nice place with free lotion. Good smelly lotion.

But women glared at me as they came in. All I had done was take off my shirt and wash my armpits with paper towels, soap and water. "What are you looking at?" I challenged the fur coat lady.

"You got a problem? I'm just washing up here." I didn't understand the look on her face, but she left quickly, so I didn't care. Checking the full length mirror, finding myself presentable, I stepped out into the store, ready to go to work, pleased with myself.

~

And there they stood, two plain clothed detectives. I knew them. Both of them. Sgt. Mike stepped forward and grabbed my arm as I tried to escape back into the ladies room. "Oh no you don't! I need to talk to you!"

"Yeah, right. You here to arrest me? Don't need any talking for that. And I haven't done anything wrong! I'm not breaking the law here, just going to the bathroom. You should let me go before I scream. I could scream and then you'd be in trouble!" I was being the boss of me and it felt good to be angry and challenge them. These big guys.

"I'm not arresting you, but stop fighting and listen to me, please," trying to shake them off, to get away. I couldn't. They were bigger and stronger. These two burly detectives ushering me down a side aisle.

"Stop trying to get away from us! You're barely eighty pounds, and maybe five feet." His smirk told me he was enjoying this and I was annoyed. They might be big and huge, both of them in their black suits and long coats. Them with their short haircuts and clean shaves. So perfect looking. Angry as I was, I couldn't break the hold they had on my arms. "All right, I'll listen, but you better talk fast, cause I got places to be, things to do."

I looked at Sgt. Mike, looked at his face, met his eyes. We had been friends, in another day, doing "Don't Use Drugs" talks together. *I know he liked me then. Maybe I should listen.* I stopped struggling.

"I've set up a methadone maintenance program for you. No, don't say it, I know it's not legal in Indiana yet, but see, you technically belong to the federal government so I've made all the arrangements. You start now, today. I don't want you out here, on the street, like this."

"I don't even know what that 'methadone' thing is, but I'm not doing it. Whatever it is."

"Methadone is a drug, pills you take every day and they block the effects of heroin. Or morphine. You shoot up and nothing happens, you never get high and you never get sick. It's just nothing. What you do get, though, is a chance at really good therapy and you get well. This is good for you. I don't want to see you back in Lexington, not again. And I don't want you on the street!"

Afraid now, I pulled away, trying to run. "No, I'm not doing it! I'm not doing it! You can't make me!" They were strong, these two detectives, towering over me, each grasping one of my arms, standing close, trapping me. I was more afraid!

They stopped listening to my protests, walked me to their car, placed me in the back seat. The back seat with no door handles. The black, unmarked car.

"I'm not going, you guys! I'm the boss and I'm not doing this and you can't make me!" I kept saying it over and over because they weren't paying attention. They weren't listening.

Looking out the window I saw the emergency room doors of the hospital, was ushered down the hall, the long hall, to a conference room. Into the room. That small room, they stood at the door, guarding it.

And then it was just me and someone called Dr.P. There he sat, in a chair, on the other side of the table, waiting for me. His grey suit a bit crumpled, his hair cut short around his ears. Professional.

He crossed his long skinny legs, leaned back in his chair, smiled. He was friendly as he explained the program to me. "First we admit you to the hospital here, we'll put you on sixty milligrams of methadone a day."

I stopped listening and leaned back in my own chair, crossed my own skinny legs, crossed my arms over my chest for emphasis, and stared at him. And Dr.P. leaned across the table, locked his eyes onto mine and the smile was gone.

"Here's the deal. When you get out of here in a few weeks, you will come to group therapy in my office every week. If you fail to show up, I will not talk to you until your scheduled time the following week. Whatever trouble you think you're in, I will not be on call for you. I understand that everybody else has been, but I won't. And you can't make me feel sorry for you so I will change my mind. I will not feel sorry for you. You could come crawling up to my door, on a cold and rainy night, you could be covered with sores, and I still would not talk to you! Oh, wait," he said, looking away thoughtfully, "I might maybe call an ambulance. But I will not talk to you." I barely listened. I only really heard, "I will not feel sorry for you."

"This is your last chance," he continued. "And, oh, by the way, you don't show up one time to get your methodone, those two detective over there, they'll come find you."

~

So there I was, in a hospital gown again, sitting on the bed, in a psych ward, waiting.

I can make him feel sorry for me, I know I can. He thinks he's so tough! But I'll show him, he'll feel sorry for me.

I sat for a few moments, and then I was afraid. *But what if I'm wrong. What if I can never get him to feel sorry for me. Then what will I do? What will I do then?*

Chapter 26 – The Little White Church

Panic stirred in the pit of my stomach and threatened to stop my heart beating and take my breath away. I was on the verge of throwing up and didn't know if it was from being truly sick or being very scared. Sitting on a bed in a bare room again, I was angry. This was a waste of time, I knew. *They think there's something worth saving here, but there isn't.*

Mr. Male Nurse marched into my room with authority. "Aw right miss, time for your meds. These six white pills are your methadone, you need to open wide to let me see that you swallowed them. The green pill will help you relax." Two little paper cups, one with pills, another with water. "Ok, get started."

Afraid to swallow them all, afraid I would gag and throw up, I took two at a time. Opened wide, moved my tongue around to prove I wasn't hiding any. It was humiliating.

I should go ahead and take them all. I should go ahead and throw up, right here in front of him. He thinks he's Mr. Bigshot, he thinks he's the boss of me, I should throw up on his shoes, yeah, I should just do that. But I didn't. I don't know why. I let him look in my mouth, under my tongue over and over, after every two pills, till we were done and he left.

My head on my pillow, blankets wrapped around me, cocoon-like I waited for the green pill to do its job and calm me. I waited for the little white pills to quiet my body's screaming need for heroin. I slept.

Clair

~

The daytime nurse, in her bright pink smock, brought my morning pills. "Oh my, look at you shivering there all wrapped up in blankets. You need this methadone. Come on now, sit up and take these." Same as the day before, swallow and open wide. I collapsed on the bed, willing her to go away. My head ached. My bones ached. "Please be quiet and go away."

"Sweetie, I'm, going to open the blinds, let the sunshine in, and tell you how Dr. P manages things. The day starts with breakfast in the community room, you have to be dressed. No hospital gown. Group therapy is at eight."

"I'm too sick, I can't go. Besides, I only have the clothes I came in. I don't want any breakfast, and I don't need any group therapy! I've had enough therapy to last a lifetime, and besides, therapy doesn't work, look at me."

"Well, he might let you skip breakfast, since you are sick. But if you don't come to therapy, he'll give you a consequence, so you might think about changing your mind."

I didn't get dressed. I went to group in my hospital gown and floppy, oversized paper slippers. I wanted to make a point. *You might be able to make me take these meds, you might be able to make me stay here or you'll put me in jail, send me back to Lexington. But I am still the boss of me. I say what I wear!*

Dr. P ignored me. The other patients, sitting on their wooden chairs, in their neat circle, fidgeted, nervous, wondering what would happen, what Dr. P would do. He still ignored me. Taking their cue from him, the patients ignored me.

Good. That's fine. You all ignore me and I'll just sit here till the time's up.

After lunch we were allowed quiet time, read, take a nap, work a jigsaw puzzle, be alone, be silent. I chose silent. I needed to think. *He says he won't feel sorry for me, but he has to. If he doesn't, if he's not on my side, he could... he could do anything to me! I have to make him like me and be sorry for me. I will be pitiful.*

So I buried the angry me, deep inside, where no one could see, and spent the afternoon remembering terrible things that had happened to me. I thought about how alone I was, because I was a bad person, "bad to the core selfish, a very selfish person" as my dad said. I thought about the dreams of home and family that were ripped away when Smitty left. I thought about my children, crying and screaming, pushed into a squad car and taken away. I thought about the clanging metal bars of Lexington, and I thought about coming back, sleeping in the park. I remembered broken ribs, and turning tricks, and using up all my veins. I remembered going to church with the Gambels and failing to make that work.

Getting up and looking at myself in the bathroom mirror, I saw a scrawny girl with half bleached blonde dirty hair. Without the anger on my face, I did indeed look very pitiful now. Staring at myself for a few moments, I felt truly very sad, and knew that was a very good thing.

For three weeks I wore those two faces. Cooperative and Sad. I ate breakfast in the dayroom with the other patients, wore real clothes to therapy every day, challenged nothing. I never argued. My movements were slow, sluggish, sad. I knew how to look desolate. I hoped he noticed. Maybe he did. I couldn't tell.

And the day came, a private meeting with Dr. P, my release date! I was overwhelmed. Where I would stay? How would I get back here every morning and every evening to take my methadone? I had no money. I had no home, no job. No car. *Probably Dr. P has a plan.* Hope blinked in my heart, a fleeting tiny second of hope.

He sat across the table from me, again, not as smug now. Explaining the process to me, he was almost friendly, almost. Two daily doses of methadone, given here at the hospital, one in the morning, one again in the evening. Once a week group therapy in his office. "You won't be able to get high because no matter how much you shoot up, the methadone will block it. If you don't show up for methadone, or group therapy, Detective M will find you. You will go to jail. This is your last chance." He looked at me to be certain I understood. I said I did.

And waited for him to continue. To tell me the plan. He said nothing. "That's it?" I ventured. "That's all?"

"I think I've covered everything. What did you expect?"

"But you can't just send me out there, I have no job or money or place to go."

Before walking out the door, he stopped to say, "Well, you poor thing. Is daddy raping his little girl again?" And he left, leaving the words to slap me with something I did not understand.

Packing my few belongings, taking my morning dose of six tiny white methadone tablets, walking through the doors, onto the street, I was on my own. Alone again.

I was hurt and angry. Of course I was. Why did he say that to me! It was mean! There must have been a good and important reason, but I didn't want to think about it. So, I walked the few miles to downtown, a few more blocks to Gypsy's.

"Hey girl, where you been? Ain't seen you around for a while. I got some good stuff here, you wanna hit?"

"No, not right now, I'm good. Maybe later." I sat on a mattress in the corner, on the floor, he lounged on another. I always liked Gypsy, this long, lanky fellow who moved as a dancer would, slow and graceful. The gentleness of his movements were in jarred contrast to the room. This room with three bare mattresses, with clothes scattered over the floor and piled in corners. With used syringes and needles tossed around.

His friends came and stayed, and left, and came back. People like me, wandering from place to place, getting high, laying around, playing cards and eating bologna sandwiches, lounging on any part of a mattress not occupied. Every day the same.

∼

I borrowed a skirt from a girl, Marie. I needed a skirt to look for a job. I went to the diner down the street and to the bar on the corner and the gas station at the end of the block. No one would hire me.

"Look I really like you, you're a nice girl, never give us any trouble. But let you work here, like behind the counter or something? Come on, you know I can't do that. I'm sorry, but I just can't." Of course they wouldn't, what was I thinking, they knew me.

~

Every day, for three days I found a ride to get my methadone, a nice fellow friend of gypsy's who had a car. I went to my first group therapy on Wednesday in Dr. P's office and listened to each person talk about how crabby and controlling their mother was, or how boring it was on their job, or how they needed a raise so they could buy that new car they really wanted. I thought they were whiney babies, but I stayed the required hour, smiled, said "thank you" and left.

And that afternoon, I lay on the mattress with Gypsy, watching him nod off, sleepy, relaxed, before waking, smiling, ready to talk. "Hey girl, you ok?"

"I think I'm ready for that hit now, if you're still offering."

"You got any works?"

"No, actually, no I don't."

"That's ok, just grab anything laying around here. I'll go get you some good stuff, you wait right here."

Grabbing the closest syringe, I found a still smooth needle and pulled water through them both, back and forth, to clean them, and waited for Gypsy.

Dr. P was wrong. Sixty milligrams of methadone did not block the high.

Hope no longer blinked, but closed its eye. I was now alone in a dark, peaceful place.

~

Every day I went to the hospital for methadone when Dr. P would not be there because I was afraid he would see me and know. Know the secret. Methadone doesn't work. I kept my group therapy appointments at his office because I did not want him to call Det. M. I went to my "aftercare-parole" lady as scheduled because I knew she didn't keep track of when I was supposed to pee in the cup.

On very cold nights, if Gypsy's house was crowded, I stayed at a Mission on Wayne Street. It was a clean bed and a warm meal, but I left the night the minister told me to bend down and tie his shoelaces for him. Life was familiar again.

Yet on cold nights, hiding out again in a gas station to keep warm, I sat in the ladies room, pulled the worn, tiny booklet about God out of my pocket and read it again and again, turning it over, looking for something, anything.

~

And then I met Jake. A man with the body of a boxer, gorgeous shiny brown skin, and a Cadillac, he took me to his house one day. A nice house.

He made coffee, sat with me and listened to my woes, looked at me with sympathetic eyes. Holding my small hand in his very large, dark one, he whispered "Honey, your troubles are over. You have met the Candy Man, and I have everything you need." It sounded like a line in a movie, and I tried to pull my hand away. He held it a little tighter, just for a second, just enough to show that he was a powerful man.

I knew then this was not a movie and he could be a dangerous man. I didn't tell him I had no place to stay or how much I was using every day. Of course I didn't! I did tell him enough to help him feel sorry for me, and flirted enough to make him like me.

But I Can Learn

"Thanks for this, it was really good stuff, you do have good drugs. You must be a really important man, but, well, I gotta go now."

"Sure, I'll drop you off wherever you want. And I'll come find you every day, check on you, just make sure you're ok, see if you need anything." And so he did, every day. Find me on my corner, Lewis Street, in front of the diner.

~

From my corner I saw it every day, the old white church down the block. Run by street-people now, the rumors said. *Maybe they'll know why going to church didn't change me.* In a moment of bravery, I walked in their door one day. Curious. Hoping they would be different from other churches.

But here were only kids running around, a table with cookies and fruity drinks, and a few white guys with short hair and shirts with button-down collars. I left.

"Excuse me miss, if you're from the Lutheran Board, can I answer some questions, show you around?" He stood at the top step, calling to me. I turned to face him.

With clean, shining black hair, framed by the white building behind him, he stood as though in a photograph and was in sharp contrast to the bleakness of this neighborhood. His bushy mustache belied the fact that he was indeed only a boy. A beautiful boy. An innocent boy.

Continuing down the steps, he stood before me, then looking at me and stopped. "Oh, sorry, I thought you were here to check us out, to see if we can keep using the building." A pause. "Sorry, I can see you're not from the Lutheran board." He stared at me, at my eyes. I saw a tenderness in his, and something else. I didn't know what it was. I knew it wasn't pity and I knew no one had ever looked at me that way before. I felt awkward and embarrassed.

We sat on the steps, the fellow with the mustache and his friends, college boys studying to be Lutheran pastors, they said.

"Well, if you all want to be Lutheran pastors, like in a church, why are you here? Ain't nobody here gonna go to your church."

"Yeah, we're figuring that out. We came here to help people, like drug addicts and alcoholics, but nobody wants to talk to us. They scowl and walk away, some do smile though, like they think we're a joke."

"Yeah, I can see that. Sure I can. You white boys with your short hair and college clothes. You look like you don't belong here, like you should be in a big office building or something. And you sure don't look like you know anything at all about life or problems or anything!"

Mr. Big Mustache shrugged his shoulders, "I know, you're right, so we just still come here and do stuff with the kids. They like us a lot." Reaching out to shake my hand, he introduced himself. "Oh, by the way, my name's Sam." The others followed, "Yeah, my name's Dave." "And I'm Tom, glad you're here." "I'm Kim, that's my car, the little green Chevy Corvair right over there." I could tell he was proud of that.

But my eyes started to water, my nose was running, and that familiar chill was creeping over my skin. I needed a hit. I needed to leave.

"Well, nice talking to you, but I gotta go. I have to be somewhere and I'm late."

Walking down the block, I turned to look back. They were still there, watching me walk away. Those six Lutheran seminary boys, trying to do good on Lewis Street. Here with dope dealers, and addicts, thieves and prostitutes. Those foolish boys.

Chapter 27 – Foolish College Boys

I stood at my corner every day. It was my corner, other girls worked other places. This was not only my corner, I claimed it as my block. Walking up and down, walking in a way that men passing by in cars had to notice me. When I was bored, I turned the corner to go around the block. I was often bored.

That back street was quiet, not much traffic. Most houses were empty, run-down, abandoned years ago. You could tell by the broken windows and front doors swinging open, and lights that never turned on. There, in the few not-empty-houses, men sat on their porch steps, smoking Camel cigarettes, sipping on bottles of Jim Beam. Calling to me. "Hey, pretty girl, come sit with me. What you doing out here all by yourself?" Bored men sitting on their porches did not pay very much, not like white men driving nice cars, cruising Lewis Street, looking for a good time. *It's better than nothing, especially cause I'm bored.*

Jake drove by several times a day, waving. Smiling. Always smiling.

Sometimes I got in his shiny black Cadillac, going back to his house for coffee and a tuna sandwiches. And always little silver packets, the ones for special friends, the ones not as cut as the others. Carrying my own set of works, I was proud. Because I was smart. Too smart to be caught without again. Too smart to use someone else's again. Too smart to get someone else's disease. Not me, no sir. I carry my own stuff!

And too smart to trust this Candy Man sitting next to me on the couch tucking a blanket around my legs, around my shoulders. Too smart to let him have any idea how many times a day I needed those silver packets, cause I knew the rule and said it often to me self every day. *Don't let anybody know how much you're using cause then they can control you!*

Every day he drove me back to my street, always. Pulling ten, sometimes twenty dollars from his wallet, pressing them into my hand, he'd smile, wink, waving a cheerful "see ya' later." And every day I watched him drive off, proud that I was still in charge, that I was the boss of this friendship. And of me.

~

I slept again that night in an empty house, two blocks over. A quiet block, abandoned, no one ever went there. A person could be alone. No one bothers you and no one wants anything from you even if they do happen to see you. The doors and windows were intact, solid. I could shut them and keep the wind away. My blankets were hidden, behind stacks of old newspapers in the corner.

Finding this place the night it snowed, the night the gas station had a new attendant, I was grateful. Cause Mr. Hot Shot New Attendant wouldn't let me sleep in the warm ladies' room anymore. Knowing this house was a good place, away from people and wind and cold, I used one tiny foil packet from Jake, hid another for later. Wrapping newspapers and blankets around my shoulders, around my feet, I slept.

A scratching noise woke me, then another! I lay very still and listened. A lot of scratching noises, close to me. I was afraid! "What is that? Is somebody here!" Alarmed, I opened my eyes, allowed them to adjust to the light from the street lamp. Sitting up, I scared dozens of rats. Scurrying off to their hiding places. Looking at the chewed newspapers at my feet, I knew my socks were next, I leaned over and threw up.

"There's no place that is safe! Not for me, anyway, not for me!" I was very sorry for myself.

~

Walking the street the next night, I watched as it came up the street slowly, towards me, the little green Chevy Corvair. Those college boys, those foolish boys! *What are they doing, driving around here during at night, they're going to find nothing but trouble.* But I couldn't help but smile at their stupid innocence.

"Hey, we found you! Been looking for ya. We're going out for pizza, wanna come?" I thought they must be joking! "You want me to get in your car, with four of you, and just go get pizza?"

"No, don't think that way! Really, we just thought you might like to get out of the cold for a while, and have some pizza."

I was cold, and could eat something. *Nobody takes me out to eat for nothing. They probably want to talk me into going to church or maybe they just want to pray for me. Well, I can trade a prayer for a meal. I can do that.* So I did. Climbed in their car, squishing in the back seat between Dave and Tom.

They ordered pitchers of beer and argued over what kind of pizza. For an hour I watched them laugh, argue, and laugh again, eat huge amounts of hot, cheesy, pizza, and drink mugs of cold, foamy beer. Waiting for the "you need to come to Jesus" speech, or the prayer, or at least the "you can change your life" talk. Those things didn't happen. They only asked what I thought about what they were talking about, and then they listened. They listened to me.

And so it went for the few next weeks. They went for pizza and beer, and took me with them. And I waited for the catch that would show me they were just like everybody else.

~

I still really needed a ride to the hospital every morning to get my methadone, but I didn't ask them. Then they'd know too much about me. That could be a bad idea.

Clair

Gypsy's friend Mac took me every evening because I had mastered the art of not actually swallowing all of my pills, saving a few for him.

No one could take me in the morning though. Wanting to be there between nine and eleven, while Dr. P was in group therapy, when I wouldn't have to see to him, I hitchhiked and wore my sad face. Pathetic girl that I was, standing with shoulders hunched over to keep out the cold, few could resist offering a ride. Few could resist waiting to take me home, wherever I said home was. I chose a run-down house six blocks from my real street, and accepted the ten or twenty dollars they offered.

"Here, let me help you with some groceries, or something."

"Oh, thank you so much, I can't believe how generous you are, to drive me and all, and now this, it's so much! You're such a good person." Allowing a few tears to fall, to show that I was truly grateful.

It happened on a Thursday morning when I couldn't get a ride, so I walked. Arriving after eleven at the hospital, I knew Dr. P could still be there, talking to the nurses, writing papers and stuff!.

So I waited in the hospital lobby, hid in the ladies' room for a while, waiting for enough time to pass. I didn't want to see him. I didn't want him to see me, so I waited for him to leave.

At noon, I crossed the lobby to the psych ward, up to the nurses station, said, "Ok, sorry I'm late, but I'm here now." Anxious to do this, get my pills, anxious to leave.

"I'll bring your meds in. Dr. P's waiting for you in the consultation room, you know where it is." *Oh no, he waited for me! I'm in trouble now!*

Sitting across the table from me, again, just as he had that first time, he was relaxed, smiling, in charge, again.

"You haven't been to group in my office the last two times. What's going on?"

"Oh, nothing, I guess I forget what day it is, me not having a calendar I carry around, you know. But I'll be there next week, I promise."

He had not called Detective M, I could tell he hadn't, and I smiled in my heart because I knew now I had made him feel sorry for me. He hadn't followed through on his threat, and I smiled because I knew victory, I had won, and it felt good. I moved to sit in the chair next to him, placed one hand on the table next to his. "Thank you for not reporting me to Detective M. I really, really appreciate it." My voice was soft and warm, my eyes sad.

Quickly standing, moving to the other side of the table, he stared at me for a moment. "Roll up your sleeves, let me see your arms."

"No!"

"Yes, come on, show me." I obeyed. I don't know why, I just did, pushing up the sleeve on each arm to expose the many colors of bruised flesh in various stages of never healing, the long lines of red dots marking a trail over each vein. Some larger than others, some scabby, some pussy sores.

He carefully studied them for a moment. "Well, I can see that you're using old needles, there must be a burr on the end. You need to use a nail file to get that off, make it sharp again. And a few of these look infected, I'll order some cream for that."

I was offended! "Well, you're just going to tell me how to do it, aren't you!"

"Can't stop you, might as well help you not hurt yourself any more than you already are." He flung the words over his shoulder as he walked out the door.

"Why are you always walking out before I can say something back!" I yelled to an empty room. I said it anyway because I knew now I had not won anything, and he was still in charge.

~

I walked fast, back to Lewis Street, my street where I was in charge of me, where no one walked out on me, where I had the last word, where I was the boss of my own life and I could be proud.

Sometimes Foolish College boys came to find me in the middle of the day. "Come on, get in, you can go through the food line out at our cafeteria. You're too skinny" I had come to like these silly boys. And I didn't know why they liked me, but they did.

They asked questions about my life, and I entertained them with a cleaned-up version. "A Day in the Life of a Heroin Addict." That sounded better than "A Day in the Life of a Junkie" or "Day in the life of a Stupid Girl." For the hour they were with me, I felt once again like the pretty waitress who wore a button that said "if it feels good I'll do it." I began to look forward to that green Corvair coming down the street.

Until the night questions became too personal, too probing, too detailed. "So where do you live? We just always pick you up out there somewhere, but where exactly do you live?"

"Oh, just around, sometimes with friends, you know, just around." I reached for a slice of pizza, trying to distract them, to appear casual.

"Come on! You have to have a place! A room you call home! You can't always be staying with friends! Where do you sleep?" They kept pushing, asking too many questions and I didn't like it!

"This is getting too personal, and you don't need to be asking so many questions." I left.

Catching up with me walking across the parking lot, they muttered apologies. "We're so sorry, we didn't mean to offend you. Don't go away."

"We don't want you to leave. Let us take you back. We'll take you wherever you want, no more questions." They were just placating me, I could tell. Telling me anything to make me stay. Trading pizza for stories.

I was angry, offended, and wanted to slap them with a harsh reality. I wanted to be mean to them.

"Ok, you all want to know where I live, where I sleep? You really want to know? Get in the car. I'll show you. You can see for yourself." I spit out the words, letting them hang in an air of silence and shock, and the boys were speechless.

We drove back to Lewis Street, to the park in the center of the busy eight block stretch. The park that was deserted late at night. They tumbled out of the car, not talking now, not as confident. They had been silent in the car, coming here, and they were silent now. I marched them across the street, into the park, past the swings and slides, to the bushes in the far back corner, my corner.

I was still angry, yet I was crying. I willed myself to stop, but couldn't. "You want to know where I live, well, here you are, now just look in there!"

I lifted a few leafless branches to expose my plastic trash bag. "You wanna see what's in the bag, well here it is!" Opening it, I threw everything out, exposing blankets, a few personal items, my toothbrush, a shirt, extra underwear, a hairbrush.

Angry at them for asking the question, angry at myself for answering it, I lashed out at them with bitter words meant to embarrass them, to shame them, because I was embarrassed and ashamed.

"Well, this is ridiculous! For goodness sake, its only April." said Tom, with indignation.

"You're right. We can't have this," Dave replied. "She should stay at the church, we have a key, and no one is there most of the time."

"Yeah right, and there's a few empty beds in my dorm, we can sneak one from there, no one will notice."

Talking fast, they stumbled over each other's words, each other's ideas. They were excited! I thought they forgot I was standing there, but they hadn't. Kim grabbed the bag, and my few belongings, pushed me back into the car. "Come on, we gotta do this tonight. You can't sleep out here."

An hour later, I stood in the small room on the second floor of the tiny, white, abandoned church they had been given to use. In the room they had chosen to give to me. A room with a bed piled high with puffy blankets and bright, colorful quilts. A table and lamp next to it. One small grey teddy bear with red and white polka dotted ears that Tom just thought I had to have. And there it was, the key they gently placed in my hand, closing my fingers over it, to show it was mine to keep.

I knew I was safe there, yet I did not want to trust it. I sat in my bed that first night, wound up in every blanket, staring at that teddy bear, reminding myself of The Rule again. *Never, ever let anyone see all of my real life, not how much I use or how I make money. Never become dependent on anyone. Be the boss of my own self.* That was The Rule. My Rule.

The Rule said not to stay in the warm room on the second floor of the little white church every night. But I stayed most nights. One overnight a week at Jake's, another at Gypsy's, just to obey The Rule.

~

It was a Thursday morning, that first week in April, when Jake showed me his new plan. I had stayed overnight, woke up to the foil packet and cup of steaming coffee, waiting for me on the nightstand. "Hey Babe, do your stuff, I got a big score for us. We're going to make some real money today." And so we did.

Driving some car into a neighborhood with nice houses, ones with mailboxes on the outside, next to the front door, he showed me how to follow the mailman, walking house to house. We watched through binoculars as he picked out welfare checks and social security checks, their bright colors showing through the small window in the envelope. Federal income tax refund checks sporting their bright turquoise color through the window of their brown envelopes. He placed each of those checks behind other mail, behind ads and letters, hiding them.

One of us on binoculars. One writing down house numbers, mailboxes that contained checks. Another to quickly lift the checks from their boxes. Pretending to be lost if a door opened.

It was easy. And dangerous. Not like when Billy Joe and I broke into people's houses when they were on vacation. Not like when I stole prescription pads from doctors. Not like anything else! This was dangerous and scary. And exciting.

And easy. Every grocery store, drug store, or gas station, cashed them, no ID required. A government check was always good!

In my room at the church, covered in those puffy blankets, I thought about what I was doing. *I'm not hurting anyone, not really stealing from those people. The government will just send them another check. I'm not hurting anybody. I'm not stealing from those people.* Turning over, adjusting the blankets, I tried to be proud of myself.

Some days Jake came to me with an occasional, really large check, over $2000, too large to cash without ID. I was the only one able to study the driver's ed booklet, pass the written test in the name of the person on the check, walking away with an ID, a beginners permit!. Then I was proud of myself because I was smarter than the rest of them. I had a talent.

~

I pretended not to see the guns or the secret meetings behind closed doors with men I had never seen. Men from Chicago and Detroit. I pretended not to notice that each week we rode with different people. To those neighborhoods looking for checks. *I'm still, after all, only staying sometimes. I have my own place at the church. He's not in charge of me. I'm still the boss of me.*

Until the morning I woke up in my room at his house to find the door locked.

Chapter 28 – The Death

Locked! It can't be locked. The door must be stuck. I pulled harder, placed my foot on the wall and put all my strength into it and it didn't move. Didn't make a sound. It was truly locked.

Sitting on the bed, I tried to understand what was happening. *Surely this is a mistake! He wouldn't really lock me in. He wouldn't lock the door!*

Standing at the door, my side of the locked door, I shouted, "Hey, you out there, you can't lock this door! I am the boss of me! You are not the boss, I am the boss. You come unlock this door. You come unlock it right now!" Only silence greeted me. Only silence. I listened carefully, listened for a creaking floor board, heavy breathing, even a chuckle at the perceived insanity of my outburst. There was none, only silence.

Dread and fear joined hands to drape a dark cloud over me. Only unbelief kept panic at bay. *This is a mistake, this isn't happening. I know Jake, he likes me, he wouldn't lock me in here, he just wouldn't. He knows I'll get sick after a while. He just wouldn't do this, not to me he wouldn't.*

And then I saw them, two silver packets on the nightstand beside my bed. My salvation wrapped neatly in tin foil. Wrapped by me the day before. *He thinks of everything! See, he likes me. He'll take care of me and this will be all right. Jake will make it all right.* I said this out loud to myself to help me not be afraid. Quickly injecting the contents of one packet into the easy-to-find vein in my groin, I relaxed. *I just know everything will be all right. I just know it will.* Grabbing for the second packet, reality burst into my brain and I remembered The Rule. "Never let anybody know how much you are using!" I desperately needed the second packet, but vowed to leave it untouched, wanting him to think I didn't need it. I tried to sleep.

When the sun no longer made shadows on my wall, I was startled by a noise at my door, the scuffle of feet, a click at the lock.

It's open, I'm not locked in anymore! Relief gave me courage to stand up, to stand and be grateful that I was not locked in. I felt that for only thirty seconds before anger took over and gave me the courage to march into the other room and assert myself.

I did. I stood before them, three men now, sitting at the table counting money, looking up from their task, all three looking at me, waiting. One held a cigar in his mouth. Not smoking it, just moving it from side to side, just pretending. His long coat hung to the floor, hiding the hugeness of him.

Next to him, the other, tall and thin, a clean shaved face and head.

I posed my body in an assertive stance, hands on hips, feet apart. I placed a scowl on my forehead. Before I could speak, before I could assert my rights, reality gripped me and I noticed the guns, there on the table, easy to reach. I saw the rifle standing against the wall in the corner. Blinds and curtains drawn. Coffee cups before them on the table, fresh coffee in the pot on the stove. Noticing that even though I had used that second packet, my nose was running and I was jittery enough for them to know that I needed more.

Now letting my arms fall to my side, forcing my body to relax, I waved my hands, trying to appear confident. "Well, I was awake earlier, I wanted to come out, just to get some coffee, you know, but my door was locked. Well, at least I think it was locked. I couldn't get it open."

The men stopped counting and looked at Jake. I saw him stop counting, turn to look at me, and say, "Yep, the door was locked. We had to go out earlier, and I don't want you going anyplace without me, so,

But I Can Learn

sure, I locked your door." Mr. Shaved Head stopped counting and stared at my eyes, laughing softly. I was annoyed.

"Well, you can't just lock me in a room! I don't have to put up with this! I'm out of here! I'm leaving!" It took me three steps to reach the front door. It took Jake one to place himself in front of me, hand on my chest. "Look, you are not going anywhere. Get this straight, you have two choices. I can carry you back to your room and lock the door again. Maybe you just need some time to think. Or you can grab some coffee and sit here and help count, be friendly like and make nice conversation. We could use a little entertainment, a little chatter, if you know what I mean."

And so the evening passed. I made silly conversation, counted money, made another pot of coffee, made tuna sandwiches and tomato soup, stopped every three hours to use the silver packet one of them placed in front of me. And was afraid, more afraid. Trapped!

Days and weeks passed. I missed the routine of my life on Lewis Street. I missed Gypsy and I missed the seminary guys in that green Chevy Corvair, and my room in the church, the room with the puffy quilts and silly teddy pair with red and white polka dot ears. Sometimes I even missed my bush in the park, the place where I could hide from the world.

Here I could not hide. Here, now, I wondered, "Am I no longer the boss of me?"

～

Taking Jake his coffee one morning, I had a plan of escape, "Hey, I know you are probably not too happy with how much of your stuff I'm using, but it could be a whole lot less if you could take me to get my methadone every day. That'd cut down your expense a lot, I think. Yeah, why don't we do that?" I made myself sound cooperative and helpful and caring. Motioning to the men around the table, he replied, "We know how much you use every day, we know it's a lot, and we know how sick you'll be without it. You see, I can make you sick and desperate enough to do anything. And you think I'm gonna let you just go walk around and do what you want? Girl, you gotta be crazy, you belong to me now and you ain't going anywhere, not without one of us, anyway."

I could not answer, there was no answer. I could only go to my room, lay on my bed, my plain bed with a thin blanket and an old smooshed pillow, in a room with no teddy bear to make me smile. My brain was dead and I knew then, "I am not the boss of me now."

~

Mr. Cigar in His Mouth came to my door. "Hey, come on now, we gotta go cash these checks." I knew the routine, we did this once a week. Divide up the checks, male or female names, cash them at drug stores or groceries, always looking away from the camera, the camera there to ID us, the camera no one paid attention to, not the cashier, not us. It was a formality. It only recorded the side or tops of our heads because we knew how to avoid it. Useless.

Mr. Cigar Person handed five checks to me, five checks with girls names. Counting fifteen with guy names, he said, "We better stop at the corner bar to pick up Tom. He's good to help with this."

Seeing him again, Tom with yellow eyes, and dark skin, and blue fingernails, I was sorry for him. Paper thin body, forever covered with an oversized army coat. I wondered if it had ever fit him. Squeezing in the front seat beside me, he smiled, and I saw that he now had even fewer teeth. Mr. Cigar Person handed him five checks to cash. As he looked at each of us gratefully,

I vowed to my own self, "I will never be that bad off."

It took two hours to drive around and get the checks cashed, before we were back at the bar, ready to drop him off.

"Hey, can I go in with him for a while? You know, just to say hi to everyone. They're probably wondering where I've been. What if they think I died, or something. You can come back and pick me up in a half hour or so."

Jake was quick to answer, "No sir, honey, you better stay right here with me. I need you here." It was Mr. Shaved Head who said, "Aw come on, Jake, we can let her do that, might be a good thing. It's Ralph behind the bar tonight, he'll watch her she don't go nowhere." It was freedom as I followed Tom into the small bar on the corner, adjusting my eyes to the barely lit room. The television announced, "Charles Manson has been sentenced to death." I didn't know who Charles Manson was. I didn't care. Scanning each face to see who was there, who could help, each person looking at me, and looking away. These were the things I cared about.

Eventually my eyes rounded to the bartender. Ralph. Ralph I remembered as the person sometimes sitting on a chair next to Jake's door. Sitting with the rifle resting across his knees. That Ralph. The Ralph with the rifle, allowing no one to enter and no one to leave, at Jakes. I looked away.

Following Tom to the backroom, to his friends who were excited over a few packets of "good heroin," I wondered where it came from. But I didn't need to know, did not want to know.

Most men in this dark and dusty, cluttered room, were content with the glass of whiskey in front of them. Content to flick the occasional cockroach off the table. Ted reached for a packet, tossed one to me. "Here, girl, you can have one too." I preferred the one in my pocket, the one from Jake. I knew it would be better.

Some new guy, Kentucky Bob he called himself, reached for a packet first. We watched as the gleam grew in his eyes, as he heated the tiny bit of liquid, drew it up into the syringe, tied off his upper arm, expertly piercing a vein, slowly drawing the blood back and forth before finally plunging it back in, one final plunge before ecstasy.

The ecstasy that never came. I watched his face, wanting to see the pleasure it brought him. I only saw him look at me before his head crashed onto the table, before blood spilled from his nose, from his ears, from his eye sockets. Before he fouled his thin pants. Before a pool of urine formed under his chair. Before panic struck every man in the room.

"Oh crap, we gotta get out of here!" Rushing to gather up their things. Afraid.

Until Ralph stood in the doorway, hands in his pockets, looking calm. Looking in charge.

"Ain't none of you leaving here till you get this mess cleaned up. I want this whole place cleaned up. And get this guy outta here. I ain't gonna be responsible for none of this crap."

And so we did. The release of fluid from Ted had stopped. One man took charge, barking orders to the rest of us. "You there," he pointed to me. "Over there, grab those towels and rags, wrap them around his head." I did so quickly, anxious to obey, to not think, to do as I was told. To be back at Jake's.

As they wrapped his coat around him to hold what had spilled there, to not leave a trail, I walked with the others as they lifted his body, out the back door to the alley, down a block, maybe two, I couldn't count, and left him there. "I wonder who's gonna find him," I wondered out loud. I didn't realize I had said it out loud until someone answered, "I don't know, who cares, just as long as it isn't some kid or something, what do I care."

Walking back to the bar, I was elated to see Jake's car parked at the side, waiting for me. It was a relief to be in his car, it smelled nice, his friends wore nice clothes, their fingernails were clean, their breath smelled nice. I smiled at Jake and said, "Take me home now, please."

∼

And so began the weeks of my non-protest days. I didn't rant and rail and pound on the door when it was locked. I didn't refuse or pout when Jake's friends came into my room. It felt good to no longer be the boss of me. And to wait for Dr. P to report me and for Det. M to rescue me.

I did often pull the little torn and worn pamphlet about God from my pocket and wonder about it, reading it over and over, still wondering where in all of those words was the secret hidden. The secret that said how all those other people had lost their addictions when they heard about God. The secret that would tell me where I missed it, why I was still a stupid junkie and why it hadn't made me the new person everyone promised me it would. Why was I still the same?

I did often wonder what happened to Detective M and Dr. P. They threatened to come find me if I missed one methadone dose or one group therapy. Where was my parole officer who should send someone to find me? "Hey, you guys!" I yelled at my empty room. "I've been here for days and weeks now, so why aren't you looking for me? You can take me to jail, and I won't fight this time. Really. Or were you just trying to scare me, with all that talk about this was my last chance and all?"

Collapsing on my bed, I knew they weren't coming. *They finally figured out I'm really not worth all that much trouble.*

~

One day it was only Jake and me in the car, only two checks to cash that one day. Large income tax refund checks. Driving to a grocery on Washington Blvd., he handed me a check, waited in the car. Always he sent me in alone. Nice blonde white girl didn't raise suspicions. Nice white girl with large black man would.

Parking near the door, he watched as I walked in, watched as I adjusted the scarf on my head to cover as much of me as I could.

I knew I was good at this. *Walk slowly, don't hurry. Stop to look at the ads posted on the wall, like you are shopping. Walk to the service counter, say "Good afternoon, how are you?" Be casual. Sign the check without looking at the front. I know my own name, after all, don't I?*

Hand it to him, look at his face, smile. If his hand moves to the camera, scrounge around in my purse, look for my grocery list. Looking down, away from the camera. It can only capture the side of face, top of my scarf. Easy.

On that day the man at the camera, stopped to say, "Now, dearie, you can't do that. You have to look here, right at the camera!"

Fear squeezed my heart, extended its hand to my stomach. My head pounded as my body rushed adrenalin to every organ, preparing my muscles to flee. And I knew I couldn't. I couldn't flee. I couldn't leave that check in his hand, turn and walk back to the car, to Jake, empty handed. I couldn't go back to the car without the check and without the $800 in hand.

Trapped, I said, "Oh, sorry sir, I was only trying to find my grocery list," I looked into the photo lens, smiled as sweetly as I could. He took my picture. A real picture of my face as I cashed a stolen federal check.

I bought a candy bar on the way out. To pretend I wasn't scared.

Sitting in the car, I handed the eight hundred dollars to Jake and watched him count it. I didn't tell him they took my photo. I did eat the chocolate candy bar.

∼

We didn't leave the house for the next two days. Everyone seemed nervous and busy. I watched as money was counted and placed in duffel bags. I watched guns loaded into other travel bags. I watched as the table for cutting heroin became two tables, then three tables. I watched all of this in silence, knowing I would be kept in my room if they noticed me. I did not ask questions.

Sitting on my bed, sometimes sitting on the floor, leaning my back against the wall, I spread out the little God paper again. This time I found a clue. All of these people had been required to give up smoking. They had to do that first. I was annoyed. "Well, if they have to give up drinking and dope, then they should at least get to smoke!" I said it out loud, to my empty room, because I wanted to argue about this. "I mean, aren't they more likely to go back to drugs if they can't even smoke? Doesn't everybody need something? Why take everything away? Besides, I ain't never even smoked one cigarette, I never smoked pot, I never smoked a regular legal cigarette, so that doesn't have anything to do with me." I was angry now, frustrated, tired of searching for answers when there were none. So I used two of the packets Jake left for me, and tried very hard not to think.

I paced the room, not caring if the men on the other side of my locked door could hear me. I was restless. Two more shiny packets were slid under the door.

Wrapping myself in my meager blanket, making a cocoon for myself, I finally slept. I slept until the sun once again pierced my window, wrapped its warmth around me to announce a new, fresh day.

It started with just a glimmer of an idea then, a random thought roaming around in my brain, urging me to sit up and make sense of it.

I don't know if God really does that stuff, if He really does anything at all except sit up there and be God of everything. I sat awhile, afraid to follow that thought, afraid to feel.

But you have to think about this, I scolded myself. *If you don't think about it you will die in here, right in this room, you will die.*

Ok, so I went to church and saw those people inviting each other out to eat together after church, hugging each other, being happy. I wanted that. If I could be part of that group, if I could get my kids back and if somebody would marry me, if I was part of their group I'd be happy and it would be easy to change. Easy to give up drugs, easy to be a nice person. But people didn't include me, they didn't invite me out to eat. I went home alone.

I sat awhile longer, remembering the sad me. I saw myself, sitting alone at my kitchen table, after church. Everybody else went out to eat. Why was I sitting here, alone?

And then I knew. Suddenly I knew the secret. The secret about God helping addicts.

I saw me, sitting there in old my kitchen, pouting, angry, wanting to punish everybody. Making a list of 'if onlys'. Blaming.

Hope opened its eye warily. My random, swirling thoughts made

Clair

a slight breeze that caused it to blink. And hope opened its eye fully and woke up.

And I knew. I knew I had tried to manipulate God and everybody to get my own way. To get what I wanted. Always what I wanted. And I knew that part was wrong, to just use God to get what I wanted.

I didn't know what was right, but I knew that was wrong.

And then, "I have to get out of here. I have to get out of here."

I spoke my first true and honest plea. "Oh, God, help me get out of here!"

Rushing to my door, I found it unlocked and my heart sank with fear. How could I convince the men in the other room that I was not worth keeping here? How could I get them to let me go?

Walking through the rooms, I found the living room empty. The kitchen empty. The house was empty! *The house is empty!*

I ran.

Chapter 29 – If Only...

    I ran. I ran as though my life depended on it. Down the alley, across the street, down another alley, between those houses. My heart racing, I could feel my pulse in my head, pounding. *There, there's a space between those two garages, a small hidden space. I can rest there, so much trash no one will see me.* Crouching between two garbage cans, pulling my coat over my knees, finally, finally I could stop and think. As my breathing slowed, as the throbbing in my head stopped, panic rested.

    I have to do something. When they come home and see that I am gone, they'll come looking for me! I can't go back there! I can't! And in a few hours I will be too sick to do anything. Wait! I searched my pockets, maybe I still had one precious silver packet stashed somewhere! With fingers cold, numb, I could barely pull the tissues from my jeans pockets. The jeans now too big for me. Jeans, coat pockets, sweater. Every pocket only full of kleenex for the runny nose of an addict. No packet of life-saving heroin. Nothing. *Oh wait! Here's my little God paper. I want to keep that.* And then my fingers found it.

    The paper, folded over many times, the paper a Foolish College Boy had given me with his phone number at the dorm. Scribbled in pencil, now fading. "Sam 321-9876".

    Walking to the gas station two blocks over I begged to use the phone. Dialed the number, waited. A strange male person answered on the fourth ring. It wasn't Sam, or anyone I knew. Struggling to be calm, to ask quietly, fearing my desperation would cause him to hang up, I said, "Sam, Sam. I have to talk to Sam," I heard my whispered voice scream into the phone.

"Hold on, don't go anywhere, I'll go find him," he promised. I waited. Hiding behind the rack of potato chips, praying that Jake wouldn't find me. Finally, it was Sam. "I'm in trouble," was all I could make myself say. All I could whisper into the phone because people were noticing me and I was afraid. I was beginning to shiver and my voice was shaky.

"I'll find someone with a car and be right there. Stay where you are, don't go anywhere." He sounded as panicked as I was.

"No, I can't stay here, it's too public, too open." I told him where else to find me. "Please hurry, I'm going to be really sick really soon!"

~

An hour later they walked with me back to the psych floor of the hospital. Into the room again with Dr. P waiting for me. The nurse handing me the familiar little paper cup with my methadone and a cup of water. No need now to examine under my tongue to see if I swallowed them!

Dr. P was soft. Placing his hand on my shoulder, he could only say, "I've upped your methadone from 60mg to 120 a day. I hope it helps." He walked away, shoulders slumped.

The nurse took me to my room, hospital gown again, floppy paper slippers. Wrist band with my name. How many times I had been here. I didn't care to count. I only wanted to hide in my bed and roll up in the blankets again.

She steered me down the hall, "We have to weigh you first." Eighty pounds! Eighty pounds of bruised arms and legs, of needle marks and infected sores. I saw myself in the mirror behind the scale. I didn't care. She made me drink something warm before letting me hide in my bed. Gave me four extra blankets, warm blankets. I thought she must have put them in the oven first. I knew that was silly. She came back with another pill, "to help you get some rest". Tucked the blankets tighter around me, brushed the hair from my face, before she left the room. The pill made me light-headed, it made my arms and legs relax, and I slept.

~

Two days later, the rules were back. No hiding in your bed. Group therapy every morning. You must be dressed. No meals in your room, only with other patients in the day room. Dr. P and the nurses wore their stern faces and voices, again. Waiting for me to be the problem person, again.

This time I liked the rules. No longer wanting to fight them. No longer angry and mean. I was glad to be there, behind locked doors. *Those doors are meant to keep me in here, so I don't escape.* I sat in the hall and watched the security. *But those doors will also keep others out!*

~

On the fourth day a nurse brought a letter to me. "A letter? Who would send me mail in here?" Reaching for the envelope, fear gripped my hand. I saw the return address: Allen County Department Children's Services.

Carefully opening it, afraid to step into that world, I read the one short paragraph. "this is to notify you that a hearing has been set for the permanent termination of your parental rights." Panicked, my heart pounding, I ran to the nurses' station. "I need to use the phone, right now!"

"Sorry, but you know that's against the rules, it's not allowed." Thrusting the letter at her, I begged. "This can't wait! I have to call my caseworker! They're still my children!" She paused only a moment before passing the phone to me.

Mrs. A was not in her office. I had to leave a message. And wait. I worked a jigsaw puzzle, made small talk with other patients, ate my lunch slowly. Trying to pass time, trying to not think, to not panic.

"My poor little children, I can't lose them forever. I just can't." I willed myself to be strong, to not cry. It wasn't until late afternoon that a nurse brought the message that came for me, written on a page torn out of the pink phone message book. "No action will be taken until you are released and can meet with us." Hope blinked again. I was determined. *They will see that this time I can really change forever. They will believe me this time. I know I can make them believe me.* I said this to myself, over and over, I said it to chase away a small tentacle of fear. Of doubt. To hold onto hope. I could not think about what it would mean if I couldn't.

∼

Days passed, then weeks. Group therapy became interesting. I listened to people talk. It was sad, so much pain in this room. Listening to their stories, I cried in my heart. For them.

Dr. P's assistant asked if I ever cried for myself, for my own story. "Of course not!" I responded with irritation. "Why would I cry for myself? Nobody did this to me, I did it to myself. There's nothing sad about my story, it's just stupid. I'm a stupid drug addict who did a lot of really bad things to a lot of people. Don't be ridiculous!" Her question annoyed me. I walked away wearing my tough posture again.

In my room, I sat on my bed, angry. *Why did she ask me that?* Tears formed in my throat, tightening, growing, threatening to spill over into my eyes. I did not want to cry, not now, and certainly not for me. Then I felt guilty that I had just been rude to a very nice lady. Leaving my bed, I walked the hall, peeking into rooms until I found her. I apologized.

∼

Sam brought a bible to me, a pad of paper and a pencil. I asked him to bring them. I wanted to write down my questions, and go over them with him, if he would keep coming to see me. I had not forgotten those moments, sitting in my locked room at Jake's, pondering why I had not become a new person when I tried church. When I used church people to get my way. The blaming and angry me had done that. I did not want to be like that now, but I wanted him to come every day. Maybe he could answer the questions I would put on my pad of paper. I wanted answers to my questions about God, but I also wanted him to be impressed with me. I was confused.

But he did come, every evening. We sat on my bed, and talked about all the things I had written that day. Days filled with reading that red bible, jotting down on the pad things we could talk about. Things I knew he would probably like to talk about. Weeks passed before I began to write down things I wanted to talk about. Weeks before I stopped needing to impress him, and began looking for answers because I really wanted to know.

~

The Foolish College Boys came to see me one afternoon. The semester at the seminary was ending. "We rented a house on Lewis Street, and we aren't going home for the summer! We're going to stay here. We can have all the neighborhood kids in for stories, and maybe some of the adults will come, like you did. You get out of here, you can come live with us to get on your feet."

They were excited! Words tumbled out, one speaking over the other. I was relieved to know what would happen to me next, when I got out of here. This time there was a plan.

Dr. P, and my parole/aftercare worker, and my children's caseworker, all were glad to know that this time I would not walk out alone, to wander the streets, carrying my belongings in a brown paper bag. This time each one smiled when they met with me. Slowly I was becoming a real person. Not an empty shell. I had stepped into a new world.

~

Until Det. Sgt. M came to see me. Walked into my room one day, manila folder tucked under his arm. Looking up from my book, I was glad to see him and smiled. He did not smile. Only tossed the folder on the bed. "Open it. Look at it, carefully."

    I did. Opened it to see photos. Photos of me. I spread them out carefully across the bed. Pictures of me cashing those checks. Photo after photo showed me turning aside to avoid the camera. And then the last picture. Me. Caught in that store when the man made me look right into the camera. When I couldn't escape. I saw then what he saw. That picture matched the others enough that he knew. He knew it was me cashing dozens of stolen government checks!

    I looked from the pictures back to him. He stood there in his black suit, black detective shoes, and black tie. He stood in his official stance, the posture that means business. The posture that stopped me from speaking because today he did not look like my friend. I could only look at him, waiting for what would come next.

    Reaching down, he gathered the photos, placing them back in the folder. Now he looked at me. Now he pointed the folder at me. "See here, see these pictures? I can tie you to all of these Federal cases. These open cases. You stole these checks. People's tax refunds, their social security checks, their welfare checks. You did that. You forged their names and then you cashed them. For heroin. You did that and I can prove it and you will go away for a long, long time."

    I could not tear my eyes away from his eyes as he spoke. I had no words. He did.

    "You know what I'm going to do? I'm going to take this folder and bury it in my desk. No one else will see it. I'm going to bury it. But if I ever see you out on the street again, I will come back to my desk and pull this folder and send you away. And you had better believe I will do it. This is your last chance."

    Tucking the folder under his arm again, still wearing his mean face, he turned and left the room. His steps were sharp, military style. He left me unable to doubt him. I believed him.

But I Can Learn

~

Three days later I moved into the house with Foolish College Boys, trying to make the house a home for them. Two bedrooms on the first floor, one for me and one for the office. The guys slept in the open attic. Beds lined up along the wall, the dorm style they were used to.

And again, two trips every day for methadone, once in the morning, again in the evening. Nurse checking now to be sure I swallowed them. Sometimes Kim drove Sam and me in his green Corvair, sometimes we bicycled, sometimes Ron loaned us his car. No longer walking the four miles alone.

I cooked supper every night. Made a lemon meringue pie that prompted Kim to leave a note for me to find in the morning, "Best Lemon Meringue Pie I ever tasted!" We made a small garden in the yard. Sam and I built a fire pit and roasted hot dogs. I helped when the neighborhood kids came for story time, served Kool-aide and cookies. These times I felt important. This is what normal people do, I said to myself every day.

But I did not like it when part time helpers came to visit. Lutheran girls eager to help in the "ministry." They came for my supper a few times a week. Laughed, flirted, had lots of stories to tell about their jobs or their church work or their school. They had long shiny hair, flipping it over their shoulder as they talked, too young and carefree. I was out of place at that table.

I had no stories to tell. My stories were of moving dead men into alleys, of stealing checks, of being sick with withdrawal, of police cars and crying children. My stories didn't fit here. I didn't fit here. When they came, I took a book and hid in the attic, laying on someone's bed, listening for when the girl visitors left. Then I could come down the steps, wash the dishes from their supper. I could sit on the couch with my red bible and pad of paper, writing down questions still, questions for someone to answer. And here I fit.

Some days, hiding in the attic, I became afraid that I really did not belong here. That it was a lie. That someday I would walk out of this house, down one block to my familiar corner, searching for that tiny silver packet that held such blessed relief in its white powder. That I would go searching for a needle and syringe and a good vein. That peace and doubt and fear would pour out of me as I pushed the plunger, sending the tiny bit of warm liquid washing over me. It wasn't that far away, just down the block. Just across the street, those guys sitting on their porch, waiting for me to cross the street to them. I was afraid these things would happen and I would be lost.

So I made more pies.

And I made a plan. If I left this house, it would be on impulse. I knew that. And I knew I would want someone to make me stop and think. Just for a moment. I decided to show the guys every place I would go. "If I turn up missing, please come get me. Remind me that there is hope, and that I am almost a real person." They agreed. For the summer, I would not be alone, I would not go anywhere without one of them. Just for the summer. And so I was a little less afraid of myself. And decided to stop calling them Foolish College Boys.

Until Jake and friends moved two blocks down the street. I saw him sitting on his porch across the street, one evening as Sam and I went for our nightly walk. He looked at me, staring, not moving from his chair, sending someone to tell me it was "time you come home." I ignored the warning, and then I looked at his messenger, and at him, in all his bigness, just sitting on the porch, glaring at me. And I was not afraid. On this side of the street, where I stood with Sam, I was not afraid. Here, this was my world, my safe world, where I now belonged. As long as I did not cross the street to his world, he had no power. I smiled to myself and I walked on.

~

That night, alone in my room, awake after a bad dream, unwilling to go back to sleep, I began to write down on my pad of paper, things I was thinking about.

Dr. P. kept asking "What do you really want?" I wanted to get married, get my children back, be a homemaker. Ruthlessly, week after week, he challenged me to think. "Well, you're never going to get that if you just walk the streets." "You'll never get it being a hooker!" Or sometimes, "You'll never get it being homeless and wearing those baggy jeans and t-shirt." On those days I didn't like him very much. I wanted him to tell me what to do instead of just what not to do. The next day I asked someone to help me find a dress.

~

Awake again the next night, I replayed the last night I had been locked in the room at Jake's house. The night I had figured out that I had not become a new person when I tried God and church because I had been just doing it to be part of that crowd, to not be alone, to get my children back. The night I had figured out that every time I didn't get what I wanted it gave me the excuse to return to the street, to sweet heroin, and it would always be somebody else's fault, not mine. I did not write about those things.

Until the night I had to. I knew I had to. I don't know why, I just did. I sat cross-legged on my bed, unable to sleep after another very bad dream. I reached for my pad of paper, took my pen and started making a list. I wrote at the top of the page, "I could be a good person if only...." "If only I had a husband." "If only I had a home." "If only I could get my children back....if only I didn't have to work and could stay home and be a mommy." I became very sad, looking at my list. I tore out that page and made a new list.

I wrote at the top of that page "I <u>will</u> be a good person! I <u>will</u> find a relationship with God even if I never..." And for several days I added things to the list.

Even if I never get married...
if I never get my kids back...
if I live alone the rest of my life...

if I never have any friends…

if I work a boring job and don't make enough money to even go to the movies…

if I go home alone every night and sit in my apartment…

if no one ever comes to visit me.

For days my list of "if onlys" grew, I cried over each one, not wanting to write it down. It was too sad and too hard. Sometimes it took days of crying before I could move on to the next "if only."

It was sad to know I could expect nothing. I could demand nothing. I would just be a good person and not do bad things. I just wouldn't. Hope was growing in my heart.

Three days after making the list, the letter came in the mailbox. The dreaded letter. The letter from child protective services.

"You are requested to attend this meeting to finalize the permanent termination of your parental rights. June 20, 1971, 3pm."

Showing the letter to no one, I quietly went to my room and shut the door. I lay on my bed and cried for a very long time. And I hugged the "if only" list tightly to my chest.

Chapter 30 – The Caseworkers

Stop crying, it doesn't change anything, it doesn't help, so stop! I forced myself to sit up on my bed, to cross my legs Indian style, to sit up straight, to blow my nose, to quiet the sob stuck in my throat. But then suddenly I couldn't breathe. Sobbing and breathing melted into one motion. *I'm going to die. I'm going to die right here, on my bed, in this room. I can't breathe and I'm going to die!*

I made myself read the "if I never" list again. The list where I vowed to learn to be a good person even if I never... I scanned the list, trying to bring myself to that place again, that place of strong will, of determination, that place of good character. But I couldn't. I fell on my pillow, sobbing. I cried for a very long time.

Looking at my list again, I didn't cry. I took a pen and circled the item half-way down the list, the part where it said "even if I never get my kids back". I sat for a while, silent. *Do I really mean this? Really, can I stay on a straight path, can I never shoot up again even if I never see my children forever? I don't know, I don't know if I can do that.* The lump in my throat threatened to turn into sobs again. I was on the verge of feeling sorry for those little children and especially sorry for myself.

I took the picture of them, the one from Lexington, I took it out of the place I hid it, the bottom drawer, under my two new pairs of jeans.

Staring at the sweet face of Matthew, always with that little smile that leaned to the left, those eyes that radiated joy even as he lived in foster care, I touched his cheek, his hair.

I looked at Michael, whose smile and eyes seemed to question what was around him. He looked happy, too. I touched his chin, his lips, put my hand on his shoulder.

And Lucy, little Lucy, my oldest. She had her arms around the boys, to hold them close, to mother them, to be a family. I could not find happy in her face. The smile seemed not real, like you have to when someone says "smile!"

Oh, my children, what have I done to you? You deserve the world and I have given you heartache.

Deep, grey fog took over my room, lay on my skin like a film. The fog was sadness and I could reach out and touch it, breathe it. The breathing of it hurt my chest. *How do I escape this overwhelming sadness, this guilt, this pity for my whole life? I don't know how to do this. What do normal people do?*

What do normal people do? I wondered again. *I guess they get out of bed and do their regular stuff. I guess I'll just do that.* And it was in that moment I knew I would be all right. I stood, placed "the list" on my pillow, their picture beside it, and new that I could learn how to do this.

Leaving my room, I went to the kitchen, looked for what I could fix the smart college boys for supper. Spaghetti would be good. And a pie, lemon meringue, of course. But the fog of sadness still followed me into the kitchen and settled there with me while I cooked.

∼

Every evening, we sat on the back steps and watched the smoldering fire, held in

place by the row of bricks and stones circling it, our makeshift fire pit. Every night we sat there, by the fire. I liked those times, everyone talking. College boys dreamed of the people they would care for after seminary. When they would be awarded churches of their own. "We won't be typical Lutheran pastors! Oh no! We'll welcome street people and drug addicts. We'll even use modern music, guitars and drums. This is the seventies, after all. Nobody relates to hymns and organ music anymore!"

But I Can Learn

Hearing their words, listening to their dreams, I didn't think it would happen. They wouldn't let me have communion and made me stay in the back pew alone while they all went to the altar. I resented it. Others would too. I said these things, but became lost in their attempts to explain why this was right.

Each night it was Sam who stayed long after the others had gone in, gone to bed. It was Sam who had a different dream, who knew there had to be something different, something better than the ritual of traditional church. I loved his dream. I loved his excited words. And I loved that he could explain all of this to me in ways that I liked. With words and ideas that the others didn't have. And so I loved him.

On the evening of the day the letter came, on that evening, sitting by the fire, I thought, *If he could love me, if he could just love me, he would marry me, we could have my children and I would make a home for all of us. I would make us a real home.*

I sat closer to him, and held his hand. He put his arm around me. I rested my head on his shoulder. He talked again of his plans to help people, to do something called "ministry." I looked in his eyes and told him how much I admired him, how right his ideas were. That I wanted to help make his dreams come true. He was impressed. He kissed me. I wore my timid self, as I kissed him back. I wore my passionate self the next night, to pull him into my world.

A world he could not enter because he was a good man. There was a line he would not cross. Sex belonged in marriage and marriage alone.

It was not an on purpose thing I did. It was not formed with words in my brain, like a thing I planned. It just came from a tiny thread of manipulation that still lived, unnoticed, in me. That thread that I could not cut because I didn't know what to do instead.

And I had begun to be afraid. *What will happen to me when college boys go back to the seminary in September? Will I have to work in a bar again? Where will I live? Can I stay in this house, here on Lewis Street alone?*

Clair

Dr. P always challenged me to think of what I really wanted, and I always became angry. "That question is for people who have choices! I don't have choices!" He smiled.

So I chose to draw Sam just a little bit over the line, not all the way, just an inch or so. Just enough that he would feel committed to me, to my children. Just enough that he would marry me. That he would love me.

Once he talked about maybe getting married the following year, when he graduated school and moved back to Canada. The following week I talked about getting married soon. "We could live here, in this house together. Keep it open for people who need help. I mean, you hate seminary and you really don't want to go back."

Taking my hand, he thought for only a moment before agreeing. "Yes! If I drop out of school, we can raise enough money to keep this house open as a halfway house. You're stronger now. We can do this together. This street needs us, the people here need us." I was pleased.

He wanted to call Vancouver, to call his parents, to tell them he was getting married. I convinced him not to. I knew they would talk him out of it. I ignored the speck of guilt taking root in my heart. I was getting married, I would just think about that.

∼

The dreaded day came, June 20. Meeting with my caseworkers. I could not eat breakfast, or lunch. I was nervous. Three o'clock took too long to come. I tried to rest, to be a strong person. Sitting on my bed, with my pad and pen, I wrote down what I would say, why they should let me have my children.

Number one: I am a new and changed person.

Number two: I have not walked the street, or stuck a needle in my arm for two months.

Three: I read the bible every day.

Four: I go to church two times every week.

And number five: I have gained weight and am healthy now."

They would have to be impressed and give my children to me, where they belonged!

With Sam coming to the meeting with me, they could see us together. *They will see how much we love each other and that we are getting married. They will see what a nice person he is!* I was hopeful.

My list was long, I hoped to remember it. Tearing the page out, I folded it many times, and stuffed it in my pocket. In the pocket of the new dress I would wear.

∼

Mrs. A. sat at her desk, motioning for us to sit. A supervisor, Mrs. P. came into the room carrying a large stack of manila folders, worn edges, papers sticking out. Those folders about my children. About me. I started to be afraid, but made myself remember that they were my children, still my children. I had their picture in my pocket. I pulled the hem of my skirt over my knees, to look modest, changed, not nervous. Normal.

Mrs. P. moved us to another room, with a long table and enough chairs for all of us. Her supervisor, Mr. M. came to stand by the door, listening.

They wanted me to sign papers, "relinquishing my rights." One paper for each child. Mrs. P. spread them on the table, looking at me with her stern face, saying, "They have been in foster care too long now, and they need to have a permanent home." Mrs. A.'s voice was softer. "A good couple, now, wants to adopt both boys together. They won't be split up. Not many families are willing to adopt older children, let alone two together. You can't let them miss this chance! If you don't sign the papers, we go to court and a judge will sign them. That could take months, and they'd lose this chance of a home where they can be together." She pushed the pen toward me.

"No! I won't do it. I can give them a home now, I'm getting married, and I haven't done drugs for about two months. I can take care of them." I kept my voice calm, and strong. Careful to not reveal the panic I felt. Mrs. A. and Mrs. P. looked at each other. I could tell they didn't believe me.

Mrs. P. opened a file from the top of her stack. "Now look here, pages and pages of what you have done, the trouble you've been in, the many chances you've had to clean up. You failed every time! And here, here is a record of how many times you missed scheduled visits with your own children. Just didn't show up. They waited for you and you just didn't come. You can't keep your children in limbo just because now you want them. And besides, you are still on a methadone maintenance program, and still have, how long, two, three years of reporting to the aftercare/parole office." Now she smiled, and laughed a little. "Two months! You've been clean only two months! You must be kidding!"

She continued reading from her list, the list of my failures to my children. Her list of how bad I was. Page after page, she read slowly and with emphasis. I did not cry. I wanted to show her my list, but I did not. I thought she would laugh.

Overwhelmed, I stared at the papers before looking up to meet her eyes. "I have to think about this. I can't do it today."

~

Walking home, I tucked the appointment card in my pocket, the pocket of my new dress, beside my own list. Two days, I had two days to decide. Sign the papers myself, or go to court.

This was a new fear, a fear I had never felt. Fear of jail, of drug withdrawal, of rape, fear of beatings, nothing matched this fear. Now I had to choose. I had to make a decision that I would never be able to change. This would last forever. This would be final.

We were silent on that walk home. Sam spoke no words of wisdom, no insights and so was silent. I was glad.

Staying in my room the rest of that day and the next, I came out only to go to the bathroom. Or to make toast. I wrote and wrote on my pad of paper, but they were just words, words that led nowhere, that were only desperate ramblings. Pages that I tore out and scrunched up and threw on the floor. I did not want to decide, how could I decide? They were my children. I wept until I was exhausted. I wept until I threw up. The fog of sadness became a storm of desolation.

On the third day, the day of my appointment, I came out of my room, made toast and coffee, and sat at the dining room table with my pen and paper. I sat quietly for a long time.

I wrote on my paper the things I had planned. "Sam will marry me. We will open a half-way house for drug addicts. The welfare department will let me have my children because they are so impressed with us." Those are the words I wrote. They looked foolish.

I thought about Sam, this gentle person that I had led down a path toward marriage. So that I would have a place to stay and to impress the welfare people. This person I had coaxed over a line he didn't want to cross, so that I could have what I wanted and because I was afraid. And because I was still manipulative.

I thought about my boys, the chance they had to be part of a real family where they would belong forever. Where they could stay together. Where they wouldn't be separated. A good home. I wanted to bring them here though, with me. They could be together here.

But in this house there was no room and the roof leaked and the neighborhood was bad. We had no money, we barely paid the rent on this old house. How long since I'd seen them, maybe a year, maybe more?

I wrote these things on my paper. And I knew I had to give them the chance to have a real home with those other people. Those people that might not wait for months for the judge to sign the paper. Those people who would love them and be there for them. Who wanted both of them. A mom who knew how to be a mom in ways that I could not imagine. *If I go to court to fight for them I will probably lose, and they'll stay in foster care for a long time till somebody else adopts them. And they won't be together. I have to let them go. I have to let them go and have their chance. It would be selfish for me to take that away from them.* I wrote all of that on my paper.

But Lucy. There was no family waiting to adopt her, and she was older, remembered me more. Some instinct told me that she would never accept a new family, that she would miss me too much. I wrote that on my paper and it looked silly. But it looked right.

On that day, sitting in the house on Lewis Street, sitting at the long table in the dining room, I made decisions. *I will sign papers for the boys. I will not sign for Lucy just yet. And I will admit to Sam that I persuaded him to marry me because I don't want to be alone and I don't want to lose my children. I will be honest and let him see this real and true manipulative me. These things I will do.* I wrote the words on my paper to make them real. I was afraid of those decisions. I was afraid of the outcome. But I was more afraid to not make them.

I wanted to go to the welfare office alone, I wanted to do this alone, but Sam walked with me, not talking, not asking questions. Only observing.

Mrs. A. and Mrs. P. smiled. "We are very proud of you, we know this is hard, but you are doing the right thing here." Spreading the two sheets before me, one for Matthew, one for Michael, handing the pen to me, holding their breath. They seemed, afraid I would change my mind at the last moment, but I didn't. I signed the papers, laid the pen on the table and looked at them. They smiled. I tried to breathe slowly, calmly.

"And here's the paper for Lucy," Mrs. A. said. I put my hand on that paper and quietly said, "No, I'm not signing that one."

They began pulling papers from their folders, showing me again the record of my failures, threatened quick court action. They pointed out the selfishness of me. "If you really love her, you will let her go, too." I was afraid they were right, but I could not sign her paper.

I had to leave the office, but my body, my legs were too heavy to move. It was painful to make my feet take me out of the building, I could only make it to the curb. There I sat, too stunned to cry or talk. There Sam stood, leaning against the light pole, waiting.

My resolve collapsed and I could hear my own words condemning me. *You are a terrible, terrible person to give your boys away. To just give them up for adoption. What have you done? You just gave your children away! Who does that? What kind of terrible, selfish person just gives her children away?*
And you want to keep Lucy? You think you can give her a good home now? Who do you think you are? You think you can make it up to her? All those years in foster care? She's eight years old now! You should have let her make a clean break!

I wanted to cry. To cry over my children, but I couldn't. I wanted to cry to show I was still a real person, but I just couldn't cry. I knew I had to stand up, away from the curb, and walk back to the house on Lewis Street. Walk with Sam, him still silent, waiting for me to talk.

I knew I still had to tell him he didn't have to marry me, that I was sorry for pushing him over his line and making him feel he had to. The pain of these things I could not bear, and my hand wanted to find a needle and syringe and the relief that heroin would bring. My hand instead reached for the list still in my pocket. I pulled it out and read it aloud. I read it to myself as we walked home. When I got to the last thing, I read it again, over and over I read the last thing. *I will be a good and strong person even if I never get married, never get my kids back, if I live alone the rest of my life, if I work a boring job, if I never have any friends, if I am alone and nobody likes me...I will still be a good person.*

And then I felt something new. Something I had never felt my whole life. I felt strong.

Chapter 31 – Court!

I woke from a deep sleep, panicked, unsure of the time, unsure of where I was. Overwhelmed by guilt. Overpowered by it. Carefully turning over, checking the bed beside me. *It's empty, no one's here. I'm alone. That's good.*

Leaping out of bed, I scanned the room for a needle, syringe, evidence that I had shot up the night before. Nothing. There was nothing there. I searched my arms, my legs, between my toes, looking for fresh needle marks. There were none. Yet overwhelming guilt hung on my shoulders. I must have done something!

Collapsing back on the bed, pulling the crumpled covers over my face, I was relieved. "I didn't do anything wrong last night. I didn't turn a trick, I slept alone, and I didn't shoot up!"

But it was still there, that familiar morning guilt. "Then why do I feel so guilty? I didn't do anything wrong! I was a good girl!"

Groggy, disoriented, confused, I left my room, hoping the familiar house would comfort me. That I'd find smart college boys sitting at the dining room table with their morning coffee. Engaged in schoolboy crazy talk.

They were not there. The house was dark and empty. I found them on the front porch, talking quietly, slowly sipping cold beers.

Tom was the first to see me standing in the open doorway. "Hey, we just made our own suppers cause we wanted to let you sleep. Did you have a good nap?"

"Wait, what? What time is it? I thought it was morning!"

It was Sam who stood, took my hand, ushering me to the top step, to sit with them. "No, you went straight to your room and shut the door when we came back from the welfare office. We figured you probably wanted to be alone, maybe take a nap. Did you sleep?"

And then I remembered. This was the eve of the day I gave my children away. I had just given them away.

I wanted to be sorry I had signed those papers. A good mother would fight for them. A mother who loved her children would sit here on this night and regret it, she would be sorry she did it. I tried to be sorry, to make myself feel it, but I couldn't. I felt guilty that I wasn't sorry. I was only sad that it had come to this, but I was not sorry for this decision.

Looking at the faces of these nice boys, sitting here with me, I knew Sam had told them. Told them I gave my children away. I was glad they knew. Glad I didn't have to tell the story. Glad I didn't have to know what they thought. If I'd done the right thing. Or if they thought I was a bad person now.

Kim came from his chair to sit beside me, on the worn top step. He held my hand. "Here's the thing, you're probably wondering what we think, but we can't know if you did the right thing or not. No one can know that. We only know that it's right for you to sit here with us and not walk across the street to those guys, on that porch over there, those guys waiting for you." I looked at my hands, not wanting him to see the tears dropping onto my cheeks. His voice sounded stern, caring. "Look at me! Not giving up is the right thing to do." I felt for the list, still in my pocket, pulled it out, all wrinkled and folded over so many times. It was a well-worn paper, smudged. *Tomorrow I will copy this onto a fresh sheet of paper and begin again.*

∼

Days passed, almost regular days like normal people have. Normal except I made a trip every morning and every evening, each time to swallow 60mg. of methadone, to open my mouth, proving I really swallowed them. Normal except that I went to therapy every week. Normal except that I had a parole/aftercare worker that made me pee in a cup twice week.

And normal except that I carried a brick in my heart, reminding me, *Don't forget! You have to tell Sam he doesn't have to marry you, that you manipulated him. You should do it today. You better do it today.*

And so finally I did. I didn't plan when, I didn't plan the best way to say it, the best way to be honest and still sound like a nice person. I didn't plan the outcome. I saw him sitting on the couch, in his jeans and white t-shirt, bare feet, drinking tea, pouring over the newspaper. Everyone else was out, we were alone. I decided in that moment to leap, to jump off the cliff and to just say it.

Taking my own cup of tea, I sat across from him, to see his face, to not hide my own. "Hey, I want to talk to you about some stuff."

"Sure, I thought maybe you did. I wondered when you would."

"So here's the thing. We talked about getting married, but..." He reached for my hand, "Yes, ...okay, what about that?"

"Wait! Let me say this. I need to say this. You need to hear me." I pulled my hand away, placing it on my teacup, holding it with two hands, so it wouldn't spill.

"You don't have to marry me. Really you don't. I made you feel like you had to, like you couldn't walk away because you'd already acted like we were a couple. I pushed you and pushed you and manipulated you and made you feel guilty and even talked you out of telling your parents. Because I was afraid. I didn't know what to do so I made you say and do things you didn't mean. So, we shouldn't get married...."

Reaching for my teacup, he placed it on the side table. He held both of my hands in his, interrupting the space between us. His words interrupted my own.

"I know all that! Do you think I didn't notice? I know you were aggressive, pushing to get married, pushing to make it happen right away. And you're right, I would have felt guilty, behaving like we were and then bailing out. I knew what you were doing and but I didn't care. I don't care. I made up my mind a long time ago that you were the person I wanted to marry."

"How can you say that? That can't be true! You can't possibly want to really marry me."

"But I do. You want to know when I decided? I knew I wanted to marry you the first time I heard you read that list. Back when you were still in the hospital. I don't know anybody who could make a list like that, not my family, not any of the people out at the seminary. Not even myself. I appreciate your confession, but that only tells me how much you are changing. Only tells me how much I do still want to marry you. This summer."

Sitting across from him, staring at the floor, I could hear his words, words falling into the empty space between us, words falling on the floor, scattered. My hands longed to pick them up and sort them out, examining each one, deciding the best thing to say next. But I didn't.

I knew I needed to face him, look in his eyes, and make him see the reality of my manipulation, the reality of who I really was.

Before I could speak, he stood, hands in his pockets. "This guy at school was getting married and I remember him telling about a jeweler who gave great discounts to seminary students, so I was thinking how I could buy rings. About how I really don't want to go back to school, how much I hate it. I didn't know I hated it this much until you said it. But it's true. When I think of school and lectures I don't believe in anymore, I dread it. But marrying you, making a half-way house, that scares me to death, but then it excites me. I'm excited. So please hear me. I knew I wanted to marry you the first time you read your list to me. I decided long before you did."

I could only stare into the eyes of my foolish college boy! *How naïve he is! He has no street sense. He doesn't know yet how hard or how tough life is.*

I looked at his innocent face, his pleading eyes, and in that moment I wanted to be foolish and naïve and without street sense. I didn't want to know how tough life could be. He held onto my hands as he stood, pulling me up from my chair. "Come on, let's go downtown and buy those rings!"

I wanted to make him sit down again, to listen to me, make him see that he really didn't have to do this. For a moment I could only stare at him. *This is probably a stupid thing to do, but this is a good man and he has a good heart, and I do love him.* So I looked into his eyes and said, "Okay!"

We walked downtown, to a little jewelry store up three flights of stairs, above the drug store on the corner. To a grey-haired jeweler sitting in a small room, polishing stones, a man who liked Lutheran school boys, a man willing to give a bargain. Showing us rings with tiny zircons that we could afford.

~

I didn't know what to say when I overheard college boys on the porch that night, telling Sam he should wait, how foolish it was to drop out of school and marry me.

I didn't know what to say when my children's casework objected. "If you think this will make us change our minds about Lucy, you're wrong, we're still going to court. This is just another example of you being foolish!"

I didn't know what to say when the aftercare/parole lady came with her list of reasons why this was a mistake.

It was only Dr. P who didn't laugh at us, who didn't object, who reached out to shake Sam's hand, congratulating us. "You've come a long way. I know you can do this because it's what you really want." And then he smiled at me. A real smile that came with sparkly eyes.

~

Clair

The ministry on Lewis Street had a board of directors. The ladies made a dress for me, not white of course, but lavender, not real silk, but something like it. Sam found a shirt, same fabric, same color. Found it in a bargain shop downtown. He wore it with his white jeans. These were our wedding clothes.

We were married in a small service at the end of the Saturday evening prayer meeting at our church. There were no announcements, no invitations. There was no one to invite. Except College Boys, we told them. At the end of the prayer meeting, the pastor simply said, "Well now you are all invited to a wedding."

∼

Our first night together was in a small apartment one block away from the Lewis Street house. The apartment of friends, loaned to us for this night. They left a roasted chicken in the fridge, and a bottle of champagne on the table. Flowers on the nightstand. Celebrating this beginning.

Sam slept soundly. I did not. Waking often, I was restless, unsure, embarrassed, thankful, hopeful, afraid, and excited. I snuck out of bed, careful not to wake him. Searching the brown paper bag, the things I had brought with me, I found my pad of paper and my pen. And my list. I took them to the kitchen table and sat for a long time. Staring at the paper sack of my few things, packed only with things for one overnight. I remembered the years I had carried another paper sack with all my belongings, the sack I kept hidden in the gas station restroom. I smiled at this new sack, this sack I did not have to hide. I smiled at the thought of my clothes, nice ones now, folded neatly in my dresser drawer, in my room in the house on Lewis Street.

I looked at my list, the list of promises I made to myself. The list that said "I will not shoot up, I will not steal, I will not turn tricks, I will be a good person even if nobody likes me, even if I am poor…" The list that went on and on, almost filling the page. I moved my finger down the list as I read them out loud to myself, until I came to the one that said "even if I never get my kids back." I paused to feel the hurt of it, to see if I could live with the pain of it, to see if I still meant it. And I did.

Moving down the list, I came to the one that said, "even if I never get married."

I took a clean sheet of paper and started another list, a list of how to be a good wife, a good homemaker. The person I had wanted to be all these past ten years.

I wrote "cook good meals" as the first one. "Always be available for sex" was the next one. And "always listen and remember what he says, what concerns him, take notes if you must, and be supportive, sympathetic." Pausing a moment, those words grabbed my heart and I was afraid. And embarrassed.

These things, the things on this list, were things I did when important men were my customers. I tore that paper out, scrunched it up, and threw it in the garbage, tucked it under some trash so no one would find it.

I sat awhile in my chair at the kitchen table, looking again at my first list, the list of "even if I never."

Taking my pen, I added one more thing to that list.

"I will be a good person, even if I fail to be a good wife, and Sam is sorry he married me and leaves me alone. I will still be a good person."

Lying in bed, later, pondering all of these things, I decided, "I have no idea how to be a good wife, no idea in the world! But I can learn! I will learn!"

Chapter 32 – This I Know For Sure

In the house on Lewis Street, I woke early one morning. Glancing at the clock in front of me, I saw it was only five am. Turning over, I found a man in my bed. It was my husband, and I smiled. Trying very hard to fall back to sleep and failing, at six am, I slipped out of bed, careful not to wake my new husband. One month. We were married one month. All the college boys had gone back to campus for the school year. We were alone in this house.

In the kitchen, I opened the cupboard doors above the sink and was delighted to see no roaches. My obsessive cleaning and washing was working. But there, on the top shelf, a cereal box was not in line with the others! I straighten it. Checking the other cabinets, I found them roach-free also. "I am learning to be a good wife with this clean kitchen." I felt proud.

While coffee brewed, I wiped the counter tops again, took the tiny bag of trash out to the alley. "Just to be safe."

Then, as I sat at the little table by the window, there in my kitchen, blue coffee mug in hand, my mind rested, then wandered, drifting to memories I could not forget. My room on Hanna Street, where the roaches covered the walls at night, invaded even the refrigerator, and crawled around the edges of the tub when I took a bath. I shuddered at the thought of it.

I remembered the apartment on Lake Avenue, the months I had a real job in a downtown office. When I had been excited for the first visit with my children. My little apartment pristine after days of scrubbing, my soup cans lined up in perfect order and my pots and pans sorted according to size. I remembered the magazine-photo perfection of my entire apartment, with the towels folded perfectly and a fresh, unused bar of soap at the sink. And then, my frantic need to make everything messy when the visit didn't go as I wanted.

Leaning back in my chair now, pulling my worn yellow robe closer around me on this chilly morning, the sun just beginning to peek through this window with a lace curtain, I pondered those things.

What does it take to make a good home, to be a good wife? Can things be out of place? Should I wash this mug and put it away as soon as I finish my coffee? Should I be dressed, hair combed, teeth brushed when Sam wakes up? Or is a good home more relaxed? Does a husband like to be greeted by a wife still in her pajamas, hair a little messy from sleep? And I said out loud to myself, "I surely have no idea. But I will learn."

Finishing the last of my now lukewarm coffee, standing to set the mug in the sink, I was overcome by a sudden wave of nausea and barely made it to the bathroom before retching violently. Lightheaded, afraid I would faint, I sat on the edge of the tub until the nausea passed, until I could walk to the bedroom to wake Sam. Maybe if we go to the hospital for my morning methadone I'll feel better. Or maybe I just have the flu. I'll feel better later, or maybe tomorrow.

~

But I didn't feel better. Serving juice and cookies to the neighborhood children during our weekly bible story hour drained any energy I had saved. I could barely do the household chores I loved so much until I had a nap. I forced myself to make the bed each morning, to cook supper every night. To listen sympathetically to the people in need, the men and women stopping by this house, open to everyone, this place of comfort. I smiled and said the nice things I knew to say, but cried on the inside of me because I knew I was not being a good wife. I felt guilty and was afraid.

Each day, several times, Sam asked, "Feeling any better today?" Or, maybe just "How are you doing this afternoon?" Sometimes I lied. "Oh yes, I'm much better today." Only to feel guilty later, going to him to say, "I lied to you! I'm so sorry, I don't know why I did it."

Only to my own self did I say, *I am confused and desperate and feeling too guilty to walk around! I just want oblivion.*

We went to the doctor instead, not Dr. P, my therapy-methadone doctor, but to Dr. R, my medical doctor, the one who always wore a white doctor coat, not regular clothes like Dr. P.

Sitting opposite us, clipboard in hand, he wore a sober expression. Sam and I reached over to hold hands.

"Well, we have a real problem here, a real problem. Because it looks like you're pregnant."

He waited, saying nothing, as though he knew we needed time to absorb the shock of it.

"But you said that would be impossible! That I was on too much methadone! Why did you say that when it's not true? How did this happen?"

"I don't know, I really don't know. It should be impossible, yet here we are. You are definitely pregnant."

I'm pregnant! Two little magic words. Guilt and fear had stalked me for days, chipping at the strong me, bleeding away the resolve that was my life's blood. Now there were two little words, "I'm pregnant," two little words pumping life into me.

I sat up straight in my chair, no longer slouching. Now excited. *What a strange thing,* I said to myself, not out loud for anyone to hear, just to my own self. *What a strange thing that me, who's labeled 'unfit' to have my own children, me who's done terrible, terrible things, that God somewhere would let me get pregnant. When it's supposed to be impossible!*

Looking at Sam, I saw his worried face. I saw White-Coat Dr. R's worried face, and yet I could only look at them and smile as I said in my most non-pretend excited voice, "I'm pregnant, I'm really pregnant!"

It was Dr. R who spoke the words, "I wouldn't be so excited. You're forgetting that you're on a high dose of methadone, which will mean this baby will be an addict. It will be born addicted to methadone and have to be withdrawn carefully. This is not good, really not good!"

"Well, so, I'll just stop taking methadone. I probably don't need it anymore anyway. I don't have to take it. I can do withdrawal, I've been through that before, I can do it in a few days."

Dr. R responded quickly, cutting me off, stopping me from saying anything more. I could hear his serious words, like flies that I tried to swat away with the wave of my hand. I wanted this moment of joy, of happiness undisturbed. I willed him to stop talking, but he kept on. I stopped listening.

Until I heard the sentence, "That's not really your decision."

Angry now, I stood, asserting myself. "What? What's not my decision? I can stop taking methadone if I want. I'm still the boss of me." I said the words because they were familiar to me, but they did not feel as comforting as they once had. I didn't know why, so I said them again. "I am still the boss of me!"

"Well, actually you're not. I could be wrong, but I think you still belong to the federal government. Didn't you get sent to Lexington for four years? And that was, let me see," he thumbed through papers in my file. "Oh yes, 1969, only two years ago. So they make the decision about methadone. I think you could get sent back if you just stop on your own. And isn't there a detective involved in this?"

I sat down, and reached for Sam's hand. Ready now to listen. Sam asked the question before I did. "So what now, what do we do next?"

Dr. R stopped looking at my chart. His worried face looked puzzled as he assured us he would meet with Dr. P. "We have to check into this, and do some research. We'll get back to you."

As we walked back to the house on Lewis Street, away from exam tables and stethoscopes and blood pressure cuffs, walking on my own street, beside my own real husband, I was not afraid of the future. I knew the doctors would find no easy plan for me. I was off the street now,

I wasn't pumping a huge amount of heroin in my veins every day, and methadone might be clean, little, legal, white pills, given by a nurse wearing a starched uniform, in a hospital, but I was still an addict. And my baby would be addicted, unless they found a solution.

I knew all of that, the hard reality of it. Yet I was happy. I wanted to skip home. I wanted to stop every person we passed on the sidewalk, I wanted to tell them, "I'm pregnant! I'm going to have a baby!" With every block I became more excited. On our block, three houses before ours, I turned into a silly child, hopping and skipping, grabbing Sam's hands, forcing him to keep pace with my dancing.

I made him smile. The worried face he'd started carrying on our long walk home, erupted first into a smile, then into a careful chuckle, then into whole-body laughing. "You silly thing, will you stop! This is serious. Be serious now!" But I knew he didn't mean it because he was smiling so big.

~

Dr. P waited for us a few days later, in the tiny conference room again. His hospital group finished, he just waited, knowing I'd come for methadone. I wondered how he had time to sit, just sit and wait, not knowing when I would be there. He looked important, sitting across the table again, in his grey suit, his long legs crossed, patient folder in hand, reading intently, as I'd seen him do so many times, the times I was in trouble. I hoped I was not in trouble today.

I wasn't. He stood when he saw us, shook hands with Sam, congratulated us. "So, you're going to be parents!" Looking at Sam, he said, "Wow, you did that fast!" He smiled and seemed to be joking. *Is this my Dr. P, making a joke?*

He motioned for us to take the chairs across from him, and began to explain The Plan. Since I was pregnant, the bosses-of-me decided to allow me to withdraw from methadone.

"But you can't do it all at once, it would be too big a shock for your body, the skinny, weak thing you are." He smiled as he said this, a smile that made the words sound affectionate, not insulting.

"And doing a quick withdrawal would probably cause you to lose your baby, so we'll do it gradually, ten milligrams at a time, hoping to have you drug-free at least six weeks before you're due. But remember, they can always put you back on methadone later, if they need to, but I don't think that will happen, do you?"

I watched his face as he said this. He looked happy, his eyes sparkly, a small smile spreading across his face, his eyes locked onto mine.

I knew I loved Dr. P then because he let me have this time of joy, because he was happy with me, and because he said "your baby" instead of "the baby".

∼

And then, there it was in my mailbox one morning. The letter giving me notice of the court hearing scheduled to terminate my parental rights in the case of Lucy. I tried very hard to not be afraid, yet I was. I looked at myself in the mirror. *How do I look? Do I still look like a stupid streetwalker-junkie person or do I look like I could maybe be a mommy now? Maybe I should dye my hair back to brown! This blonde is too, I don't know, but not motherly, not respectable-looking.*

Practicing how to stand, how to sit, I hoped the judge would see a good person, not the one the welfare department would testify about. I hoped he would not listen to the 'seven page- single spaced' list of my bad acts. The list they threatened to use when I wouldn't sign their paper giving my rights away. I hoped he would stop them and say, "Okay, I get the point, but I can see those things are no longer true."

I wanted him to say, "I can't sign these termination papers because I can see this is a changed girl and she deserves to have her daughter with her." Every day I practiced how to stand straight and how to sit like a lady, and rehearsed what I would say to the judge. I wanted to wash all my words free of anger or helplessness. I wanted to sound strong, even if I had to pretend I was strong, not scared.

He did not refuse to sign the paper on that day, the day of the hearing, but he did continue the case sixty days, and he did order visitation. Every other weekend Lucy would come now to spend a day and night with us. Outside the courtroom I sat on a bench, then, and cried with relief.

If he was letting her come to visit, I knew he did not intend to ever sign it. As long as I behaved, as long as I didn't mess up again. And I knew I wouldn't mess up. I'd already decided. It was on my list of 'I will never, even ifs'.

It seemed to take forever, arranging that first visit, for Lucy to spend a day and an overnight with us. The caseworker didn't think it was a good idea, her supervisor was angry. Her foster parents were afraid and prepared this child for the dangers she could face in the home of heathen people.

Three weeks later objections came to a halt, the Saturday my sweet daughter walked up the steps of our porch, carrying her little suitcase, ready for an overnight with her mommy. Mrs. Caseworker stood by her car at the curb, silent, not talking, not waving goodbye.

This ramshackle house, our house on Lewis Street, home to anyone who needed help or rest or a little conversation, this often empty house, came alive with a bouncy, happy girl. We curled our hair, colored pictures with crayons, new crayons, went to the grocery to find her favorite things. Mostly we sat together and held each other, reading stories in bed.

Morning came too quickly, and we played the scene in reverse. Mrs. Caseworker waited at the curb, next to her car, as Lucy walked down our porch steps, out to her car. I watched them drive away, content, knowing we had done well and would be granted another visit in two weeks. And then another.

Clair

~

And so it was, the next morning, coffee cups at hand, Sam and I sat with paper and pen and checkbook. He wore the worried look again, and I knew skipping and dancing would not make him smile now.

"I don't know how we are going to do this. As an intern at the church, I get paid very little. We're not good at fundraising, so there's not much money in the bank." He wrote those dollar amounts on the paper. "Then later we'll get a small check for Lucy since she's still a ward of the court." We sat in silence as he wrote "gas, electric, rent, food" in a new column on the right side of the paper, the lined yellow page torn from the pad. One column of our income, another of our bills. Staring at the paper, the numbers, he could only say, "We can't do it! It will never work. There's only one solution."

I held my breath, waiting, waiting for him to say I couldn't be a stay at home mommy, that I had to get a job.

Tossing the pen aside, not placing it on the table calmly, but flinging it with a force that caused it to bounce to the floor, he paced the room. Back and forth he marched, my eyes following him. I waited, afraid to speak, unwilling to hear those next words. "You'll have to get a job, too."

I couldn't bear to hear his next words, sounding angry and disappointed.

"That's it! My internship will be over in a few weeks so then I'll get a regular job. I have to stop thinking we're missionaries to this street. We're not doing any good here anyway. Nobody wants to talk to us except the little kids and they only come for the cookies."

It was my fault, this giving up of his dream. The death of it broke my heart. Quietly I said, "I could get a job."

He stopped pacing, walked back to the table, sat in his chair again, sat very still, with his head bowed, and did not talk for a long time.

"You can't do that, look at you, you are still terribly thin, you're just beginning to feel the effect of them cutting back your methadone. And you're pregnant. And you have a police record. No, I don't want you to get a job. It's not a problem, I'll just finish my internship and get ordained, then I'll find a regular job somewhere. This will be better, we need to shut down this house anyway and move. What was I thinking? We can't live here. With Jake down the street and junkies across the street, I can't bring a baby and a little girl here."

I stood, knowing I needed to make him stop saying these things, I wanted to make things right for him, to help him keep his dream, to make him happy, all these things a good wife does. But I didn't because I had no words, I didn't know how to fix this, to make it right for him.

It's not fair. I get to stay home and be mommy, I get to live my dream, but he has to go work in a factory or something.

Feeling helpless and guilty, I knew only one thing to do. I went to the kitchen, searched the cupboards and fridge for flour, butter, eggs, and a package of lemon pudding. I made a lemon meringue pie. For him.

"I may not be able to leave the house and get a job, but I can do this one thing and I will do it well. A good wife comforts her husband any way she can."

∼

By the end of his internship I knew he was right. My methadone dose was so low that I was in a long, painful withdrawal. For months we counted the hours during the night, waiting until I could get the morning dose. Rushing home to soak in the bathtub, filled with enough hot water to soothe my painful skin and muscles and joints. Electric heater poised on the toilet seat, aimed at me to stop the shaking. Tring to eat something before Sam went to work. Often vomiting before I could finish it. Holding my pregnant belly, I threw up and peed my pants.

Sam left an hour later, when I was calmer. When I could lay on the floor near the register, with a blanket to make a tent over me to keep the heat in when the furnace turned on. Counting the hours again until I could claim my evening meds. Living the routine again the next day and the next. Week after week, marching to the end of methadone and to baby day.

Friends brought their old baby bassinette, filled with their daughter's infant clothes. Wrapped in plastic. "You'll have to wash all this stuff, it's been in the attic for years!" I could not climb the basement stairs to wash them. I did not spread them on the bed to fondle them as I had done with my firstborn. I was too tired.

And then it happened. I stood in the hall, in front of the nurses' station. They were all there, most of them, these nurses I had seen every day. Miss Puffy Hair smiled as she handed me my last pill. This was it. I made it to the end and I was very proud of myself.

∼

The following week, as my strength began to return, I stood in the basement to fold towels, towels fresh from the dryer. They were warm, smelled of fabric softener. I held them close to my face to enjoy the moment before folding them in my usual pattern. Piling them high in the basket.

Starting up the steps, I saw it. There it was tucked, behind the paint cans. My paper bag of belongings. The one I kept hid in the gas station bathroom when I worked the street. All I had owned, there in that bag. When had I put it there? I couldn't remember.

Backed down the stairs, setting the basket on the floor, I retrieved my bag. Taking it to a table, I opened it carefully. *Why can't I remember what's in here? Has it been that long?*

Here, my short skirt. And now here, an extra t-shirt, a sweater, a small blanket. Thinking the bag was empty, I tossed it in the trash. And I heard the noise, items in the bag, still there in the bottom, small items.

Turning the bag upside down, I shook them onto the table. Two things landed with barely a sound. Small things. My needle and syringe, my 'works.' I'd had a version of them with me almost always for ten years or so. They were part of me, like an arm or a hand. They belonged to my body. I picked them up, simply holding them in my hand, feeling the shape as I turned them over, brought a flood of memories. My comforters.

I looked at the second item, a small, round piece of metal, about the size of a nickel. Turning it over, I saw my button, the pin-on one I wore when I worked in the nightclub, the red one with white letters proclaiming, "If it feels good, I'll do it." I had worn that button proudly and enjoyed the attention it brought.

I held them both tightly, the button and the needle and syringe. Climbed the stairs, leaving the towels sit in their basket on the basement floor. Went to the kitchen, pulled out all the papers from the trash, took a box of matches from the drawer on the left, walked outside to the fire pit.

Scrunching up the newspaper, placing it in the center, adding my things, the needle and syringe and the button, I lit the fire and watched them burn.

I know I'll never need them again, but this is to be sure. Just to be sure. I watched them burn and absorbed the stink of plastic. *I want to remember this smell, the smell of them. This foul smell.*

I buried the ashes. And didn't tell anyone. I don't know why.

∼

I marked days on the calendar, six weeks till baby day, then five weeks. It was the beginning of 'four weeks till baby' that I thought I was in labor.

No, it can't be, I'll lay in bed today, maybe it will stop. It can't be now, only two weeks after methadone! It has to stop. I went to bed and lay very still. It didn't help. I called Sam.

"Maybe if we go to the hospital, they can make it stop. It's too early, we need another four weeks."

∼

Clair

That evening baby boy, Jonathan was born, weighing almost a bit over six pounds. His fingers and toes were perfect, his face was perfect, everything was perfect. A little black hair made him look especially beautiful. Did I say he was perfect? I did. Because he was, a perfect baby, not an addict baby. Not an addict baby.

I held him in my arms, him all wrapped in a soft blanket, sleeping peacefully. I watched him sleep, his eyelids fluttering, his lips moving a little. Holding him close to my chest then, this tiny boy, his hair touching my cheek.

I will learn to be a good mother now. To this boy babe and to my little Lucy. I don't know exactly what that means, but I don't care. Whatever it takes, whatever sacrifices are needed, I will do them. I will learn all that needs to be learned.

I can do these things, because I am strong. I am a real person, not a pretend person anymore. I have won this fight and will continue to win. These things I know for sure.

Epilogue

And I did learn! Now, fifty years later, I am still married to that "silly college boy." It has been a hard marriage, him the proper seminary non-risk taking, afraid of failure, defensive man; and me, the street-wise, afraid of nothing defensive person that I am. We are both broken people, not just me. He could rescue me, even while needing to be rescued himself. It took me a long time to understand that. Never willing to give up, we still, even today are finding ways to "make this work." It's called commitment.

We made two sons and those boys are amazing grown men now, each with his own unique personality and with families of their own. They give their lives to helping those in need, while maintaining the balance necessary to be good husbands and fathers. I am very proud of them!

While my daughter and I have had a rocky re-connecting, we have done it! She is her own person and will never be the helpless person I was! I am so very proud of her also!

I have a very long dining room table and still remember sitting at the head of that table, looking down its length to see my children, their spouses, my grandchildren and great-grandchildren and knowing what it was to finally find home. I had wanted God to restore to me that born-into family and it hadn't happened. Yet as I looked over these sitting at this table, it came to me that He had given me everything I ever wanted. This. This here is my family. My real family! There is peace here, and acceptance, and laughter, and safety. And arguments and making up and debating and letting go. This is the family I have always wanted and I have it. I am so grateful!

My story after the one you have just read has not been easy; it was not a "come to Jesus" moment that magically made everything work. Recovery and healing are hard. Really, really hard work. Getting off drugs is easy compared to the years of self-awareness needed to learn to be a good person. How to live life with these people in a way that is true and not manipulative. In a way that values honesty and integrity over anger and pity and selfishness.

To know myself, what I like and don't like, what I am good at and what I'm not good at. And to be okay with the "am not good at " part. To love my own imperfect self, to live in the present, in the today of my life. Only then can I truly love those around me. I am learning these things, too!

I am now nearing my eightyth birthday and am still learning!

I have also learned to be happy! And maybe that's the best part!